Drupal 6 Theming Cookbook

Over 100 clear, step-by-step recipes to create powerful, great-looking Drupal themes

Karthik Kumar

[PACKT] open source✲
PUBLISHING   community experience distilled

BIRMINGHAM - MUMBAI

Drupal 6 Theming Cookbook

First published: November 2010

Production Reference: 1081110

Published by Packt Publishing Ltd.
32 Lincoln Road
Olton
Birmingham, B27 6PA, UK.

ISBN 978-1-847198-68-6

www.packtpub.com

Cover Image by Vinayak Chittar (vinayak.chittar@gmail.com)

Credits

Author

Karthik Kumar

Reviewers

Peter Brady

Kevin Davison

Sheena Donnelly

Richard Eriksson

Jake Strawn

Acquisition Editor

Sarah Cullington

Development Editor

Wilson D'Souza

Technical Editors

Manasi Poonthottam

Rupal Pravin Joshi

Indexer

Hemangini Bari

Editorial Team Leader

Mithun Sehgal

Project Team Leader

Lata Basantani

Project Coordinator

Leena Purkait

Proofreader

Joanna McMahon

Graphics

Nilesh Mohite

Production Coordinator

Adline Swetha Jesuthas

Cover Work

Adline Swetha Jesuthas

About the Author

Karthik Kumar is a Drupal developer residing in Chennai, India. He first came across Drupal in late 2004 and has been a fan ever since. He maintains a number of modules on `http://drupal.org` under the moniker Zen (`http://drupal.org/user/21209`), and has also made substantial contributions towards the development of Drupal core.

Acknowledgements to the reviewers—Peter Brady, Kevin Davison, Sheena Donnelly, Richard Eriksson, and Jake Strawn—for their careful scrutiny. To all the people at Packt involved in the publishing of this book—Sarah Cullington, Wilson D'Souza, Sunny Kansara, Priya Mukherji, Leena Purkait, Sudha Rao, and Patricia Weir—for their guidance and patience. To Dries and the Drupal developer community for making Drupal what it is today.

Finally, this book is dedicated to my parents for all freedoms given.

About the Reviewers

Kevin Davison is a Web Generalist, Content Strategist, "Drupaler", and Owner of Quevin, LLC in San Francisco, California. Since Netscape Navigator 2.0, Kevin has built hundreds of dynamic websites and he recently finished a Technical Writing degree at SFSU. His experience with Drupal began as an experiment on `Quevin.com`, and now it has become his passion. Find Kevin actively involved at DrupalCon SF, SFDUG, Drupal.org support, Quevin, and with the Drupal community on IRC (Quevin).

Quevin—the business—stands for a system of web production methodologies and iterative development interactions to help ensure the success of complex website projects. Quevin, LLC isn't a large company, although it has produced like one since 2007.

Thanks to the Drupal community for making all of this possible, and to Dries for having the vision. Packt Publishing has made this a great learning opportunity. And thanks to my wife especially for her support.

Richard Eriksson has been a member of the Drupal community since 2004. Richard worked on the community support and systems administration team at Bryght, the first commercial Drupal venture, and subsequently Raincity Studios. He has since struck out on his own with his consultancy, Ethical Detergent.

Jake Strawn has been working with the web since 1998, and started with a brief background in HTML/CSS, moving into PHP/MySQL and web application programming. After almost eight years of PHP/MySQL programming, he discovered Drupal, and his life changed forever, making complex tasks simple with a framework built for extensibility and efficiency. Jake has extensive experience with the Drupal framework with over 800 commits to his name (`http://drupal.org/user/159141`). He has been a speaker at many Drupal events including DrupalCons, and DrupalCamps evolved his programming background to include design capabilities to create and deliver amazing looking sites.

Jake works almost exclusively with Drupal 7 now and has invested hundreds of hours into learning and expanding on the new Drupal 7 APIs, including upgrading his Omega base theme (`http://drupal.org/project/omega`), which promises to be one of the most powerful base themes in Drupal 7.

Jake is also a contributing author on the *Definitive Guide to Drupal 7* set to be published shortly after an official release of D7. Jake is writing the jQuery and AJAX chapter, which deals with changes to jQuery in D7, and also the new AJAX system.

Jake also recently relaunched his blog (`http://himerus.com`) on Drupal 7.

Table of Contents

Preface

Themes are among the most powerful and flexible features available when it comes to the presentation of a website. The greatest strength of Drupal lies in its design which, when done correctly, allows developers and designers to customize and micromanage each and every aspect of the site. Furthermore, the Drupal theming system and its APIs allow for the design of custom themes that are easy to administer and maintain.

This book provides a plethora of solutions that enable Drupal theme designers to make full use of all its features and its inherent extensibility to style their sites just the way they want to. It covers numerous aspects from using contributed and custom themes to leveraging the powerful CCK, Views, and Panels triad of modules to create rich designs that are easy to administer and maintain.

Structured as a collection of recipes to perform a wide variety of practical tasks, this book will systematically guide readers towards solutions that are central to Drupal theming. Each recipe is divided into the following sections:

- ▶ An *Introduction* that explains what the recipe is about
- ▶ *Getting ready* lists any prerequisite steps required for the recipe to work
- ▶ *How to do it* describes how to implement the recipe
- ▶ *How it works* explains how the recipe works
- ▶ *There's more* catalogs useful information related to the recipe

While it is recommended that readers follow the recipes in each chapter in sequence, it is also possible to sift through the recipes at random. Special attention should always be paid to the *Getting ready* section of each recipe which provides information on preliminary steps that need to be performed, and in some cases, specify if the recipe builds on the result of earlier recipes in the same chapter.

What this book covers

Chapter 1, Drupal Theme Basics, introduces the reader to the basic elements of Drupal theming, such as downloading and installing a contributed theme, and learning how to add and customize blocks.

Chapter 2, Beyond the Basics, explains the concept of theme engines and sub-themes and briefly introduces the topic of template overrides. It also includes essentials recipes dealing with adding and optimizing CSS files.

Chapter 3, Custom Themes and Zen, focuses on starter themes, specifically Zen.

Chapter 4, Templating Basics, details how to customize page elements and content by overriding template files.

Chapter 5, Development and Debugging Tools, provides essential information on debugging and expediting development through the use of a number of tools.

Chapter 6, Advanced Templating, explores the PHPTemplate theme engine further and delves into using techniques such as variable manipulation and preprocess hooks to customize various theme elements.

Chapter 7, JavaScript in Themes, covers the use of JavaScript and jQuery in Drupal themes.

Chapter 8, Navigation, contains recipes which focus on theming navigational elements in a Drupal theme such as menus, breadcrumbs, pagers, and so on.

Chapter 9, Form Design, discusses the Drupal Forms API from a theming point of view.

Chapter 10, Customizing CCK, demonstrates how to theme CCK nodes and fields and also covers the use of customization of the ImageField and ImageCache modules, to display and style images to suit the theme.

Chapter 11, Views Theming, focuses on the Views module from a themer's perspective.

Chapter 12, Rapid Layouts with Panels, shows how to create complex layouts using the Panels module and demonstrates its use in conjunction with the CCK and Views modules.

What you need for this book

A standard Drupal 6 development site is all that is required to run through the recipes in this book. The system requirements for Drupal is available at `http://drupal.org/requirements`. Since this book deals with theming, it is assumed that this test site is already up and running.

Who this book is for

This book is written for Drupal developers who want to refresh the look and feel of their sites. If you are a Drupal site administrator who is looking to go beyond the basics and customize the presentational aspects of your Drupal site, then this book is for you. It assumes that readers are familiar with rudimentary PHP and acquainted with Drupal installation and general usage. Readers are also expected to have knowledge of CSS and XHTML.

Conventions

In this book, you will find a number of styles of text that distinguish between different kinds of information. Here are some examples of these styles, and an explanation of their meaning.

Code words in text are shown as follows: "$path denotes the path to the CSS file relative to the `base_path()`".

A block of code is set as follows:

```php
<?php

/**
 * Implementation of hook_init().
 */
function mysite_init()mysite_init() {
  // Display a message on every page load.
  drupal_set_message("Welcome to MySite!");
}
```

When we wish to draw your attention to a particular part of a code block, the relevant lines or items are set in bold:

```
stylesheets[all][] = css/html-reset.css
stylesheets[all][] = css/wireframes.css
stylesheets[all][] = css/layout-fixed.css
stylesheets[all][] = css/page-backgrounds.css
stylesheets[all][] = css/tabs.css
stylesheets[all][] = css/messages.css
```

New terms and **important words** are shown in bold. Words that you see on the screen, in menus or dialog boxes for example, appear in the text like this: "Click on the **Save configuration** button at the bottom of the page to ensure that any vestiges of the setting are also cleared from the database".

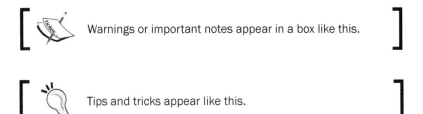

Warnings or important notes appear in a box like this.

Tips and tricks appear like this.

Reader feedback

Feedback from our readers is always welcome. Let us know what you think about this book—what you liked or may have disliked. Reader feedback is important for us to develop titles that you really get the most out of.

To send us general feedback, simply send an e-mail to feedback@packtpub.com, and mention the book title via the subject of your message.

If there is a book that you need and would like to see us publish, please send us a note in the **SUGGEST A TITLE** form on www.packtpub.com or e-mail suggest@packtpub.com.

If there is a topic that you have expertise in and you are interested in either writing or contributing to a book, see our author guide on www.packtpub.com/authors.

Customer support

Now that you are the proud owner of a Packt book, we have a number of things to help you to get the most from your purchase.

Downloading the example code for this book

You can download the example code files for all Packt books you have purchased from your account at http://www.PacktPub.com. If you purchased this book elsewhere, you can visit http://www.PacktPub.com/support and register to have the files e-mailed directly to you.

Errata

Although we have taken every care to ensure the accuracy of our content, mistakes do happen. If you find a mistake in one of our books—maybe a mistake in the text or the code—we would be grateful if you would report this to us. By doing so, you can save other readers from frustration and help us improve subsequent versions of this book. If you find any errata, please report them by visiting http://www.packtpub.com/support, selecting your book, clicking on the **errata submission form** link, and entering the details of your errata. Once your errata are verified, your submission will be accepted and the errata will be uploaded on our website, or added to any list of existing errata, under the Errata section of that title. Any existing errata can be viewed by selecting your title from http://www.packtpub.com/support.

Piracy

Piracy of copyright material on the Internet is an ongoing problem across all media. At Packt, we take the protection of our copyright and licenses very seriously. If you come across any illegal copies of our works, in any form, on the Internet, please provide us with the location address or website name immediately so that we can pursue a remedy.

Please contact us at copyright@packtpub.com with a link to the suspected pirated material.

We appreciate your help in protecting our authors, and our ability to bring you valuable content.

Questions

You can contact us at questions@packtpub.com if you are having a problem with any aspect of the book, and we will do our best to address it.

1
Drupal Theme Basics

We will be covering the following recipes in this chapter:

- Installing and enabling a theme
- Uploading a new logo
- Uploading a new favicon
- Adding a slogan to the theme
- Allowing users to choose from multiple themes
- Displaying a different theme for administration
- Adding an existing block to the theme
- Adding a custom block to the theme
- Displaying a block only on the front page
- Controlling block visibility based on user role
- Controlling block visibility based on node type

Introduction

Drupal is designed to separate logic from presentation with the former usually handled through the use of modules and the latter via themes. Although this separation is not absolute, it is distinct enough to facilitate quick and efficient customization and deployment of websites. This especially holds true when the site is developed in a team environment as it enables developers, designers, and content managers to work independently of each other.

Themes are synonymous with *skins* in other applications and control the look and feel of a website. Each theme can consist of a variety of files ranging from a `.info` configuration file which registers the theme with Drupal to `.tpl.php` template files accompanied by CSS, JavaScript, and other files that determine the layout and style of the content. Depending on the nature of the site and its requirements, developers can choose from the slew of themes available on `http://drupal.org` as contributed themes or, instead, decide to roll their own.

Contributed themes are, as the name suggests, themes which have been contributed by the Drupal community at large. They usually tend to be the designs that have been developed by a user for a site and then shared with the community, or designs from other packages or sites which have been ported over to Drupal. Consequently, while they are ready-to-wear, they are generic in nature and lack uniqueness. Furthermore, the quality of these themes vary significantly from one to the other with some being excellent and others well below par. Contributed themes are primarily used for sites which require rapid deployment or in hobby sites with basic requirements where uniqueness is not a factor.

Custom themes, on the other hand, are a necessity for sites with unique requirements in layout, usability, and design. While they are often built from the ground up, it is now established practice to use special *starter themes* as a base on which they can be extended.

Contributed themes can be accessed at `http://drupal.org/project/themes`. This page, by default, lists all available themes and provides filters, to narrow down on those which are compatible with Drupal 6, and sorting options to peruse contributions based on popularity, update status, and other criteria. More information about a particular theme can be accessed by clicking on its **Find out more** link.

Prior to choosing a contributed theme, there are a few considerations to keep in mind. Firstly, it is important to have a general idea of the layout required for the site with the chief concern usually being the column layout of the theme. Most themes support a three-column (with two sidebars and a content area) layout which also work as two-column layouts (one sidebar) if no content is added to one of the sidebars. The more exotic ones support four or more columns and are only really a viable option for special cases.

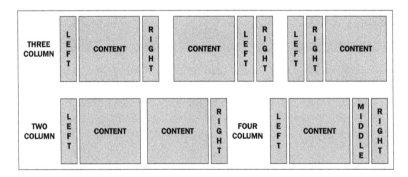

Secondly, while fewer themes nowadays are being laid out using tables, they are still around. Unless there is no other recourse, these should be avoided in favor of CSS layouts.

Next, check to see whether the theme is a **fixed-width** or a **fluid theme** or supports both types. Fixed-width themes, as the name suggests, maintain a predefined width irrespective of the user's screen resolution. As a result, the site has a consistent appearance. Fluid layouts, or liquid layouts as they are sometimes referred to, grow according to the user's screen size and consequently make better use of the available real estate. The question of which to use is generally decided on a case by case basis.

The Drupal theme system also supports the use of different **theme engines** to render the design. Each engine uses a different process by which the designer can interact with Drupal to implement a design. The **PHPTemplate** engine is built into Drupal and is by far the most popular of the ones available. The vast majority of contributed themes available are compatible with PHPTemplate. Nevertheless, it is prudent to check the specifications of the theme to ensure that it does not require a different theme engine. Contributed theme engines can, if necessary, be downloaded from `http://drupal.org/project/theme+engines`.

Every theme's project page usually provides screenshots and explicitly specifies layout and other useful information. A number of them also link to a demonstration page—as in the following screenshot—where the theme can be previewed and tested using different browsers, screen resolutions, and so on. A third-party site `http://themegarden.org`, which showcases various contributed themes, comes in very handy for the same reason.

Downloads			
Recommended releases			
Version	**Downloads**	**Date**	**Links**
6.x-3.0-beta1	Download (102.37 KB)	2010-May-04	Notes
Other releases			
Version	**Downloads**	**Date**	**Links**
6.x-2.0	Download (147.65 KB)	2009-Dec-28	Notes

- View all releases

Resources	**Development**
• Home page	• View pending patches
• Read documentation	• Browse the CVS repository
• Try out a demonstration	• View CVS messages
• Look at screenshots	• Report a security issue
• View usage statistics	
• View project translations	

Additionally, project pages customarily link to their CVS repositories where files within the theme can be viewed prior to downloading. It is also worth exploring the issue queue of a theme to see if bugs have been reported and are being addressed in a timely manner.

CVS is a tool used by Drupal developers to manage their code and control their releases. It is effectively a repository for modules, themes, and Drupal itself. More information on CVS is available at `http://drupal.org/handbook/cvs`.

Once the list of candidate themes has been narrowed down to a short list, the only way to test them further is to download and install them. The theme project page lists available downloads based on version and stability along with release notes which might be useful to glance through as well. Download the latest release recommended for Drupal 6. The recipes in this chapter will address the installation and configuration of a downloaded theme.

Installing and enabling a theme

This recipe will cover the steps required to install and enable a downloaded theme.

Getting ready

Downloaded themes are usually in `tar.gz` format. These files can be extracted using archive programs such as **7-Zip** (`http://www.7-zip.org`) as well as commercial packages such as **WinZip** (`http://www.winzip.com`) and **WinRAR** (`http://www.rarlabs.com`).

How to do it...

To install a theme, open Windows Explorer and navigate to the Drupal installation.

1. Browse to `sites/all` and create a sub-folder named `themes`.
2. Extract the downloaded theme into a sub-folder inside this folder. In other words, if the theme is called `mytheme`, the folder `sites/all/themes/mytheme` should contain all the files of the theme.

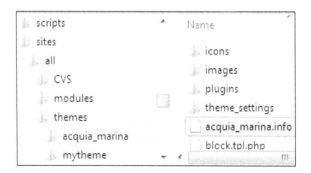

In the last screenshot, we see the Acquia Marina theme's installation folder situated within `sites/all/themes`. Themes also occasionally contain a `README.txt` file which provides documentation which is worth a read-through.

File structure options

In this recipe, we have chosen to use the folder `sites/all/themes/mytheme` to store our theme. By positioning our theme inside `sites/all`, we are stating that the theme is to be available to *all* sites using this Drupal installation. In other words, this enables multi-site setups to share modules and themes. In case we want to restrict access to the theme solely to one particular site, we would position its folder within `sites/foo.example.com/themes/` where `foo.example.com` is the site in question.

3. Access the Drupal site in a browser and navigate to `admin/build/themes` (**Home | Administer | Site building | Themes**).

4. The newly installed theme should now be listed on this page. Check the associated **Enabled** checkbox and **Default** radio button.

In the last screenshot, we can see that the contributed theme **Acquia Marina** has been enabled and is set to be the default theme for the site. Drupal comes packaged with six **core themes** including **Bluemarine** shown in the last screenshot.

Click on **Save configuration** to enable the new theme and also set it as the default theme for the site.

How it works...

Drupal scans folders within `sites/all/themes` and, in particular, looks for files with the extension `.info`. This file contains information about the theme such as its name, description, version compatibility, and so on. If the theme is compatible, it is listed on the theme administration page.

A site can have multiple themes enabled. Out of these, only one can be chosen as the default theme. The default theme is, as the name suggests, the primary theme for the website. When more than one theme has been enabled, users with the **select different theme** permission can optionally select one of the other available options as their personal theme.

There's more...

Drupal makes it easier for us to manage our site by following preset naming conventions when it comes to the folder structure of the site.

Folder structure

Themes do not necessarily have to be placed at the root of the `sites/all/themes` folder. For organizational purposes, it might be useful to create `sites/all/themes/contrib` and `sites/all/themes/custom`. This will allow us to differentiate between downloaded themes and custom themes.

 Since Drupal's *core* themes are located within the root `themes` folder, we might be led to believe that this might also be a good place to store our contributed or custom themes. While this will certainly work, it will prove to be a bad decision in the long run as it is never a good idea to mix core files with custom files. The chief reason for this separation is manageability—it is far easier to maintain and update Drupal when there is a clear distinction between the core installation, and contributed modules and themes.

Uploading a new logo

Most websites incorporate a logo into their design, usually accompanying the site name in the header. For example, the Drupal logo or "Druplicon" in the following screenshot represents the default logo displayed for every core theme that comes packaged with Drupal.

These logos tend to play an important role in the branding and identity of the site and are frequently an important facet in the overall design of the theme. This recipe details the steps involved in changing the logo displayed in a theme.

Getting ready

The new logo should be in a suitable format and should balance quality with size. The usual rule of thumb is as follows:

- **PNG**: For high quality images which contain transparencies.
- **JPEG**: For detailed photographic logos which do not involve transparencies.
- **GIF**: For simple line-art.

How to do it...

Adding a custom logo to a theme can be done using the following steps:

1. Navigate to `admin/build/themes` (**Home | Administer | Site building | Themes**).
2. Click on the **Configure** link next to the theme in question.
3. Look for the **Logo image settings** fieldset. Within, uncheck the **Use default logo** checkbox as we want to use a custom image.

4. Using the **Upload logo image** field, browse and select the logo file in the filesystem.
5. Finally, click on the **Save configuration** button below to upload and save the changes.

How it works...

The uploaded file is saved in the Drupal filesystem and the path to the logo is registered as a configuration setting in the database. During display, the theme uses this setting to embed the logo within the Drupal page. The following screenshot displays the Bluemarine core theme with its default logo replaced with a custom PNG.

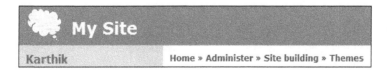

There's more...

Besides specifying the logo file via a theme's configuration page, there are other avenues which can also be pursued.

Directly linking to image files

Alternatively, instead of uploading the logo via Drupal, use the **Path to custom logo** textfield to point to an existing logo file on the server. A third option is to just place the logo file in the theme's folder and rename it as `logo.png`. Provided that the **Use the default logo** field is checked, the theme will automatically look for this file in its folder and use it as its logo.

Uploading a new favicon

This recipe details the steps involved in changing the **favicon** displayed with the theme. A favicon, dubbed as a **shortcut icon** in the Drupal interface, is an image which is particular to a site and is displayed in the address bar of the browser next to the site URL as well as the browser tab. It also makes its presence felt if the site is bookmarked in the browser as in the following screenshot:

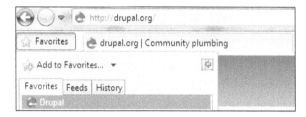

Getting ready

We are going to need the icon file to be added which is recommended to be of size 32x32 pixels or higher. An example icon file named `favicon.ico` can be seen in the `misc` folder in the Drupal installation.

How to do it...

Adding a custom favicon to the theme can be done by performing the following steps:

1. Navigate to `admin/build/themes` (**Home | Administer | Site building | Themes**).
2. Click on the **Configure** link next to the theme in question.
3. Look for the **Shortcut icon settings** fieldset.

4. Within, uncheck the **Use default shortcut icon** checkbox as we want to use a custom icon.

5. Using the **Upload icon image** field, browse and select the icon file in the filesystem.

6. Finally, click on the **Save configuration** button below to upload and save the changes.

How it works...

The uploaded file is saved in the Drupal filesystem and the path to the icon is registered as a theme setting in the database. When a page is being rendered, the Drupal theme system designates this `.ico` file as the favicon for the site.

In the following screenshot, we can see the logo image added in the previous recipe also being used as the basis for a favicon:

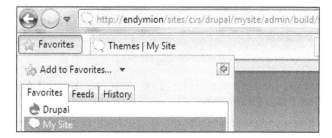

There's more...

Besides manually uploading the icon file via the theme's configuration page, other options exist to perform the same task.

Alternative methods

Alternatively, instead of uploading the icon file via Drupal, use the **Path to custom icon** textbox to point to the icon file on the server. A third option is to place the icon file in the theme's folder and rename it `favicon.ico`. Provided that the **Use the default shortcut icon** field is checked, the theme will automatically look for this file in its folder and use it as its favicon. Not specifying a favicon will result in the site using Drupal's default icon, **Druplicon**, instead.

 Other formats besides the ICO format are also supported by some, but not all browsers. More information is available at `http://en.wikipedia.org/wiki/Favicon#Browser_support`.

Adding a slogan to the theme

This recipe details the steps involved in adding a **slogan** to the theme. Site slogans are a common feature on most sites and are typically witty or involve clever wordplay. They are synonymous with catchphrases, tag-lines, mottoes, and so on.

Drupal offers a global setting to store the site slogan which is customarily displayed by themes near the site logo or site name, and is also regularly added to news feeds and site e-mails as part of the site's identity.

Getting ready

Think up a good slogan! This is the biggest stumbling block to getting this recipe right.

How to do it...

Adding a slogan to a theme involves the following steps:

1. Navigate to `admin/settings/site-information` (**Home | Administer | Site configuration | Site information**).

2. Locate the **Slogan** textfield and add the slogan here as shown in the following screenshot:

Site information

Name: *

My Site

The name of this website.

E-mail address: *

mysite@example.com

The *From* address in automated e-mails sent during registration and new password requests, prevent this e-mail being flagged as spam.)

Slogan:

Mysite's slogan is to be as witty as can be

Your site's motto, tag line, or catchphrase (often displayed alongside the title of the site).

Mission:

Mysite's mission is to be displayed prominently on the front page.

3. Click on the **Save configuration** button at the bottom of the page to save our changes.

4. Now, navigate to `admin/build/themes` (**Home | Administer | Site building | Themes**).

5. Click on the **Configure** tab at the top of the page.

   The resulting page should have multiple tabs: one titled Global settings which affects all themes and others representing each enabled theme. Configuration options under the **Global settings** tab serve as the site's default settings for all themes while equivalent settings within each theme's tab work as overrides for the global settings.

6. On the **Global settings** page, look for the **Site slogan** setting in the **Toggle display** section and ensure that it is checked.

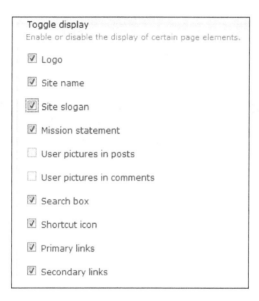

7. Click on the **Save configuration** button to save our changes.

 If any of the themes have overridden the global settings, then the **Site slogan** checkbox will also need to be checked in its respective theme tab.

How it works...

Drupal saves the provided slogan as a configuration setting in the database. The theme system makes this setting available as a variable to the theme which outputs it accordingly when the page is being rendered.

In the following screenshot, we can see that the slogan is enabled and is displayed below the logo and name of the site.

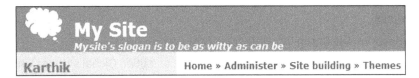

There's more...

Besides the site slogan, other site variables are also available on the theme configuration pages.

Similar settings

The Drupal **Site Information** page seen in this recipe also contains fields for other settings such as the site name, mission, and footer which are also similarly exposed by themes.

Allowing users to choose from multiple themes

This recipe details the steps involved in enabling users to choose which theme they wish to use when they are viewing the site. For example, users with accessibility issues might prefer to view the site using a high-contrast theme, or those viewing the site via monitors with low resolutions might prefer a theme which uses a fluid layout.

Drupal's flexible approach to themes includes the ability to allow theme-specific block arrangements. As a result, this allows us to, for example, have a separate theme for site contributors with, perhaps, an extra sidebar equipped with a contributor-specific block arrangement.

Getting ready

Since we are going to be working with multiple themes in this recipe, we will need at least two themes to have been enabled on the site. This can be done via the theme administration page at `admin/build/themes` (**Home | Administer | Site building | Themes**) as seen earlier in this chapter.

How to do it...

We can enable users to choose between the different themes which are available through the following steps:

1. Navigate to `admin/user/permissions` (**Home | Administer | Users | Permissions**).

2. Scroll down to the section titled **system module** dealing with system-level permissions.

3. Check the box labeled **Select different theme** for the **authenticated user** role.

4. Click on the **Save permissions** button to save our changes.

5. Now, visit the **My account** page at the path `user` and click on the **Edit** tab at the top.

6. Locate the newly available section titled **Theme configuration**.

7. Choose the preferred theme by selecting the associated radio button as in the following screenshot:

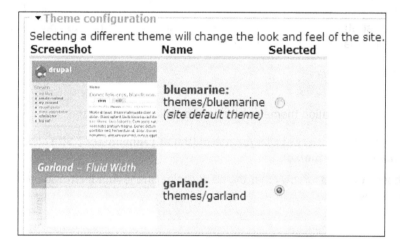

8. Click on the **Save** button at the bottom of the page to register our changes.

How it works...

Drupal saves the users' choice as a configuration setting in the database. When a page is to be displayed, Drupal notices this setting and themes the page using the specified theme instead of the site's default theme.

Displaying a different theme for administration

This recipe describes how to set up Drupal to use a different theme only for administration pages. This is a frequent requirement especially on brochure sites which have a limited number of regions where blocks can be placed, or have missing page elements such as breadcrumbs which reduces usability. Having a separate administration theme also comes in handy during custom theme design as the site could well be largely unusable during the initial stages of development. A stable administration interface will therefore ensure that administrative tasks can still be performed effortlessly until the new theme becomes ready.

Getting ready

Depending on the amount of real estate required, it will be worthwhile to put some thought into deciding on the right theme to use as the administration theme. Themes such as the aptly named **Administration theme** (`http://drupal.org/project/admin_theme`) and **RootCandy** (`http://drupal.org/project/rootcandy`) have been designed specifically with the administration pages in mind. That said, if the requirement is temporary, using a core theme such as Garland will usually suffice.

How to do it...

Specifying an administration theme can be done by following these steps:

1. Navigate to `admin/settings/admin` (**Home | Administer | Site configuration | Administration theme**).

2. Choose **Garland** (or any other theme of choice) in the **Administration theme** drop-down list.

Home » Administer » Site configuration

Administration theme

Administration theme:

Garland   ▾

Choose which theme the administration pages should display in. If you choose "System default" the administration pages will use the same theme as the rest of the site.

☐ Use administration theme for content editing
Use the administration theme when editing existing posts or creating new ones.

[Save configuration]   [Reset to defaults]

In situations where only administrators have permissions to add and edit content, it might be handy to also check the **Use administration theme for content editing** checkbox seen in the previous screenshot.

3. Click on the **Save configuration** button to save our changes in the database.

Viewing an administration page should confirm that the specified administration theme is being used in preference to the default theme.

How it works...

Every time a page is displayed, Drupal checks to see if the URL of the page begins with `admin`. If it does, and if we have specified an administration theme, Drupal overrides the default theme being used with the specified theme.

 Since the administration theme is something of a special case, Drupal does not require the theme to be enabled for it to be available as an option.

Adding an existing block to the theme

Drupal's page layout is customarily divided into a content area and a number of **regions** which are laid out differently from theme to theme. For example, a theme could have a region named **Left sidebar** and **Right sidebar** which will be displayed to the left and right-hand side of the content respectively. Regions serve as containers for **blocks**.

Blocks are self-contained elements which are located within regions and typically contain information or functionality which is repeated consistently across multiple pages. They can contain contextual information which complements the actual content of a page, such as a block which outputs information about the author of the node currently being displayed, or static information, such as a login form block or a block which displays advertisements.

This recipe details the steps involved in adding an existing block to a region of a theme.

Getting ready

For this example, we will be adding a **Who's online** block to the **left sidebar** region (assuming that the theme has declared such a region). The position of a block both in terms of region as well as its weight (which determines its order among other blocks in the same region) can prove to be very important in terms of usability and exposure.

How to do it...

The **Who's online** block can be added by following these steps:

1. Navigate to `admin/build/block` (**Home | Administer | Site building | Blocks**).

2. If more than one theme is enabled on the site, choose the appropriate tab at the top of the page.

3. Look for the **Who's online** block under the **Disabled** section.

4. Click on the cross-hairs icon to its left and drag the block to the **Left sidebar** region.

   Alternatively, we could have simply chosen the **Left sidebar** in the **Region** dropdown and then used the cross-hairs to order the block within the region. This is the quicker option when there are a lot of blocks and regions to deal with on this page.

5. Click on the **Save blocks** button at the bottom of the page to save our changes.

The block should now be visible in the left sidebar as can be seen with the Garland theme as follows:

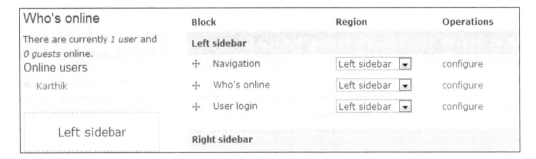

How it works...

Drupal maintains a table named `blocks` in its database which contains a list of all the blocks exposed by the modules in its installation. By moving the **Who's online** block to the **Left sidebar** region, we are effectively just manipulating this table in the database. When a page is displayed, Drupal uses this table to determine the status and location of each block for the current theme and the theme system positions them accordingly.

There's more...

Block layouts are particular to each theme and can therefore be customized accordingly.

Theme-specific block layouts

Seeing as to how each theme is laid out differently with its own set of regions, it stands to reason that a block can also be positioned in different regions for different themes. For example, the **Who's online** block seen in this recipe can be positioned in the **Left sidebar** region of the Garland theme and the **Right sidebar** of another theme such as Bluemarine. Taking this idea further, we can also have the block enabled only for Garland and not for Bluemarine.

The block layout for each theme can be managed by clicking on the appropriate theme tab at the top of the block management page at `admin/build/block` (**Home | Administer | Site building | Blocks**). The page will be rendered using the theme being configured, thereby providing a preview of the theme and its regions.

Adding a custom block to the theme

This recipe details the steps involved in adding a block with custom content to the theme. Drupal blocks can either be declared using a module or, as we are doing here, added manually via the block administration interface.

Getting ready

For this recipe, we will be adding a simple welcome message in a custom block within a predetermined region. As with standard blocks, position matters!

How to do it...

The following procedure outlines the steps required to add a custom block to a theme:

1. Navigate to `admin/build/block` (**Home | Administer | Site building | Blocks**).
2. Click on the **Add block** tab at the top of the page.
3. In the **Block specific settings** fieldset, type **Welcome message** in the **Block description** text field.

   This description field comes in handy on the Block administration page when trying to differentiate between blocks with identical titles, or as is frequently the case, no titles.

4. Next, if the block requires a title to be displayed above its content, add one via the **Block title** textfield. In this case, we do not need one as we are just looking to display a welcome message.

5. Enter the following text into the **Block body** textarea: **Welcome to Mysite. Enjoy your stay!**.

Similar to most other textareas in Drupal, a linked **Input format** should be available to filter the content appropriately.

6. Finally, click on **Save block** to create the block.

How it works...

Just as with standard blocks, Drupal maintains a table named `boxes` which tracks all custom blocks including their content and input format. Once a custom block is enabled, it is added to the `blocks` table and tracked as if it was a standard block.

When created, a custom block appears in the block list and can be treated just like any other block. It can be dragged around different regions, have its visibility settings controlled, and so on. The following screenshot displays our newly created welcome block:

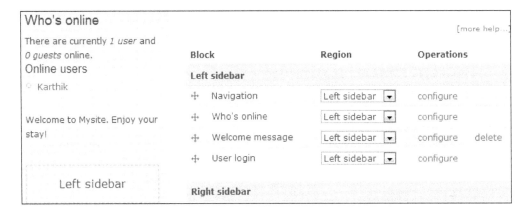

 An easy way to identify custom blocks on the block management page is by their telltale **delete** links. Only custom blocks feature a delete option.

There's more...

Custom blocks are useful in rendering more than just simple text strings.

Doing more with custom blocks

Custom blocks can be very handy to not only add visible content, but also to execute short code snippets on specific pages, provided the appropriate input format has been selected. For example, we could embed some custom JavaScript required only for a few specific page nodes, by adding it to a custom block—equipped with a suitable input format—which is set to be displayed only with the aforementioned page nodes.

That said, if a more optimal solution is available—such as using a module to hold our code—then it should be pursued instead of inserting code into blocks and thereby into the database.

Displaying a block only on the front page

This recipe details the steps involved in displaying a block only on a certain page, which in this case, is the front page. We will be displaying the welcome message block created in the previous recipe as an example.

Getting ready

The front page is a special case on most sites as it usually showcases the rest of the site. Manipulating block visibility for front page blocks is a frequent requirement and, in our case, we are going to ensure that the welcome message block is only going to be displayed on the front page and nowhere else.

How to do it...

Block visibility is controlled from the block's configuration page as follows:

1. Navigate to `admin/build/block` (**Home | Administer | Site building | Blocks**).

2. Locate the block which needs to be configured—the `Welcome message` block—and click on the **Configure** link next to it.

3. On the configuration page, scroll down to the **Page specific visibility settings** section and select the **Show on only the listed pages** radio button.

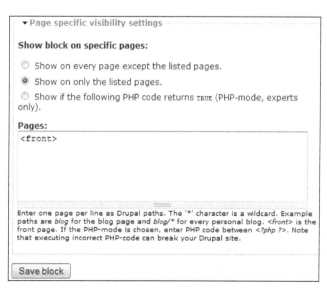

4. Further down in the textarea titled **Pages**, add the word `<front>`.

5. Click on the **Save block** button at the bottom of the page to save the changes.

How it works...

Whenever a block is to be displayed, Drupal checks to see if we have any visibility settings applied to it. In this case, we have **Show on only the listed pages** switched on. As a result, Drupal checks the **Pages** textarea to see which pages have been listed. The use of the `<front>` keyword, which is a special indicator that represents the front page of the site, tells Drupal that unless this is the root of the site, this block should not be displayed.

This is all done before the content of the block is processed by Drupal thereby improving performance and making this method cleaner and more efficient than hiding the block using CSS or elsewhere in the theme.

There's more...

Drupal offers a number of page-matching options to further help refine when and where we display our blocks.

Multiple pages

Multiple pages can be specified in the **Pages** textarea. For example, if the block is to be displayed on the front page and on user pages only, the list would be the following:

```
<front>
user/*
```

Drupal will now compare the path of the page against each entry in this list and decide to display the block only if there is a match.

Wildcards

The use of the asterisk wildcard in `user/*` states that the match should be performed against all paths beginning with `user`. This ensures that the block is displayed for all pages within every user's **My account** section.

Matching against URL aliases

Drupal's **Path** module allows users to specify aliases for nodes and system paths. While this might lead to the conundrum of which paths to use while specifying a block's page-visibility settings, the Block module's page-matching code intelligently compares against both possibilities. For example, consider the following table which specifies the internal paths and corresponding aliases for three nodes:

Internal path	URL alias
node/1	products/foo
node/13	products/bar
node/22	products/baz

If we wanted to match against all three nodes, we could specify the three node paths directly:

- node/1
- node/13
- node/22

Or, we could specify the three aliases as follows:

- products/foo
- products/bar
- products/baz

Alternatively, we could simply use the aliases with a wildcard:

> products/*

Exclusive display

This recipe can also be similarly applied to display a block on all pages but the front page. This involves choosing the **Show on every page except the listed pages** option in the **Page specific visibility settings** section.

Controlling block visibility based on user role

This recipe details the steps involved in toggling block visibility based on which type of user is viewing the page. For example, a block displaying advertisements might only need to be visible for anonymous users and not for authenticated users.

Getting ready

For this recipe, we will be configuring the welcome message block which we created in an earlier recipe in this chapter, to only be visible to authenticated users.

How to do it...

Controlling block visibility is handled from the block administration pages as outlined in the following:

1. Navigate to `admin/build/block` (**Home | Administer | Site building | Blocks**).
2. Locate the block which needs to be configured—the `Welcome message` block—and click on the **Configure** link next to it.
3. On the configure screen, scroll down to **Role specific visibility settings**.
4. Check the box corresponding to the **authenticated user** role which should have access to the block.

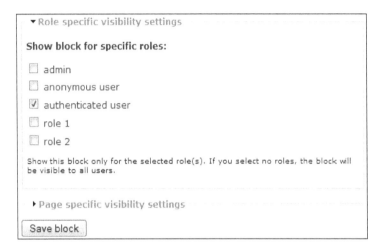

5. Click on the **Save block** button at the bottom of the page to save the changes.

How it works...

Drupal maintains a table named `block_roles` which keeps track of role-specific settings for all blocks. Changes made to role settings on the block configuration page are stored in this table. When an anonymous user now visits the site, Drupal will not display the `Welcome message` block.

Controlling block visibility based on node type

Thus far in this chapter, we have looked at controlling block visibility based on the path of the page and the role of the user. In this recipe, we will look to configure a block to be displayed based on the node type of the content on the page.

Getting ready

We will be configuring the **Recent comments** block—which is provided by the **Comment** module—to only be visible for the `story` and `blog` node types. While the `story` type is enabled by default, the `blog` type is created only upon enabling the **Blog** module from the module administration page at `admin/build/modules` (**Home | Administer | Site building | Modules**).

It is assumed that both the Blog and Comment modules have been enabled, and sample nodes and associated comments have been created.

How to do it...

Block visibility can be configured from the block's configuration page as per the following steps:

1. Navigate to `admin/build/block` (**Home | Administer | Site building | Blocks**).

2. Look for the block which needs to be configured—**Recent Comments**—and click on the **Configure** link next to it.

3. Navigate down to the **Page specific visibility settings** section.

4. Select **Show if the following PHP code returns TRUE** and enter the following code in the **Pages** textarea below:

```php
<?php
  // Array of allowed types.
  $types = array('blog', 'story');

  // Check if the current page is a node.
  if ((arg(0) == 'node') && is_numeric(arg(1))) {
    $node = node_load(arg(1));
    return in_array($node->type, $types);
  }
?>
```

5. Click on the **Save block** button to save the changes.

6. Back on the block administration page, ensure that the block has been enabled and added to one of the current theme's available regions such as the left or right sidebar.

How it works...

Since we have chosen to control block visibility using PHP, Drupal evaluates the code within the **Pages** text area and only displays the block if it returns the value `TRUE`.

The variable `$types` contains the list of allowed node types. This list is populated with the *internal* names of each node type which can be accessed via the **Content types** page at `admin/content/types` (**Home | Administer | Content | Content types**).

Name	Type	Description	Operations
Blog entry	blog	A *blog entry* is a single post to an online journal, or *blog*.	edit
Company	company	A company for inclusion in the company registry.	edit delete
Page	page	A *page*, similar in form to a *story*, is a simple method for creating and displaying information that rarely changes, such as an "About us" section of a website. By default, a *page* entry does not allow visitor comments and is not featured on the site's initial home page.	edit delete
Product	product		edit delete
Story	story	A *story*, similar in form to a *page*, is ideal for creating and displaying content that informs or engages website visitors. Press releases, site announcements, and informal blog-like entries may all be created with a *story* entry. By default, a *story* entry is automatically featured on the site's initial home page, and provides the ability to post comments.	edit delete
» Add a new content type			

In the previous screenshot, the internal names of each type are listed under the column titled **Type**.

Since blocks are not restricted to only be visible on node pages, we need to ascertain if the page that is currently being viewed is a node page. We do this by checking the path to see if it matches the pattern `node/node-id`. In other words, we only consider displaying the block if the path involves the word node followed by the node ID, an integer.

Once we have ensured that we are viewing a node, we need to get Drupal to load the node using the `node_load()` function so that we can check if its type matches one of the types that we have allowed.

If the type of the node being viewed is in this list of allowed types, then the `in_array()` call returns `TRUE` and the block is displayed. Else, it returns `FALSE` which leads to the block not being displayed.

Good practice

Always add comments to code. If the code snippet has been taken from a website or a book, add a comment mentioning the URL or page number for future reference.

2
Beyond the Basics

We will be covering the following recipes in this chapter:

- ► Understanding the anatomy of a theme
- ► Creating a sub-theme based on a core theme
- ► Overriding base theme elements in a sub-theme
- ► Changing the screenshot image of a theme
- ► Including a CSS file in a theme
- ► Enabling CSS optimization
- ► Creating the mysite module to hold our tweaks
- ► Adding a CSS file from a module
- ► Displaying a different theme for each day of the week
- ► Creating a fresh look using the color module

Introduction

One of the more prevalent adages with respect to Drupal development and theming is:

> *Do not hack core!*

Modules, themes, and other files which come with a stock Drupal installation should never be edited directly. In other words, we really should not need to modify anything outside the `sites` folder which is designed to contain all our changes and customizations. The reasoning behind this is that most, if not all, aspects of core are accessible and modifiable through a clean and non-invasive process using Drupal's APIs. Therefore, hacking core modules and themes to get things done is almost always unnecessary and ill-advised.

Another reason why *directly* editing core modules and themes, or for that matter, even contributed modules and themes, is that whenever an upgrade of Drupal or said modules and themes takes place, we will very likely be overwriting the changes we have made, or at the very least, make the upgrade a trying exercise.

With respect to themes, let us take the example of a core theme such as Garland. As previously mentioned, it is a poor practice to edit the theme directly. The Drupal way is to extend the existing core theme using a sub-theme which, by default, is more or less an identical copy. This sub-theme can then be extended further and customized by overriding elements of the base theme,such as its stylesheets, template files, template variables, and so on.

In this chapter, we will look at the building blocks of a basic theme and then familiarize ourselves with the concept of the sub-theme and the various techniques available to extend, override and modify it according to our requirements.

Understanding the anatomy of a theme

Drupal themes can consist of a multitude of files each with its own purpose, format, and syntax. This recipe will introduce each of these types with an explanation of what they do.

Getting ready

It will be useful to navigate to the Garland folder at `themes/garland` to browse and view the files inside a typical, fully featured theme. Garland also uses the **PHPTemplate theming engine** which is the most commonly used and recommended engine across Drupal's core and contributed themes.

How to do it...

The following table outlines the types of files typically found inside a theme's folder and the naming conventions to be followed for some of them.

Type	Mandatory?	Description
`mytheme.info`	Yes	Configuration file which provides information to Drupal about a theme named mytheme.
`page.tpl.php`	Yes	A template file which determines the layout of all Drupal pages.
`node.tpl.php`	No	A template file which determines the layout of a node inside a Drupal page.
`block.tpl.php`	No	A template file which determines the layout of a block.
`*.tpl.php`	No	Other template files which allow the customization and styling of themable aspects of Drupal.

Type	Mandatory?	Description
style.css	No	CSS stylesheet—if this file exists, it will be automatically included in the theme.
script.js	No	Javascript file—if this file exists, it will be automatically included in the theme.
*.js	No	Other Javascript files which will need to be explicitly included in the .info file.
favicon.ico	No	Shortcut icon—if this file exists, it will be automatically included in the theme unless overridden from within Drupal.
logo.png	No	Site logo—if this file exists, it will be automatically included in the theme unless overridden from within Drupal.
screenshot.png	No	Theme preview image—if this file exists, it will be automatically included in the theme.
template.php	No	PHPTemplate master file where some of the more complicated and powerful tweaks and overrides occur.

Perusing the contents of each of the available files will prove very useful as we go along developing our theme.

How it works...

When a theme is added, Drupal first parses its .info file. This file, as its extension suggests, provides information about the theme such as its name, Drupal version compatibility, regions declared, CSS stylesheets used, JavaScript files included, and so on. In other words, Drupal uses it to find out the configuration and features of a theme.

The .info file also specifies the theming engine being used by the theme which, by default, is PHPTemplate. Theme engines allow theme developers to communicate with Drupal using a simpler and more convenient interface commonly via template files. A number of them also introduce their own language formats for use in these template files.

Template files in PHPTemplate themes are those that use the .tpl.php extension. Unlike other engines, these files just use PHP and HTML and do not rely on any special markup languages.

There's more...

Other theme engines besides PHPTemplate are also available. However, only a handful of themes in Drupal's contribution repository rely on them.

Other theme engine types

The PHPTemplate engine is the most widely prevalent theming engine used in the Drupal ecosystem and is a part of the Drupal core package. Themes using other engines such as Smarty or Xtemplate are rare and will be structured quite differently. A list of engines can be found at `http://drupal.org/project/Theme+engines`.

Engine-less theme

The Chameleon theme which is a part of core is a theme which does not use a templating engine and relies on straight PHP to get things done.

Creating a sub-theme based on a core theme

This recipe details the steps involved in creating a sub-theme of an existing core theme.

Getting ready

Create a folder named `mytheme` inside `sites/all/themes`. This name is usually also the name of the new theme and it is best to keep things uncomplicated by not using spaces and special characters. While `mytheme` is suitable for the purpose of this recipe, it will be a good idea to give the theme a unique and pertinent name based on its design and use. It is also important to ensure that there are no name-conflicts with other existing core or contributed themes.

How to do it...

A sub-theme of a core theme can be created through the following procedure:

1. Create a file named `mytheme.info` inside the `mytheme` folder.

2. Edit this new file and add the following code inside it:

```
name = Mytheme
description = My new sub-theme (CSS, phptemplate, 3-col)
base theme = garland
core = 6.x
```

```
engine = phptemplate
stylesheets[all][] = mytheme.css
```

 It is useful to add an informative `description` field as it will be visible in the theme administration page. Specifying the key characteristics of the theme can save time and effort as the administrator gets a quick overview of the design.

3. Save the file.

4. Create an empty CSS file named `mytheme.css` inside the `mytheme` folder.

5. Next, visit `admin/build/themes` (**Home | Administer | Site building | Themes**) to check if our new theme is available.

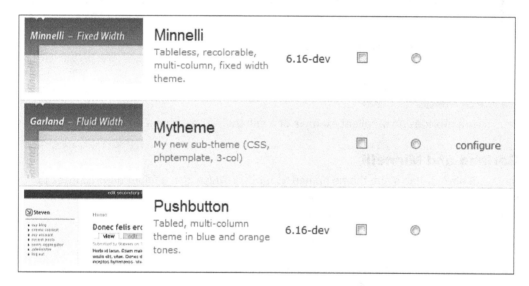

As the preceding screenshot attests, the theme administration page should now include our new theme—**Mytheme**. Enabling it should confirm that it is more or less identical to Garland and can now be extended further as per our requirements.

How it works...

Drupal uses the `.info` file to learn about our new sub-theme. The `name` and `description` variables, rather unsurprisingly, represent the name of the theme and a description that customarily includes details about the layout of the theme.

The `base theme` variable denotes the parent theme which our sub-theme is based on. By using this variable, we are informing Drupal that it should use the layout and styling of the base theme—in this case `Garland`—unless we indicate otherwise. This process is commonly referred to as **overriding** the base theme.

Finally, the `core` variable denotes the compatibility of our theme with Drupal 6, while `engine` indicates that the theme uses PHPTemplate as its templating engine. PHPTemplate is the most widely used system. Other engines, which include **Smarty, PHPTal**, and **Xtemplate**, are seldom used and themes using them are few and far between.

The `stylesheets` variable declares the CSS stylesheets to be included with the theme. When it comes to sub-themes, the stylesheets of base themes are automatically included unless explicitly overridden. However, due to a quirk in Drupal's theming system, base theme stylesheets are not inherited by the sub-theme unless the latter declares at least one stylesheet of its own. We have worked around this by including an empty stylesheet named `mytheme.css`.

There's more...

Drupal core provides an excellent example of a sub-theme based on a core theme.

Garland and Minnelli

`Garland` already has a sub-theme named `Minnelli` which is in a folder titled `minnelli` inside `themes/garland`. The difference between the two is that Garland uses a fluid layout while Minnelli is a fixed-width version of the same theme.

Chaining

Sub-themes can be **chained**, if necessary. For example, our `mytheme` could have used `Minnelli` as the base theme even though it is a sub-theme itself.

Overriding base theme elements in a sub-theme

This recipe details the steps involved in overriding a base theme template file. We will be restructuring the layout of a Drupal node by modifying the `node.tpl.php` template.

Getting ready

We will be using the `mytheme` sub-theme which was created in the previous recipe.

How to do it...

As we are dealing with a sub-theme here, it is by default relying on the template files of its base theme. To override the base file used to theme the layout of a node, copy the `node.tpl.php` file from the base theme's folder—`themes/garland`—to the `sites/themes/mytheme` folder. Opening the new file in an editor should bring up something similar to the following:

```php
<?php
// $Id: node.tpl.php,v 1.5 2007/10/11 09:51:29 goba Exp $
?>
<div id="node-<?php print $node->nid; ?>" class="node<?php if
($sticky) { print ' sticky'; } ?><?php if (!$status) { print ' node-
unpublished'; } ?>">

<?php print $picture ?>

<?php if ($page == 0): ?>
  <h2><a href="<?php print $node_url ?>" title="<?php print $title
?>"><?php print $title ?></a></h2>
<?php endif; ?>

  <?php if ($submitted): ?>
    <span class="submitted"><?php print $submitted; ?></span>
  <?php endif; ?>

  <div class="content clear-block">
    <?php print $content ?>
  </div>

  <div class="clear-block">
    <div class="meta">
    <?php if ($taxonomy): ?>
      <div class="terms"><?php print $terms ?></div>
    <?php endif;?>
    </div>

    <?php if ($links): ?>
      <div class="links"><?php print $links; ?></div>
    <?php endif; ?>
  </div>

</div>
```

The highlighted lines in the preceding code excerpt indicate the code we are looking to modify. To elaborate, we are going to move the *taxonomy terms* DIV from the bottom to a position further above, right next to the *submitted* DIV. Doing so will result in the `node.tpl.php` file now looking like this:

```php
<?php
// $Id: node.tpl.php,v 1.5 2007/10/11 09:51:29 goba Exp $
?>
<div id="node-<?php print $node->nid; ?>" class="node<?php if
($sticky) { print ' sticky'; } ?><?php if (!$status) { print ' node-
unpublished'; } ?>">

<?php print $picture ?>

<?php if ($page == 0): ?>
  <h2><a href="<?php print $node_url ?>" title="<?php print $title
?>"><?php print $title ?></a></h2>
<?php endif; ?>

  <?php if ($submitted): ?>
    <span class="submitted"><?php print $submitted; ?></span>
  <?php endif; ?>

  <?php if ($taxonomy): ?>
    <div class="terms"><?php print $terms ?></div>
  <?php endif;?>

  <div class="content clear-block">
    <?php print $content ?>
  </div>
  <div class="clear-block">
    <?php if ($links): ?>
      <div class="links"><?php print $links; ?></div>
    <?php endif; ?>
  </div>
</div>
```

Once this has been done, save the file and exit the editor. As we have made changes to the template system, we will need to rebuild the theme registry, or as is recommended throughout this book, simply clear the entire Drupal cache.

How it works...

For performance purposes, Drupal maintains a registry of all the stylesheets which have been included, the template files which are available, the theme functions which have been declared, and so on. As our theme initially had no `node.tpl.php` file in the `mytheme` folder, Drupal fell back to the `node.tpl.php` file of the base theme which, in this case, is `Garland`. However, once we added one to the `mytheme` folder, we needed to rebuild this registry so that Drupal became aware of our changes. Once this was done, Drupal used the updated `node.tpl.php` file the next time a node was displayed.

The following screenshots provide a before and after comparison of an example node:

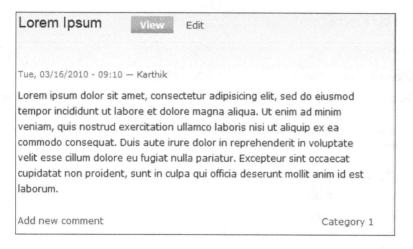

In the following screenshot, we can see our modified template file in action as the position of the taxonomy term **Category 1** has moved from the bottom to the top of the node.

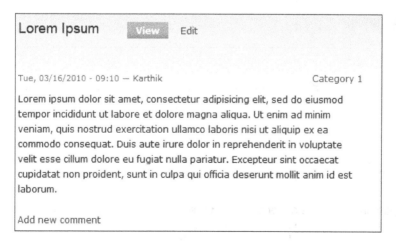

There's more...

The non-invasive technique of extending base themes using sub-themes allows for smooth upgrades.

Clean upgrades

If we had modified the `node.tpl.php` file inside Garland, the next time our Drupal installation is upgraded, we would have very likely forgotten about our changes and overwritten them during the upgrade process. By using a sub-theme, we can now upgrade Drupal without any fear of losing any changes we have made.

Another positive is that if bugs have been fixed in Garland, they will seamlessly propagate downriver to our sub-theme.

Changing the screenshot image of a theme

This recipe details the steps involved in changing the screenshot image associated with a theme. This image provides the user with a preview of what the site will look like when the theme is enabled. This is normally only required when we are working with a sub-theme or a custom theme.

Getting ready

Once the theme is just about ready to go, visit the front page of the site to take the screenshot. Since we are providing a snapshot of the theme, temporarily swap the name of the site with the name of the theme. It might also be useful to prepare some example content for display on the front page to obtain an accurate representation of the style and layout of our theme.

How to do it...

Adding a screenshot for our theme can be done via the following steps:

1. On the front page, press *ALT + Print Screen* to take a screenshot of the active window.

    Mac users can use *Command + Shift + 3* while Linux users should be able to bring up the screenshot utility relevant to their distribution by pressing *Print Screen*.

2. Open up a graphics editor and paste the screenshot within.

3. Make a wide selection of the theme incorporating different elements such as the position of the logo, breadcrumb, fonts, node styles, and so on.

4. Crop and resize to 150x90 pixels which is the standard size for theme screenshots.

5. Save the image as a PNG file named `screenshot.png`.

6. Finally, copy the file to the theme's folder.

Visiting `admin/build/themes` (**Home | Administer | Site building | Themes**) should confirm that `screenshot.png` is being used to represent our theme.

How it works...

Drupal automatically looks for a file named `screenshot.png` in the theme's folder and, if found, includes that image as a preview of the theme on the theme management page.

There's more...

Each theme's `.info` file provides the syntax required to specify many of the theme's configuration settings. This also includes nominating the screenshot file to be used.

Using the .info file

The screenshot image can also be specified in the theme's `.info` file using the following syntax:

```
screenshot = mytheme.png
```

where `mytheme.png` is the name of the screenshot file.

Including a CSS file in a theme

This recipe details the steps involved in adding a CSS file to the theme via its `.info` file. In this case, we will be adding a CSS file to the mytheme sub-theme which we created earlier in this chapter.

Getting ready

Create a CSS file inside the theme's folder named `mytheme.css` and add the following example rule to it:

```
* {
  color: #996633 !important;
}
```

This rule should override and change the color of all text on the page to a brownish hue.

How to do it...

Adding a CSS file to a theme is best accomplished via its `.info` file. Navigate to the theme's folder at `sites/all/themes/mytheme` and open the `mytheme.info` file in an editor. Add the following line to this file to include our CSS:

```
stylesheets[all][] = mytheme.css
```

> If the CSS file is stored along with other stylesheets in a sub-folder named `css`, the syntax would include the relative path to the file as follows: `stylesheets[all][] = css/mytheme.css`.

Once done, save the file and exit the editor. Since we have modified the `.info` file and introduced a new file, our changes will not take effect until the theme registry is rebuilt. Therefore, clear the Drupal cache and view the site to confirm that our new stylesheet has been included correctly. The theme should now display all text in brown.

How it works...

Drupal checks the `.info` file and notes that we have declared stylesheets using the `stylesheets` variable. The syntax of this variable is similar to that of an array in PHP. The `all` index in the syntax represents the media type as used in CSS declarations.

The next screenshot displays a section of the source code of a page which confirms the inclusion of the new stylesheet, `mytheme.css`. We can also see that our sub-theme is including the stylesheets declared by its base theme—Garland—as well as its own stylesheets.

```
<link href="/mysite/modules/node/node.css?e" rel="stylesheet" type="text/css" media="all"/>
<link href="/mysite/modules/system/defaults.css?e" rel="stylesheet" type="text/css" media="all"/>
<link href="/mysite/modules/system/system.css?e" rel="stylesheet" type="text/css" media="all"/>
<link href="/mysite/modules/system/system-menus.css?e" rel="stylesheet" type="text/css" media="all"/>
<link href="/mysite/modules/user/user.css?e" rel="stylesheet" type="text/css" media="all"/>
<link href="/mysite/themes/garland/style.css?e" rel="stylesheet" type="text/css" media="all"/>
<link href="/mysite/sites/all/themes/mytheme/mytheme.css?e" rel="stylesheet" type="text/css" media="all"/>
<link href="/mysite/themes/garland/print.css?e" rel="stylesheet" type="text/css" media="print"/>
```

In the preceding screenshot, we can see that Drupal references each stylesheet along with a query string. For example, `mytheme.css` is included as `mytheme.css?e`. This rather quirky suffix is a trick used by Drupal to ensure that browsers do not use stale copies of a cached CSS file while rendering our site.

We can test this by clearing the Drupal cache and viewing the source code once again. Now, our stylesheets should have a different suffix— perhaps, something like `mytheme.css?A`—thereby tricking browsers into believing that these are different files and using them instead of their cached copies.

There's more...

One of the advantages of using a sub-theme is that we can easily override elements of the base theme. This includes stylesheets as well.

Overriding the base theme's stylesheet

If the base theme includes a stylesheet named `layout.css`, adding a stylesheet of the same name in the sub-theme will override the base theme's stylesheet. In other words, Drupal will include the sub-theme's stylesheet instead of that of the base theme.

Enabling CSS optimization

CSS optimization in Drupal is accomplished through two steps—aggregation and compression. This optimization provides a significant boost to performance both on the server as well as for the user. This recipe details the steps to be performed to enable this feature in Drupal.

Getting ready

CSS optimization is a requirement only when a site is ready to go live. Until such time, it is recommended that it be left switched off as CSS changes during development will not take effect unless the Drupal cache is cleared.

How to do it...

Optimization and other performance-related features are sequestered within `admin/ settings/performance` (**Home | Administer | Site configuration | Performance**). This performance configuration page should have a section titled **Bandwidth optimizations** which should contain options for CSS and Javascript optimization. Look for the setting named **Optimize CSS files** and set it to **Enabled** as in the following screenshot:

Bandwidth optimizations

Drupal can automatically optimize external resources like CSS and JavaScript, which can reduce both the size and number of requests made to your website. CSS files can be aggregated and compressed into a single file, while JavaScript files are aggregated (but not compressed). These optional optimizations may reduce server load, bandwidth requirements, and page loading times.

These options are disabled if you have not set up your files directory, or if your download method is set to private.

Optimize CSS files:

◯ Disabled

◉ Enabled

This option can interfere with theme development and should only be enabled in a production environment.

Public File system

As the screenshot states, the optimized CSS file is cached using Drupal's file system which needs to be set to public to ensure that the user's browser can access and download it. Therefore, it is necessary to set **Download method** of the Drupal file system to **Public**. This can be done via `admin/settings/file-system` (**Home | Administer | Site configuration | File system**).

Once done, click on the **Save configuration** button at the bottom of the page to save our changes.

How it works...

Aggregation involves the collating and joining of multiple CSS files into a single stylesheet, while compression reduces the resulting file to a smaller size by trimming out unnecessary elements such as whitespace. The former helps in reducing the number of files that the server has to load and serve. The latter saves on bandwidth and time.

```
<link href="/mysite/modules/node/node.css?e" rel="stylesheet" type="text/css" media="all"/>
<link href="/mysite/modules/system/admin.css?e" rel="stylesheet" type="text/css" media="all"/>
<link href="/mysite/modules/system/defaults.css?e" rel="stylesheet" type="text/css" media="all"/>
<link href="/mysite/modules/system/system.css?e" rel="stylesheet" type="text/css" media="all"/>
<link href="/mysite/modules/system/system-menus.css?e" rel="stylesheet" type="text/css" media="all"/>
<link href="/mysite/modules/user/user.css?e" rel="stylesheet" type="text/css" media="all"/>
<link href="/mysite/themes/garland/style.css?e" rel="stylesheet" type="text/css" media="all"/>
<link href="/mysite/themes/garland/print.css?e" rel="stylesheet" type="text/css" media="print"/>
```

The previous and following screenshots demonstrate CSS optimization at work. The previous screenshot is a snippet of the HTML source of a Drupal page running on a stock Garland theme. As displayed, this involves the server performing look-ups and serving eight separate CSS files—seven for `all` media types and a `print` stylesheet—for each and every page served. If this is extrapolated to sites of greater complexity, the number of files and, consequently, the server and bandwidth load, begin to take on significant proportions and can seriously impact performance.

```
<link href="/mysite/sites/default/files/css/css_88b7141151b02488dea23fb3f2832c0c.css" rel="stylesheet" type="text/css" media="all"/>
<link href="/mysite/sites/default/files/css/css_3161b4ddf57e420d3017ffc42ce58eb6.css" rel="stylesheet" type="text/css" media="print"/>
```

The preceding screenshot is of the same page as before with one difference—CSS optimization is now turned on. The number of CSS files has now been reduced to only two—one for `all` media types and the other being the `print` media type. These stylesheets are stored in the `files` folder and are cached copies. As a result, each page load now only involves the webserver serving two files instead of the previous eight.

There's more...

CSS optimization and other performance improvements should be used with care.

When to use it

CSS optimization is only necessary to improve performance on production sites. Enabling it beforehand will only hinder theme development.

Enabling optimization can sometimes be handy when working on sites which are using more than 31 stylesheets—a not too infrequent occurrence on sites using a plethora of modules and an elaborate theme—as this is an upper-bound for Internet Explorer. IE will only load the first 31 stylesheets and ignore the rest. Drupal's CSS optimization feature reduces this number to one, thereby conveniently working around the issue. An alternative is to use modules such as IE CSS Optimizer (`http://drupal.org/project/ie_css_optimizer`).

Other optimizations

Other optimization settings can also be configured on the performance page. These include page caching, block caching, and JavaScript optimization. It is also worthwhile browsing the caching and performance modules that are available as contributed modules via `http://drupal.org/project/modules` under the category **Performance and scalability**.

Creating the mysite module to hold our tweaks

In the course of developing our site, we will frequently come across situations where various elements of the site need to be tweaked in PHP using Drupal's APIs. While a lot of theme-specific cases can be stored in template files, certain tweaks which are theme-agnostic require that we store them in a module to ensure that they are available to all themes.

This recipe covers the creation of a module to hold all these bits and pieces.

Getting ready

Create a folder inside `sites/all` named `modules`. This is where custom and contributed modules are usually housed.

How to do it...

The following list details the procedure involved in creating a module named `mysite` to hold our theme-agnostic customizations and other odds and ends:

1. Create a folder inside `sites/all/modules` named `mysite` where mysite refers to the name of our site.

2. Create a file named `mysite.info` within the `mysite` folder.

3. Edit this file and add the following code inside:

```
name = Mysite
description = A module to hold odds and ends for mysite.
core = 6.x
```

4. Save the file.

5. Create another file named `mysite.module` which will hold our odds and ends.

6. Save and exit the editor.

7. Finally, enable the module via the module administration page at `admin/build/modules` (**Home | Administer | Site building | Modules**).

How it works...

Just as with themes, modules require a `.info` file which provides information to Drupal on compatibility, dependencies, and so on. Once Drupal ascertains that the module is compatible with the version installed, it loads the `.module` file of the same name and processes it accordingly.

We can test if the module is working by adding a snippet such as the following:

```php
<?php

/**
 * Implementation of hook_init().
 */
function mysite_init(){
  // Display a message on every page load.
  drupal_set_message("Welcome to MySite!");
}
```

As the comment suggests, the preceding snippet will display a welcome message on every page load.

There's more...

The Drupal community routinely comes up with modules to ease the pain of development.

Module builder

There's a module available named **Module builder** which can be used to generate a skeleton of a general module. This can subsequently be populated as per our requirements. It is available at `http://drupal.org/project/module_builder`.

Adding a CSS file from a module

Situations arise where CSS files or CSS rules are to be added from a module. This recipe covers the steps required to do so.

Getting ready

We will be adding the CSS to the `mysite` module as created in the previous recipe. Create two CSS files named `mysite.css` and `mysite_special.css` inside the `mysite` module's folder and populate them with some sample rules.

How to do it...

Add the following code to the `mysite` module:

```
/**
 * Implementation of hook_init().
 */
function mysite_init() {
  // The path to the mysite module.
  $path = drupal_get_path('module', 'mysite');

  // Include mysite.css.
  drupal_add_css($path . '/mysite.css');

  // Include mysite_special.css, but do not preprocess.
  drupal_add_css($path . '/mysite_special.css', 'module', 'all',
FALSE);
}
```

Save the file and visit the site to check if the two CSS files are now included.

How it works...

The `drupal_add_css()` function is used to add CSS files from a module. Its syntax is as follows:

```
drupal_add_css($path = NULL, $type = 'module', $media = 'all',
$preprocess = TRUE)
```

The documentation for this function explains each of the parameters:

 ▸ `$path` denotes the path to the CSS file relative to the `base_path()`.

 ▸ `$type` indicates the type of stylesheet that is being added—a module stylesheet or a theme stylesheet with module being the default.

 ▸ `$media` sets the media type for the stylesheet which can include `all`, `print`, `screen`, and so on.

 ▸ Lastly, `$preprocess` specifies if the CSS file should be aggregated and compressed if this feature has been turned on.

In our snippet, we first get the path to the `mysite` module using `drupal_get_path()` and with the result, can obtain the complete path to `mysite.css`. We can now add this CSS file using `drupal_add_css()`.

The next CSS file—mysite_special.css—is as the name suggests, a special file, that we do not want to be preprocessed. This could be because we are going to be including it conditionally, or perhaps, because we have encountered quirks in certain browsers when this file is aggregated. Consequently, we can use the following syntax to instruct Drupal to avoid preprocessing this file.

```
drupal_add_css($path . '/mysite_special.css', 'module', 'all', FALSE);
```

Looking at the source code of a typical page on the site when CSS optimization is enabled, we should see the stylesheets included similar to the following transcription:

```
<link rel="shortcut icon" href="/mysite/misc/favicon.ico" type="image/
x-icon" />
<link type="text/css" rel="stylesheet" media="all" href="/mysite/
sites/all/modules/mysite/mysite_special?8.css" />
<link type="text/css" rel="stylesheet" media="all" href="/mysite/
sites/default/files/css/css_32c93f4662aecdab9e9b87330ae5f157.css" />
<link type="text/css" rel="stylesheet" media="print" href="/mysite/
sites/default/files/css/css_456756789c4eab1267644ab3f147a231.css" />
```

As the preceding markup attests, the mysite_special.css file is never aggregated while plain old mysite.css is always aggregated.

Drupal API documentation

Drupal documentation for drupal_add_css(), drupal_get_path(), and every other function is available at http://api.drupal.org.

There's more...

Besides adding external stylesheets, the Drupal API also allows for adding inline CSS.

Adding inline CSS

Inline CSS can be added with the drupal_set_html_head() function which can insert just about anything between the HEAD tags of an HTML document.

```
drupal_set_html_head('<style type="text/css">body { color: #000; }</
style>');
```

Displaying a different theme for each day of the week

This recipe provides the PHP code that allows the rotation of themes based on the day of the week.

Getting ready

As we have seen in other recipes in this chapter, a number of sites use an "odds and ends" module to handle tweaks and customizations particular to the site. We will be using the `mysite.module` created earlier in this chapter to hold our customizations. It is assumed that the module is available and already enabled.

How to do it...

Open the `mysite` module file and paste the following code into it:

```
/**
 * Implementation of hook_init().
 */
function mysite_init() {
  global $custom_theme;

  // An array of themes for each day of the week.
  // These themes do not have to be enabled.
  $themes = array();
  $themes[0] = 'garland';
  $themes[1] = 'minnelli';
  $themes[2] = 'bluemarine';
  $themes[3] = 'pushbutton';
  $themes[4] = 'chameleon';
  $themes[5] = 'marvin';
  $themes[6] = 'mytheme';

  // Get the current day of the week in numerical form.
  $day = date("w");

  // Override current theme based on day of the week.
  $custom_theme = $themes[$day];

}
```

If the module is named something else, the function `mysite_init()` will need to be renamed appropriately. In case the module already contains an existing `hook_init()` function, the contents of the function below will need to be integrated appropriately to the end of the existing function.

Save the file and then refresh the page on the Drupal site to see this snippet at work. Due to the nature of this feature, it might be necessary to fiddle with the computer's date settings to simulate different days of the week during testing.

How it works...

The function `hook_init ()` is run on every page without exception. It is also run before Drupal gets to the theming stage when it displays every page. Consequently, this is the best place to override the theme to use.

We are overriding the site's theme by manipulating a global variable named `$custom_theme`. If it is set, then Drupal changes the theme being used to the value in this variable. Now that we know how to change the theme, it is just a question of when to do it. Since we are looking to change it based on the day of the week, we are going to take advantage of a feature of PHP's `date()` function which returns the day of the week as a number between zero and six.

```
// Get the current day of the week in numerical form.
$day = date("w");
```

We now map the `$day` variable to the `$themes` array which also has elements from 0 to 6 associated with seven enabled themes and, as a result, we obtain the equivalent theme for that day of the week. Finally, assigning our result to the `$custom_theme` variable overrides the default theme with the theme for the current day of the week.

There's more...

The PHP code used in this recipe can be easily modified to display a random theme on every page load.

Displaying a random theme

Instead of displaying a preset theme for each day of the week, integrating the following snippet into the `mysite_init()` function will display a random theme on every page load:

```
// Override current theme randomly.
$custom_theme = $themes[array_rand($themes)];
```

Creating a fresh look using the color module

The color module allows the administrator to easily change the color scheme of themes that support it. This facilitates a fresh look for the site without having to create a new theme or sub-theme. Drupal's default theme, Garland, supports the color module and, in this recipe, we will be covering the steps required to change its color scheme to something unique.

Getting ready

Ensure that the color module is enabled in `admin/build/modules` (**Home | Administer | Build | Modules**). Since we are going to change the color scheme of the Garland theme, ensure that it is set as the current theme.

How to do it...

Colorizing the Garland theme can be accomplished by following these steps:

1. Navigate to `admin/build/themes` (**Home | Administer | Build | Themes**).

2. Look for the **Garland** theme and click on the **configure** link next to it.

3. Look for the section titled **Color scheme**.

4. In this section, the **Color set** drop-down lists available presets. Choosing any of the presets will change the color scheme of the preview section further below.

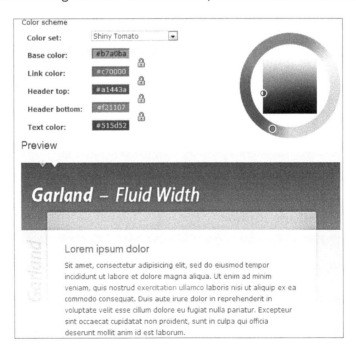

5. Once satisfied, click on the **Save configuration** button at the bottom of the page to save our changes.

How it works...

The color module works by generating stylesheets using the new color scheme which effectively replace the existing stylesheet during runtime. The generated CSS file is stored in the site's `files` directory in a folder named `color`. In addition to the stylesheets, the color module, when configured correctly as with the Garland theme, can also blend the theme's image assets to suit the new color scheme.

 The color module creates a new stylesheet which is a customized copy of the theme's original CSS file. Since it is a copy, fixes and updates to the original file are not automatically propagated to it. Therefore, whenever changes are made to the original file, It is recommended that the stylesheet be regenerated by simply saving the customized color settings once again.

There's more...

We are not restricted to the inbuilt presets provided by the color module and can also create our own.

Custom presets

If the provided presets are unsatisfactory, clicking on the textfields below the drop-down will allow further customization. Once a textfield has focus, the color wheel on the right can also be clicked and used to select different palettes at will. These new settings are saved as the **Custom** preset as demonstrated in the following screenshot:

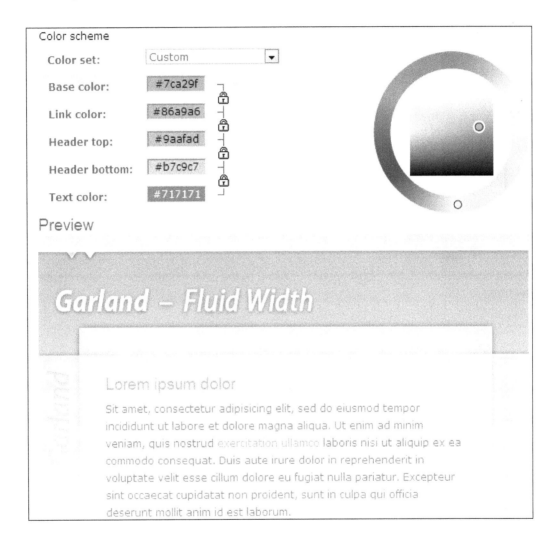

3
Custom Themes and Zen

We will be covering the following recipes in this chapter:

- ▶ Clearing the theme registry
- ▶ Creating a theme from scratch
- ▶ Creating myzen, a Zen-based theme
- ▶ Choosing a CSS layout for myzen
- ▶ Overriding Zen template files with myzen
- ▶ Adding a custom region to myzen
- ▶ Adding a background image to the theme
- ▶ Adding a conditional stylesheet in Zen
- ▶ Modifying myzen's theme settings

Introduction

While, as detailed in the previous chapter, sub-themes of core and contributed themes are convenient and efficient in modifying and reusing elements of their base themes, circumstances often require a completely unique approach specific to our site. Custom themes are the solution for websites which demand a fresh look, using complex layouts, or need so much customization that it would be prudent to start with a clean slate.

Custom themes are the equivalent of handcrafted pieces of art as the themer controls every piece of the puzzle from a design or implementational point of view. This includes setting up the theme using `.info` files, choosing the layout, implementing it in a page template, adding regions, styling nodes using node templates, blocks using block templates, and so on. But over time, developers have identified a list of common tasks, characteristic layouts, and file and folder hierarchies which are logical, efficient, and promote reuse. This has evolved into what have been dubbed starter themes, themes upon which custom themes are built, usually as sub-themes.

The most popular starter theme for Drupal is **Zen**. As advertised on its project page, the Zen theme is a flexible standards-compliant and semantically correct XHTML theme that can be highly modified through CSS and an enhanced version of Drupal's template system. It is designed in modular fashion making it straightforward to change layouts, override templates and theme functions, and to add or remove features. Additionally, the Zen theme comes with extensive documentation within each file which make things all the more convenient.

With respect to CSS, Zen maintains a number of well documented CSS files segregated by functionality or location. For example, layout rules are contained within a dedicated `layout.css` (or similar) file and page backgrounds are styled within `page-backgrounds.css` and so on. This makes it convenient when it comes to managing and tracking code changes.

In addition to the standard files we have encountered while customizing themes in earlier chapters, a Zen-based theme contains the following file and folder structure:

File/folder name	Purpose
`template.php`	A file where theme overrides and other theme and engine-related code is placed.
`theme-settings.php`	A file where settings particular to a theme can be placed. These settings are usually exposed on the theme's configuration page.
`css/`	A folder to store stylesheets.
`images/`	A folder to store images used in the theme.
`images-source/`	The folder where the source files for the optimized images in the images folder are available.
`js/`	A folder to store JavaScript files.
`templates/`	A folder where `tpl.php` template files are to be placed.

There are a number of other starter themes available on `drupal.org`. Some of the more popular ones include **Fusion** (`http://drupal.org/project/fusion`), **Blueprint** (`http://drupal.org/project/blueprint`), **Ninesixty** (`http://drupal.org/project/ninesixty`), and **Adaptivetheme** (`http://drupal.org/project/adaptivetheme`). We will be looking only at the Zen starter theme in this book.

Clearing the theme registry

Before we begin, we need to familiarize ourselves with a seemingly trivial yet crucial task that needs to be performed on a routine basis during theme development—clearing the **theme registry**. The theme registry is essentially a table that Drupal uses to list and track the files and features of a theme, as well as the theme functions which are being exposed by modules and the theme itself.

While it is recommended practice to turn on Drupal's cache feature only for production sites, the theme registry is built and cached regardless of other caching options. As a result, any changes that affect the structure of the theme will necessitate the clearing of the theme registry.

Getting ready

Rebuilding the registry is an intensive operation which is required only when changes have been made to the theme's files.

How to do it...

There are a number of ways of clearing the registry. In a stock Drupal installation, visiting `admin/settings/performance` (**Home | Administer | Site configuration | Performance**) and clicking on the **Clear cached data** button will clear *all* cached data, including the registry, and force a rebuild.

> **A shortcut**
>
> It is sometimes handy to know that the cache and registry can also be cleared by visiting `admin/build/themes` (**Home | Administer | Site building | Themes**) and just clicking the **Save configuration** button.

However, during development or debugging, we will want to clear the registry with great regularity. Rather than having to do so manually, it is often handy to be able to instruct Drupal to perform this operation automatically on every page load. Some themes, including the Zen-based theme which we will be familiarizing ourselves with later in this chapter, offer an option on their configuration pages to rebuild the registry on every page load. While this is certainly convenient, the recommended method of managing this and other development-oriented operations is through the use of the **Devel** module.

As the name suggests, the Devel module is one which is tailor-made for use during development. It can be downloaded from `http://drupal.org/project/devel`. Once the module has been downloaded and installed, navigate to `admin/settings/devel` (**Home | Administer | Site configuration | Devel settings**) where the option to **Rebuild the theme registry on every page load** can be enabled.

How it works...

Drupal maintains a cache of all `.info` files, template files, and theme functions in the theme registry. This registry is a part of the `cache` table in the Drupal database. When we click on the **Clear cache data** button in the performance settings page, all Drupal is doing is clearing this entry in the cache table, which automatically forces a rebuild of the registry. The Devel module does the same thing when the **Rebuild the theme registry on every page load** setting is enabled, except that it does this automatically on every page view.

 It is important to keep in mind that rebuilding the registry, or for that matter, clearing any of the caches is an expensive operation which adversely affects the performance of the site. Therefore, it is recommended that this setting only be enabled during development and not in production sites.

Clearing the registry is an important factor to keep in mind during development and especially during debugging. More information on development and debugging tools including the Devel module is available in *Chapter 5, Development and debugging tools*.

There's more...

The Devel module also provides a block with handy shortcuts to oft-used areas of the site.

Clearing the cache using the Development block

The Devel module provides a **Development** block which can be enabled via the block management page at `admin/build/blocks` (**Home | Administer | Site building | Blocks**). Once enabled, the block lists, as in the following screenshot, a number of links to perform operations such as emptying the Drupal cache, rebuilding the menu cache, and even reinstalling modules. Emptying the cache will also force a rebuild of the theme registry.

Creating a theme from scratch

While we have previously looked at installing contributed themes and extending base themes using sub-themes, this recipe will outline the steps required to create a custom theme.

Getting ready

It is assumed that the `sites/all/themes` folder has already been created. This is the recommended location to place custom and contributed themes.

How to do it...

Creating a brand new custom theme is not unlike what we did in *Chapter 2, Beyond the Basics*, in creating a sub-theme for a core theme. The main difference is that there is no base theme and that files such as `page.tpl.php` will need to be explicitly defined.

1. Create a folder with the new theme's name inside the `sites/all/themes` folder. In this example, we are going to call our theme `mytheme`.

2. Create a file named `mytheme.info` and open it in an editor.

3. Add details about the theme as follows:

   ```
   name = My theme
   description = My custom theme
   core = 6.x
   engine = phptemplate
   ```

4. Save the file.

5. Visit the theme administration page at `admin/build/themes` (**Home | Administer | Site building | Themes**) and we should be able to see a new entry for our theme.

Screenshot	Name	Version	Enabled	Default	Operations
Minnelli – Fixed Width	**Minnelli** Tableless, recolorable, multi-column, fixed width theme.	6.16-dev	☑	○	configure
no screenshot	**My theme** My custom theme		☑	◉	configure

6. Enable the theme by checking its **Enabled** checkbox.

7. Also, set it as the default theme by selecting its **Default** radio button.

8. Click the **Save configuration** button at the bottom of the page to save the changes.

How it works...

Just as with other themes, Drupal scans the `sites/all/themes` folder looking for `.info` files which indicate the presence of a theme. Seeing `mytheme.info`, it parses the file and loads the details of the theme, and saves them in the database.

When the new theme is enabled, what we will see is largely unstyled content not unlike the following screenshot. The problem here is that we have not specified any CSS stylesheets to lay out the page. The only styles being loaded are those that are module-specific as opposed to theme-specific.

The styles being used in the preceding screenshot are as follows:

```
<link type="text/css" rel="stylesheet" media="all"
href="/mysite/modules/node/node.css?u" />
<link type="text/css" rel="stylesheet" media="all"
href="/mysite/modules/system/defaults.css?u" />
<link type="text/css" rel="stylesheet" media="all"
```

```
href="/mysite/modules/system/system.css?u" />
<link type="text/css" rel="stylesheet" media="all"
href="/mysite/modules/system/system-menus.css?u" />
<link type="text/css" rel="stylesheet" media="all"
href="/mysite/modules/user/user.css?u" />
```

As we can see, the only stylesheets in evidence are those belonging to core modules and none from our theme. In addition, Drupal has noticed that we do not have any template files in our theme, most notably, `page.tpl.php`. Therefore, it has loaded an inbuilt page template file from `modules/system/page.tpl.php` and used it instead. Similarly, it is using the `node.tpl.php` file from `modules/node/` as the basis for each node's layout.

In other words, we have a lot of work ahead of us in getting things up and running especially if our eventual requirements are going to be complicated. As we will see in the next recipe, this is one of the reasons why most themers prefer to use a starter theme and hit the ground running.

Creating myzen, a Zen-based theme

While building a custom theme from scratch is great, most themers prefer to use starter themes as the base for their designs. Starter themes save time and effort as we do not have to perform tedious repetitive tasks and can rely on a tried and tested structure to use as a foundation for our theme.

In this recipe, we will be looking at creating a theme based on the most popular of all starter themes available on drupal.org, `Zen`.

Getting ready

Download the theme from `http://drupal.org/project/zen` and install it following the instructions in the first recipe from *Chapter 1, Drupal Theme Basics*.

How to do it...

The Zen theme provides a starter kit which can be used to kick-start our theme.

1. Navigate to the newly installed Zen theme's folder at `sites/all/themes/zen`. Copy the `STARTERKIT` folder inside it.

2. Paste this folder into `sites/all/themes`. Rename the folder to the name of our new theme which, in this case, is `myzen`.

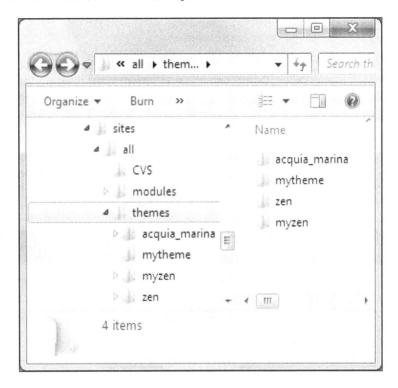

3. Within this folder, rename the file `STARTERKIT.info.txt` to `myzen.info`.

4. Open the `.info` file in an editor.

5. Update the name field to the name of the theme which in this case is **My Zen**.

6. Update the description field to **My custom zen sub-theme**.

7. Save and exit this file.

8. Open `template.php` in an editor and replace all occurrences of `STARTERKIT_` with `myzen` using the find and replace all function.

9. Save and exit this file.

10. Repeat the above find and replace operation for the file `theme-settings.php` as well.

11. Save and exit this file.

Visiting the theme administration page at `admin/build/themes` (**Home | Administer | Site building | Themes**) should now display our new theme. Screenshots, favicons, and other niceties can be configured just like for any other theme.

How it works...

The Zen theme contains a folder named STARTERKIT which is effectively a skeleton theme containing files and folders which can be readily customized to create a new theme. Once we have made a copy of this folder and renamed its .info file with the name of our theme, Drupal will recognize our new entry, which is now registered as a sub-theme of Zen as seen in the following screenshot.

 While the Zen theme needs to be available, it does not need to be enabled for myzen to function.

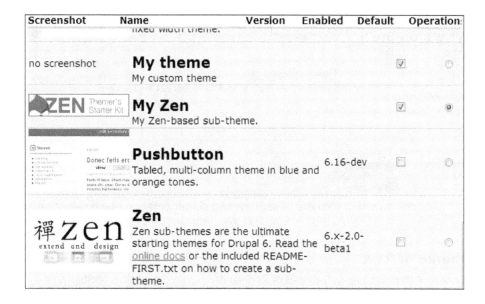

Once enabled, the front page of the site will look something like the following screenshot. It is worthwhile comparing the screenshots in this recipe with those from the *Creating a theme from scratch* recipe earlier in this chapter. The essential difference is that we have a slightly fleshed-out skeleton to work with when we use Zen with a lot of the right pieces already in the right place.

There's more...

The Zen theme comes with a plethora of settings and documentation which can at times, be a little overwhelming. But the rewards of familiarizing ourselves with them are worth our time.

Sub-theme of Zen

We can confirm that this is a sub-theme of Zen via its `.info` file which specifies that

```
base = zen
```

As mentioned in the last chapter, if we need another theme similar to myzen, we can create one with `base = myzen` and save ourselves a whole host of repeated operations.

RTFM

Just about every folder which comes with Zen contains a `README.txt` file which is filled to the brim with copious documentation. It is a good idea to always read through these files. prior to diving in head-first

Rebuild theme registry automatically

The Zen theme contains a setting which rebuilds the theme registry automatically on every page load. This setting is exposed in the `.info` file as `settings[zen_rebuild_registry]` and also via the theme configuration page.

Choosing a CSS layout for myzen

Layouts decide how elements on a page, customarily contained in DIVs, are positioned. Zen comes with a couple of preset layouts which can be used. If neither of them is suitable, a custom layout can be created. In this recipe, we will be replacing the default fixed-width layout with a liquid layout, which we discussed in *Chapter 1, Drupal Theme Basics*.

Getting ready

We are going to assume that the myzen theme from earlier in this chapter is enabled and the current default. It is also important to decide on the type of layout required for the site during the design stage.

How to do it...

All we are going to do here is replace one of the stylesheets used in myzen with another.

1. Open `myzen.info` in an editor.
2. In the section pertaining to stylesheet declarations, look for the line that declares the fixed-width layout which should usually be `stylesheets[all][] = css/layout-fixed.css`.
3. Replace this with `stylesheets[all][] = css/layout-liquid.css`.
4. Save the file.
5. As usual, clear the theme registry for our changes to take effect.

How it works...

The default fixed-width layout is, as the name suggests, of a fixed width. The positioning of the content does not vary based on the dimensions of the browser. By replacing the `layout-fixed.css` stylesheet in the `myzen.info` file, Drupal will now load the `layout-liquid.css` file instead. As a result, when we refresh the front page, we should now see that the layout of the site occupies the full width of the screen and will flow and reposition itself as we resize the browser window.

There's more...

Zen and its sub-themes take care while displaying content and ensure that the markup is clean and semantically correct. Furthermore, in light of the growing internationalization of the web, it provides **RTL** support out of the box.

Sidebar support

The Zen theme, by default, comes with two sidebars—left and right—and it automatically displays the sidebar markup only if it contains content within.

RTL

A number of CSS files in Zen and other themes are often in two variants—one with an `rtl` suffix and the other without. RTL is an acronym for Right-To-Left and is used to signify that the stylesheet will be used when RTL mode is enabled, customarily for sites with content in languages such as Hebrew and Arabic.

Custom layouts

There are various advantages and disadvantages to using a fixed-width or a liquid layout, and a variety of ways to accomplish these very same layouts which are drastically different from the way Zen implements them. If a custom layout is being used, add the necessary rules and styles to a separate CSS file such as layout-custom.css.

Overriding Zen template files with myzen

Zen sub-themes, by default, use the page, node, and other template files directly from the base theme. In other words, we do not need to specify template files in our myzen theme unless we have to.

In this recipe, we are going to override the base theme's `page.tpl.php` template file with our own copy and make changes to it. As an example, let us see if we can reposition the status messages element which is usually represented by the `$messages` variable.

Getting ready

We are going to assume that the myzen sub-theme is already created and available.

How to do it...

The following steps outline the procedure to import a template file from the base theme to the sub-theme:

1. Navigate to the `sites/all/themes/zen/templates` folder which contains the default templates.

2. Copy the `page.tpl.php` file.

3. Paste it into the `sites/all/themes/myzen/templates` folder.

4. Open this file in an editor.

5. Scroll down looking for any usage of the $messages variable. It should be located in a code block not dissimilar to the following:

```php
<?php print $breadcrumb; ?>
<?php if ($title): ?>
  <h1 class="title"><?php print $title; ?></h1>
<?php endif; ?>
<?php print $messages; ?>
<?php if ($tabs): ?>
  <div class="tabs"><?php print $tabs; ?></div>
<?php endif; ?>
<?php print $help; ?
```

6. What we are looking to do is to move the status messages to a more prominent location above the title and the breadcrumb. After moving the relevant line of code further above, this block should look something like the following:

```php
<?php print $messages; ?>
<?php print $breadcrumb; ?>
<?php if ($title): ?>
  <h1 class="title"><?php print $title; ?></h1>
<?php endif; ?>
<?php if ($tabs): ?>
  <div class="tabs"><?php print $tabs; ?></div>
<?php endif; ?>
<?php print $help; ?
```

7. Save the file and exit.

8. As we have imported a template file, we also need to clear the theme registry.

We should now be able to see our changes in effect when a node, for example, is updated.

How it works...

Once we copied the template file from Zen to myzen and subsequently cleared the registry, Drupal was alerted during the theme registry rebuilding process that a new `page.tpl.php` file was available. Due to the fact that this template file was located in the myzen theme's folder, it took precedence over the version contained within the Zen theme's folder leading to our updates taking effect.

> It is interesting to note that while the `page.tpl.php` template file in myzen took precedence over the file in the `Zen` folder, the latter was already overriding the equivalent template file in Drupal's system module folder.

The following screenshots should offer a before and after comparison of this recipe in action:

In the preceding screenshot, we can see that the status message is being displayed below the title of the node. However, with our new template file in action, we can see that the status message is now displayed above the title and the breadcrumb as shown in the following screenshot:

Adding a custom region to myzen

Regions are essentially containers for Drupal blocks. The layout of regions in a page effectively dictates the layout of the site.

The myzen theme contains the following regions by default:

- First sidebar
- Second sidebar
- Navigation bar
- Highlighted content
- Content top
- Content bottom
- Header
- Footer
- Page closure

In this recipe, we will be looking to replace the existing **Content bottom** region with two separate regions named **Content bottom 1** and **Content bottom 2** respectively.

Getting ready

We are going to assume that the myzen theme from earlier in this chapter is enabled and the current default. We will be updating the default `page.tpl.php` template file that is used by myzen. If this file does not exist in `sites/all/themes/myzen/templates`, it will need to be imported into this folder from `sites/all/themes/zen/templates/page.tpl.php`.

How to do it...

First up, we will be updating the regions list in the `.info` file.

1. Open the `myzen.info` file in an editor.
2. Scroll down to the section dealing with regions.
3. Look for the following declaration:

   ```
   regions[content_bottom] = Content bottom
   ```

4. Replace the declaration in step 3 with the following:

   ```
   regions[content_bottom1] = Content bottom 1
   regions[content_bottom2] = Content bottom 2
   ```

5. Save the file and exit.

Now that we have added our new regions, we need to ensure that Drupal uses them by updating the `page.tpl.php` template.

6. Open myzen's `page.tpl.php` file in an editor.

7. Scroll down and look for the following line of code:

    ```
    <?php print $content_bottom; ?>
    ```

8. Replace the line in step 2 with the following two:

    ```
    <?php print $content_bottom1; ?>
    <?php print $content_bottom2; ?>
    ```

9. Save the file and exit.

10. Clear the theme registry as per usual.

The new regions should now be visible if we navigate to the blocks administration page at `admin/build/blocks` (**Home | Administer | Site building | Blocks**).

How it works...

The following two screenshots should offer a before-and-after comparison of the blocks administration page. Each region in the layout is depicted by a yellow bar containing the name of the region.

Block	Region	Operations
No blocks in this region		
Content bottom		
No blocks in this region		
Header		
No blocks in this region		
Footer		
No blocks in this region		
Page closure		
No blocks in this region		
Disabled		
⊹ Powered by Drupal	\<none\>	configure
⊹ Primary links	\<none\>	configure
⊹ Recent comments	\<none\>	configure
⊹ Secondary links	\<none\>	configure
⊹ Syndicate	\<none\>	configure
⊹ Who's new	\<none\>	configure

Save blocks

Content bottom

Footer

Page closure

In the original layout, as displayed in the previous screenshot, we can see the regions highlighted in yellow. These regions include the lone **Content bottom**, situated below the content of the page. By simply editing the `.info` file, we have been able to replace this single option with two new regions, **Content bottom 1** and **Content bottom 2**, as seen in the following screenshot.

Block	Region	Operations
Content bottom 1		
No blocks in this region		
Content bottom 2		
No blocks in this region		
Header		
No blocks in this region		
Footer		
No blocks in this region		
Page closure		
No blocks in this region		
Disabled		
⊹ Powered by Drupal	\<none\> ▾	configure
⊹ Primary links	\<none\> ▾	configure
⊹ Recent comments	\<none\> ▾	configure
⊹ Secondary links	\<none\> ▾	configure
⊹ Syndicate	\<none\> ▾	configure
⊹ Who's new	\<none\> ▾	configure

Save blocks

Content bottom 1

Content bottom 2

Footer

Page closure

Adding a background image to the theme

Zen-based themes come with a plethora of stylesheets separated logically by functionality. In this recipe, we will be exploring their use by adding a background image to our myzen theme.

Getting ready

As usual, we are going to assume that myzen is enabled and is the current default theme. Since we are going to be using a background image in this recipe, it will also be a good idea to ensure that the myzen theme is using a fixed-width layout to improve the visibility of the background.

The background image to be used should be optimized and saved in the `sites/all/themes/myzen/images/` folder. In this recipe, we will be setting the image file named `body-bg.png` as the background and repeating it along both the X and Y axes.

How to do it...

As Zen-based themes use stylesheets partitioned based on their functionality, we can add our rules to the file `page-backgrounds.css` as follows:

1. Navigate to the `sites/all/themes/myzen/css` folder which contains a set of stylesheets available for customization.

2. Look for the file named `page-backgrounds.css` and open it in an editor.

3. The first rule which we are concerned with is the one for the `body` tag. Locate it and add the following highlighted rule to set the background image:

```
body {
   background: url(../images/body-bg.png) repeat;
}
```

 Since the CSS file is within the `css` folder, we need to use the `../images/body-bg.png` syntax to reference the file within the `images` folder.

4. The next element we are going to be styling is the `DIV` with `id="#page"` which contains the regions of the layout. Look for the entry for `#page` and add the following rule to it:

```
#page {
   background: #EEE;
}
```

5. Save the file and exit.

How it works...

The `page-backgrounds.css` file is added to the theme via its `.info` file. The `myzen.info` file will, by default, have a whole host of CSS files included not unlike the following list:

```
stylesheets[all][]    = css/html-reset.css
stylesheets[all][]    = css/wireframes.css
stylesheets[all][]    = css/layout-fixed.css
stylesheets[all][]    = css/page-backgrounds.css
stylesheets[all][]    = css/tabs.css
stylesheets[all][]    = css/messages.css
stylesheets[all][]    = css/pages.css
stylesheets[all][]    = css/block-editing.css
stylesheets[all][]    = css/blocks.css
stylesheets[all][]    = css/navigation.css
stylesheets[all][]    = css/views-styles.css
stylesheets[all][]    = css/nodes.css
stylesheets[all][]    = css/comments.css
stylesheets[all][]    = css/forms.css
stylesheets[all][]    = css/fields.css
stylesheets[print][]  = css/print.css
; stylesheets[handheld][] = css/mobile.css
; stylesheets[only screen and (max-device-width: 480px)][] = css/
iphone.css
```

> **Commented code**
>
> In the preceding excerpt from the `.info` file, lines prefixed with a semicolon are deemed to have been commented out and are not considered.

Most of the CSS files referenced in the file are skeleton stylesheets, each with its own functionality and purpose. They are usually littered with a lot of documentation and examples to get us started. In this case, the `page-backgrounds.css` file is already included and our rules should take effect automatically. It is important that we limit our changes in this stylesheet to rules pertaining to page element backgrounds. Including extraneous styles will defeat the purpose of partitioning the CSS based on functionality.

The resulting front page should now have a tiled background image for its body and a gray background for its content as demonstrated in the following screenshot:

There's more...

Stylesheet management can sometimes be an involved process and is largely dependent on our own personal preferences.

Custom file structures

Some themers are uncomfortable with managing the multitude of CSS files that come with Zen and other themes. They either prefer their own logical structures or use a single monolithic stylesheet containing all the rules. There is nothing really wrong with this and it is simply a question of comfort and ease of use.

Unused stylesheets

Once we are done styling our theme, we will usually find that there are a number of stylesheets included in `myzen.info` which are empty or never used. Rather than deleting the relevant lines, it is prudent to just comment them out by prefixing them with a semicolon.

Adding a conditional stylesheet in Zen

Conditional stylesheets are a frequent requirement to accommodate hacks and workarounds specific to versions of the Internet Explorer browser. While other themes would require us to conditionally introduce said stylesheets either using a module or by inserting the appropriate HTML directly in the `page.tpl.php` template, Zen-based themes offer a straightforward alternative.

In this recipe, we will be looking at the procedure involved in adding a conditional stylesheet which is loaded only if the browser is Internet Explorer (IE). Furthermore, the version of the browser has to be 7 (IE7) or greater.

Getting ready

This recipe centers around the myzen sub-theme which is assumed to have been created, enabled and set as the default theme. A CSS file named `ie7.css` should be created and saved inside myzen's `css` folder. Hacks and workarounds particular to IE7 are to be added to this file.

How to do it...

Adding a conditional stylesheet to the myzen theme can be accomplished as follows:

1. Navigate to the `sites/all/themes/myzen` folder.

2. Open the `myzen.info` file in an editor.

3. Scroll down to the section dealing with conditional stylesheets. The default configuration should look something like the following:

    ```
    conditional-stylesheets[if IE][all][]        = css/ie.css
    conditional-stylesheets[if lte IE 6][all][] = css/ie6.cs
    ```

4. Add the following statement to this section:

    ```
    conditional-stylesheets[if IE gte 7][all][] = css/ie7.cs
    ```

 `lte` and `gte` in the code above stand for "lesser than or equal to" and "greater than or equal to". More information and a list of other operators can be found at `http://msdn.microsoft.com/en-us/library/ms537512.aspx`.

5. Save the file and exit.

6. Since we have made changes to the `.info` file, the theme registry needs to be rebuilt.

When the site is now viewed in IE7, the `ie7.css` stylesheet will also be loaded.

How it works...

When the HTML source for a sample page is now viewed, the conditional stylesheets declaration used in this recipe will have translated to something like the following:

```
<!--[if IE]>
<link type="text/css" rel="stylesheet" media="all" href="/mysite/
sites/all/themes/myzen/css/ie.css?J" />
<![endif]-->
<!--[if lte IE 6]>
<link type="text/css" rel="stylesheet" media="all" href="/mysite/
sites/all/themes/myzen/css/ie6.css?J" />
```

```
<![endif]-->
<!--[if IE 7]>
<link type="text/css" rel="stylesheet" media="all" href="/mysite/
sites/all/themes/myzen/css/ie7.css?J" />
<![endif]-->
```

As evident from the preceding source, Zen translates our entries in the `.info` file to conditional comments and inserts them as markup. The conditional comments are only triggered in Internet Explorer which includes the appropriate stylesheet accordingly.

There's more...

The maintainers of the Zen theme have made this functionality available to other themes as well through the use of a dedicated module.

Conditional stylesheets for other themes

The conditional stylesheets module (`http://drupal.org/project/conditional_styles`) provides similar functionality for non-Zen themes. A number of themes rely on this module to simplify the process of adding conditional comments.

Modifying myzen's theme settings

Visiting the theme configuration page for the myzen theme created earlier in this chapter should reveal a number of theme-specific settings. In this recipe, we are going to learn how these settings are added and then, rather than creating our own setting, we will familiarize ourselves with their structure by learning how to remove an existing setting.

Getting ready

As we are working with the myzen theme, it should be enabled and set as the site's default theme. Furthermore, as detailed in the recipe where myzen was created, all instances of `STARTERKIT` in the `theme-settings.php` file should be replaced by `myzen`. Once this is done, the theme configuration page for the myzen theme should include theme-specific settings as in the following screenshot.

Theme-specific settings

These settings only exist for the *My Zen* theme and all the styles based on it.

☑ Show block editing on hover
When hovering over a block, privileged users will see block editing links.

Breadcrumb settings

Display breadcrumb: Yes   ▼

Breadcrumb separator: >
Text only. Don't forget to include spaces.

☑ Show home page link in breadcrumb

☑ Append a separator to the end of the breadcrumb
Useful when the breadcrumb is placed just before the title.

☐ Append the content title to the end of the breadcrumb
Useful when the breadcrumb is not placed just before the title.

Theme development settings

Theme registry: ☐ Rebuild theme registry on every page.
During theme development, it can be very useful to continuously rebuild the theme registry. WARNING: this is a huge performance penalty and must be turned off on production websites.

Wireframes: ☐ Display borders around main layout elements
Wireframes are useful when prototyping a website.

How to do it...

The setting that we will be removing is the **Show block editing on hover** checkbox. To do so, we will be working with three different files—myzen's `theme-settings.php`, `myzen.info`, and Zen's `theme-settings.php`.

1. Load all three files in three separate editors.

2. Comparing myzen's `theme-settings.php` and Zen's `theme-settings.php`, we can tell that all the settings in the preceding screenshot are exported by Zen via a function named `zen_settings()`. myzen gets access to these settings as it is a sub-theme of Zen.

   The block editing links setting appears in the following block of code:

```
$form['zen_block_editing'] = array(
'#type'           => 'checkbox',
'#title'          => t('Show block editing on hover'),
```

```
'#description'   => t('When hovering over a block, privileged
users will see block editing links.'),
'#default_value' => $settings['zen_block_editing'],
);
```

3. As highlighted, the setting is stored in an index named `zen_block_editing`. Therefore to remove this setting, we just need to clear this index.

4. Switch to myzen's `theme-settings.php` file and look in the `myzen_settings()` function for the following code:

```
// Remove some of the base theme's settings.
unset($form['themedev']['zen_layout']);
```

5. We are doing something similar to a different variable. Add the following code under the block in step 4:

```
// Remove the setting for block editing links.
unset($form['zen_block_editing']);
```

6. Save the file and exit.

7. Navigate back to myzen's theme configuration page at `admin/build/themes/settings/myzen` (**Home | Administer | Site building | Themes | Configure**) and refresh the page to confirm that the **Show block editing on hover** checkbox is no longer present.

8. Click on the **Save configuration** button at the bottom of the page to ensure that any vestiges of the setting are also cleared from the database.

We still have a little more work to do. Even though the checkbox appears to have vanished, hovering over a nearby block will result in a block edit link appearing.

The culprit is the following block of code in `myzen_settings`:

```
// Get the default values from the .info file.
$defaults = zen_theme_get_default_settings('myzen');
// Merge the saved variables and their default values.
$settings = array_merge($defaults, $saved_settings);
```

What is happening is that default settings from the `myzen.info` file are being loaded as well. Looking at the file in an editor the following telltale entry appears to be the one responsible:

```
settings[zen_block_editing]         = 1
```

Commenting out this line of code and subsequently, clearing the theme registry should sort our problem out.

How it works...

The Zen theme exports a set of variables and allows its sub-theme, myzen, to act upon them by updating their values, adding new settings, or removing existing ones. The addition of new settings can be achieved through the use of the Forms API while removal of existing settings is performed using an `unset()` operation. Furthermore, default values for each settings can be added or removed via `myzen.info` as well.

4
Templating Basics

We will be covering the following recipes in this chapter:

- ▶ Changing the layout of a page using `page.tpl.php`
- ▶ Customizing the appearance of a particular node type
- ▶ Customizing the appearance of a specific node
- ▶ Theming made easy using the Devel module
- ▶ Theme overrides using the Theme developer module
- ▶ Listing all available variables in a template file
- ▶ Displaying the profile name instead of a user name
- ▶ Theming the maintenance page

Introduction

Drupal's design stresses the separation of logic from presentation with the former being handled by modules and the latter by themes. Theme functions, commonly those that are prefixed with `theme_`, and theme template files act as a bridge between the two as they are designed to be overrideable. All theme functions and template files are tracked by Drupal's theme system and cataloged in a theme registry. Modules and themes are expected to declare their theme functions and templates through the use of a function named `hook_theme()`. This function is parsed for each module and theme and the resulting registry is cached in the database.

What this registry does is allow developers to modify and override existing theme implementations with their own customizations. If the registry states that for task `foo`, theme function `bar()` has to be used, we can modify the registry to point to our own function named `baz()` instead of `bar()` which does something entirely different.

For example, let us consider the following snippet of code from Drupal's user module which is located at `modules/user/user.module`:

```
/**
 * Theme output of user signature.
 *
 * @ingroup themeable
 */
function theme_user_signature($signature)
{
  $output = '';
  if ($signature) {
    $output .= '<div class="clear">';
    $output .= '<div>—</div>';
    $output .= $signature;
    $output .= '</div>';
  }

  return $output;
}
```

The preceding code snippet is a theme function used to insert the markup required to display a user's signature in a comment. This piece of code is expressly isolated in this function so that it can be modified from the theme layer.

When we want to modify the output of the user signature and incorporate our own markup into it, we need to override `theme_user_signature()` with our own implementation. Doing so can be as simple as creating a function named `myzen_user_signature()` inside the `template.php` of our theme, which in this example is `myzen`. Once the registry is rebuilt, Drupal will become aware of this new function which will supersede `theme_user_signature()` and use it instead of the original when displaying a user's signature.

Similar to the last theme function, the `modules/user` folder contains a collection of `.tpl.php` template files including one named `user-picture.tpl.php` with the following content:

```
<div class="picture">
  <?php print $picture; ?>
</div>
```

This template file specifies the markup to be used when displaying a user's avatar image and can be overridden through the use of, for example, a new template file in the theme's directory with the same name. Once the theme registry is rebuilt after our change, Drupal will notice this new file and use it instead of the original.

In this chapter, we will be using this and other techniques to add our customizations to our theme.

Changing the layout of a page using page.tpl.php

As we have seen in earlier chapters, the page template file, `page.tpl.php`, is responsible for the overall layout and markup of a Drupal page. Besides the basic HTML headers, various elements common to all pages in the site, such as the layout of regions, headers, footers, logos, slogans, breadcrumbs, and so on are, all positioned here.

In this recipe, we will look at modifying the page template file in order to move the search form—another element which is normally present across all pages—from the header to the footer.

Getting ready

It is possible that some themes will not have a `page.tpl.php` file of their own. This is usually because they are sub-themes and the template file will need to be imported from the base theme, as we saw in the last chapter. In other cases, using `modules/system/page.tpl.php` as a foundation is usually a good idea. Themers looking for a little adventure can, of course, create one from scratch!

The search module needs to be enabled if the search form is to be visible.

Missing search box?

Some themes, by default, disable the search form. This can be rectified via their configuration screens.

How to do it...

The following is an abbreviated snippet from a typical page template file. The highlighted search box field is in the DIV titled `header` and is displayed at the top of the page.

```
<div id="header"><div class="section clearfix">

  <?php if ($logo): ?>
    <a href="<?php print $front_page; ?>" title="<?php print
t('Home'); ?>" rel="home" id="logo"><img src="<?php print $logo; ?>"
alt="<?php print t('Home'); ?>" /></a>
  <?php endif; ?>
  <?php if ($search_box): ?>
    <div id="search-box"><?php print $search_box; ?></div>
```

```
    <?php endif; ?>

    <?php print $header; ?>
</div></div> <!-- /.section, /#header -->
<div id="main-wrapper"><div id="main" class="clearfix<?php if
($primary_links || $navigation) { print ' with-navigation'; } ?>">

    <div id="content" class="column"><div class="section">
    <!-- Content related code which has been trimmed -->

    </div></div> <!-- /.section, /#content -->
</div></div> <!-- /#main, /#main-wrapper -->

<?php if ($footer || $footer_message || $secondary_links): ?>
    <div id="footer"><div class="section">

        <?php print theme('links', $secondary_links, array('id' =>
'secondary-menu', 'class' => 'links clearfix')); ?>

        <?php if ($footer_message): ?>
          <div id="footer-message"><?php print $footer_message; ?></div>
        <?php endif; ?>

        <?php print $footer; ?>

    </div></div> <!-- /.section, /#footer -->
```

Using the Bluemarine theme as a guide, the preceding snippet will result in the search box being displayed at the top along with the logo, site name, and other fields as in the following screenshot.

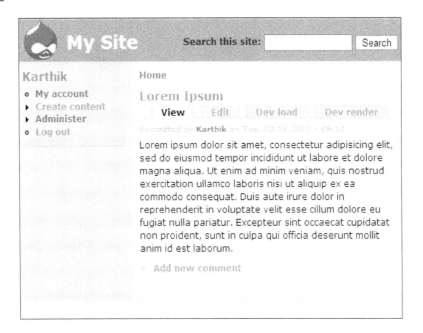

To move the search box from the top of the page to the bottom, all we need to do is to move the highlighted block of code from its current position inside the `header` DIV to the `footer` DIV. Subsequently, the block of code will now look like:

```
<div id="header"><div class="section clearfix">

  <?php if ($logo): ?>
    <a href="<?php print $front_page; ?>" title="<?php print
t('Home'); ?>" rel="home" id="logo"><img src="<?php print $logo; ?>"
alt="<?php print t('Home'); ?>" /></a>
  <?php endif; ?>

  <?php print $header; ?>
</div></div> <!-- /.section, /#header  -->
<div id="main-wrapper"><div id="main" class="clearfix<?php if
($primary_links || $navigation) { print ' with-navigation'; } ?>">

  <div id="content" class="column"><div class="section">
  <!-- Content related code which has been trimmed -->

  </div></div> <!-- /.section, /#content -->
</div></div> <!-- /#main, /#main-wrapper -->
<?php if ($footer || $footer_message || $secondary_links): ?>
  <div id="footer"><div class="section">

    <?php print theme('links', $secondary_links, array('id' =>
'secondary-menu', 'class' => 'links clearfix')); ?>

    <?php if ($footer_message): ?>
      <div id="footer-message"><?php print $footer_message; ?></div>
    <?php endif; ?>

    <?php print $footer; ?>

    <?php if ($search_box): ?>
      <div id="search-box"><?php print $search_box; ?></div>
    <?php endif; ?>

  </div></div> <!-- /.section, /#footer -->
```

How it works...

Once the file is saved and the page refreshed, the search box should now be relocated as evident from the following screenshot:

We can also see that the styling of the search box is now altered as it is located inside the footer DIV and consequently, some of the pre-existing rules might no longer apply.

Looking at the block of code that we moved, it is interesting to note that the markup for the search form is ensconced within an IF block. Moreover, looking through the rest of `page.tpl.php` or even other template files, we can confirm that this is something of a recurring theme. This practice ensures that our markup is not riddled with a bunch of empty tags which, besides being unsightly can potentially affect the style of the page. For example, consider the situation where we have disabled the search box via the configuration page of our theme. If the IF check was not utilized as in this recipe, we would have been stuck with an empty tag in the form of `<div id="search-box"></div>`. If this DIV had some CSS applied to it in the form of padding or margins, they would still adversely affect the style of the page even though we are not displaying the search box at all.

Customizing the appearance of a particular node type

Drupal's PHPTemplate theming engine uses naming conventions to easily theme nodes. While the standard template used is named `node.tpl.php`, other naming conventions are available to target specific subsets of nodes. Here, we will be looking at specifically theming content of a particular node type—`story`—by removing information about its categories and submission fields during display.

Getting ready

This recipe uses the myzen theme created earlier in this book as an example theme. As we are targeting particular node types, it will be a good idea to have more than one node type enabled along with sample content for each.

How to do it...

The following steps are performed in the theme folder, which in this recipe is `sites/all/themes/myzen`. Zen-based themes store their template files in a `templates` folder while others might choose to store them in the base folder.

1. myzen's `templates` folder should contain a `node.tpl.php` file. If this is not available, import it from the Zen theme as described in recipes in the previous chapter.

2. Make a copy of this file within the same folder.

3. Name the copy `node-story.tpl.php` where `story` signifies the internal name of the node type.

 The internal or machine-readable names of node types can be discerned via the **Content types** page at `admin/content/types` (**Home | Administer | Content management | Content types**). They are listed under the column named **Type**.

4. Open this file in an editor.

5. The default template code should look like the following:

```
<div id="node-<?php print $node->nid; ?>" class="<?php print
$classes; ?> clearfix">
  <?php print $user_picture; ?>
  <?php if (!$page): ?>
    <h2 class="title"><a href="<?php print $node_url; ?>"><?php
print $title; ?></a></h2>
```

```
    <?php endif; ?>

    <?php if ($unpublished): ?>
       <div class="unpublished"><?php print t('Unpublished'); ?></
    div>
      <?php endif; ?>

    <?php if ($display_submitted || $terms): ?>
       <div class="meta">
         <?php if ($display_submitted): ?>
           <span class="submitted">
             <?php
               print t('Submitted by !username on !datetime',
                  array('!username' => $name, '!datetime' => $date));
             ?>
           </span>
         <?php endif; ?>

    <?php if ($terms): ?>
       <div class="terms terms-inline"><?php print $terms; ?></div>
    <?php endif; ?>
    </div>
    <?php endif; ?>

      <div class="content">
        <?php print $content; ?>
      </div>

      <?php print $links; ?>
    </div> <!-- /.node -->
```

6. Delete the lines which are highlighted in the preceding block of code.

7. Save the file and exit the editor.

8. Clear the theme registry as we have added a new template file.

9. Visit a story node to confirm that submission and taxonomy information are no longer being displayed.

10. Visit a page node to verify that its display is untouched.

How it works...

The following screenshot displays a typical node layout with the submission information and taxonomy terms displayed along with the body of the node:

Drupal's theme system is designed to be overridden. As soon as we create the `node-story.tpl.php` file in this recipe and, importantly, clear the theme registry, Drupal updates the registry to account for this new addition. Subsequently, whenever a story node is displayed, it is aware of the presence of this new file which supersedes the default `node.tpl.php` file and uses it instead. It gets a little complicated with our myzen recipe as it is actually a Zen sub-theme. As a result, we are overriding Zen's own template files which, in turn, are overriding the default Drupal files.

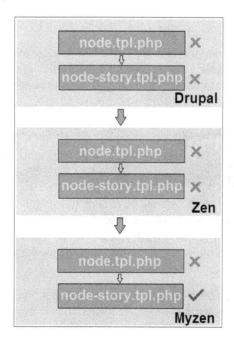

The preceding chart lists the template hierarchy in an increasing order of precedence with `node-story.tpl.php` always overriding `node.tpl.php`, and the template files of the myzen theme being preferred over those of Zen and Drupal.

The result of our machinations is evident in the following screenshot which demonstrates our typical story node now being laid out using the `node-story.tpl.php` template file with the submission information and taxonomy terms removed.

There's more...

If we are looking to modify the display settings across all themes, the theme management page provides a section where global changes can be implemented.

Hiding submission information

Technically, we could have used the theme global settings page at `admin/build/themes/settings` (**Home | Administer | Site building | Themes | Configure | Global settings**) to toggle the display of post information. However, as the name suggests, this is a global setting and affects all themes which is not always what we are after.

Customizing the appearance of a specific node

In a similar vein to an earlier recipe, we will be looking at using the Drupal theme system's naming scheme to customize specific pieces of content. While the previous recipe targeted nodes of a particular node type, here we are going to target a single node based on its node ID. However, Drupal does not support this particular naming convention out of the box. So we have to do the next best thing—add it ourselves.

The customization we will be performing on the node in question is that it should only display its content and links to authenticated users. In other words, anonymous users will only be able to see its title.

Getting ready

There are two places where we can add our new template suggestion. We can do it either in our theme or in a custom module similar to the one we created in *Chapter 2, Beyond the Basics*. We will be using the myzen theme created earlier in the book as the example theme in this recipe. The significant difference between Zen-based themes and others is that template files are stored inside a separate folder titled `templates`. It is also assumed that a `node.tpl.php` file already exists in this folder.

Additionally, since we are going to be targeting a particular node based on its node ID, we will need to obtain this number from the node in question. This can be discerned from the URL of the node which should, by default, be of the form `node/123` where 123 signifies the node ID. If the node has a URL alias enabled, this ID can be obtained by clicking on the **Edit** link of the node which should lead us to a URL containing the node ID.

How to do it...

Navigate to the `sites/all/myzen` folder and perform the following steps:

1. Open the `template.php` file in an editor.
2. Add the following code to the end of the file:

```
function myzen_preprocess_node(&$vars) {
    $vars['template_files'][] = 'node-'. $vars['nid'];
    return $vars;
}
```

   If a function named `myzen_preprocess_node()` already exists, merge the highlighted line of code into it.

3. Save the file and exit the editor.
4. Move to the `templates` folder.
5. Create a copy of the file `node.tpl.php`.
6. Name the new file `node-123.tpl.php` where *123* signifies the node ID of the node that we want to customize.
7. Open this file in an editor. The default `node.tpl.php` should look something like the following:

```
<div id="node-<?php print $node->nid; ?>" class="<?php print
$classes; ?> clearfix">
  <?php print $user_picture; ?>

  <?php if (!$page): ?>
    <h2 class="title"><a href="<?php print $node_url; ?>"><?php
      print $title; ?></a></h2>
```

```
<?php endif; ?>

<?php if ($unpublished): ?>
  <div class="unpublished"><?php print t('Unpublished');
  ?></div>
<?php endif; ?>

<?php if ($display_submitted || $terms): ?>
  <div class="meta">
  <?php if ($display_submitted): ?>
  <span class="submitted">
<?php
  print t('Submitted by !username on !datetime',
  array('!username' => $name, '!datetime' => $date));
  ?>
  </span>
<?php endif; ?>

<?php if ($terms): ?>
  <div class="terms terms-inline"><?php print $terms; ?></div>
  <?php endif; ?>
  </div>
<?php endif; ?>
<div class="content">
  <?php print $content; ?>
</div>
<?php print $links; ?>
</div> <!-- /.node -->
```

8. What we want to do is wrap the highlighted code in the previous step inside an `if` statement so that the resulting block looks something like the following:

```
<?php if ($logged_in): ?>
  <div class="content">
    <?php print $content; ?>
  </div>

  <?php print $links; ?>
<?php endif; ?>
```

9. Save the file and exit the editor.

10. Clear the theme registry as we have added a new template file.

11. Visit `node/123` both as an anonymous and as an authenticated user to verify if our changes have taken effect.

12. Confirm that other nodes are unaffected.

How it works...

While we will be looking at the `preprocess_node()` function in greater detail in the next chapter, what we have effectively done is add a new pattern into an array that holds a list of possible template file candidates. The statement:

```
$vars['template_files'][] = 'node-'. $vars['nid'];
```

states that if a file named `node-NID.tpl.php` exists where `NID` is the node ID of the page currently being visited, then that file should be used. Once Drupal is aware of this, it uses our new template file whenever the node corresponding to the file name is to be displayed.

The change that we have made to the contents of the template file uses the built-in variable named `$logged_in` which is `FALSE` when the current user is anonymous and `TRUE` otherwise. Displaying the content of the node only when this variable is TRUE ensures that it is only inserted when the user is logged in.

Theming made easy using the Devel module

While it is entirely fine to develop and theme sites without the use of the Devel module and related modules such as **Theme developer**, they are highly recommended as they save time and effort and will eventually seem indispensable. This recipe will outline the setup process and relevant features of the Devel module.

Getting ready

The `Devel` module can be downloaded from `http://drupal.org/project/devel`. Once downloaded, install and enable it via the module administration page.

How to do it...

From a themer's point of view, there are two primary features of importance which are provided by the Devel module. The first is the **development** block which can be enabled from the block administration page at `admin/build/block` (**Home | Administer | Site building | Blocks**).

Development

- Devel settings
- Empty cache
- Enable Theme developer
- Execute PHP Code
- Function reference
- Hook_elements()
- PHPinfo()
- Rebuild menus
- Reinstall modules
- Run cron
- Session viewer
- Theme registry
- Variable editor

In the preceding development block, the most frequently used option is usually the **Empty cache**. Clicking this link will empty Drupal's cache as well as clear and rebuild the theme registry. In other words, it is a regular port of call during most debugging sessions.

The **Enable Theme developer** link is only pertinent when the Theme developer (`devel_themer`) module is available. It is a complementary module which is useful when it comes to overriding existing theme functions to introduce custom changes, as we will see during the rest of this chapter. Additionally, the **Theme registry** option links to a page listing all theme functions registered with Drupal.

Lastly, the **Devel settings** link is a handy shortcut to the Devel module's settings page at `admin/settings/devel` (**Home | Administer | Site configuration | Devel settings**). Of immediate importance to us on this page is the setting right at the bottom—a checkbox titled **Rebuild the theme registry on every page load**. When checked, the registry does not need to be manually emptied and rebuilt as it will be done automatically by the Devel module.

Theme registry rebuilding is an intensive operation and automatically rebuilding it on every page load will severely affect performance if used in a production site. Remember to turn this off!

How it works...

The Devel module is a crucial component of every Drupal developer's toolkit whether it be module or theme development. As just demonstrated, from a theme developer's point of view, it provides a number of handy tools to speed up development as well as aid debugging.

The Devel module, as its name suggests, is a module tailored towards development and, as such, is not intended for production environments. That said, circumstances might sometimes demand its use in debugging issues on the production server. In such cases, it is important to only enable it temporarily and strictly control access to its features via the **Permissions** page at `admin/user/permissions` (**Home | Administer | User management | Permissions**).

Theme overrides using the Theme developer module

This recipe will outline the features of the Theme developer module. We will use it to demonstrate the steps to be followed to locate the theme function or template being used to display a particular element in a page.

Getting ready

The Theme developer module can be downloaded from `http://drupal.org/project/ devel_themer`. It depends on the Devel module which we looked at in the previous recipe. Both of these modules need to be downloaded, installed, and enabled.

Once Devel has been installed, we will also need to enable the **Development** block in order to readily access all of its features including those pertaining to Theme developer. This can be done from the block administration page at `admin/build/block` (**Home | Administer | Site building | Blocks**).

How to do it...

Once the modules and block have been enabled we should have a page which looks something like the following screenshot.

As we saw in an earlier recipe, there are three items which are of particular interest to us in the development block, namely the **Enable/Disable Theme developer**, **Empty cache**, and **Theme registry** links. The first is a handily accessible option that allows us to enable and disable the theme developer at will. The **Empty cache** link, as the name suggests, clears the Drupal cache and theme registry when clicked. Lastly, the **Theme registry** link provides a directory of currently available theme functions which are stored in the registry.

When the **Enable Theme developer** link is clicked, the **Themer info** checkbox appears on the top left of the screen. This checkbox is always disabled by default upon every page load and needs to be checked only when we want to find out information about a particular element in our theme. For example, if we want to obtain details about the theme function responsible for the display of an author's name in a node, all we need to do is check the **Themer info** checkbox and then click on the author's name. This will load details about the theme function or template file involved in an overlay along with a list of arguments passed to the function.

 The Drupal Themer Information overlay can be dragged. If it blocks elements of the page, it can be dragged it to a more convenient location.

How it works...

The Theme developer module makes use of a function named `hook_theme_registry_alter()` which allows it to intercept and track the use of theme functions and template files in each page. With a little Javascript, the module compares the clicked element with a stored list which displays theme-related information about the element.

In the previous screenshot, we can see that the **Parents** hierarchy list provides information about the template file used to display the author's name, which in this case is `node.tpl.php` which in turn is embedded in `page.tpl.php`.

Below the parents list, we are given the name of the theme function—theme_username()—which was used to theme the username field. Further below, we are provided with a list of arguments, just one in this case, which have been passed to this function. The arguments can be expanded to list their contents which will prove very handy.

Lastly, and crucially, we are also provided with a list of candidate function names which can be used to override the currently used function. In other words, rather than editing theme_username() to add our changes, we can use one of myzen_username() or phptemplate_username(), or zen_username() to hold our changes depending on our scope and requirements.

 If the element is not displayed by way of a theme function, Theme developer just shows the template file involved in the display process and lists candidate template files which can be used to override the existing file.

There's more...

The Theme developer module besides providing information on theme functions and template files also links to their documentation pages.

Drupal API documentation

Theme developer will link Drupal's core functions, such as theme_username() in the recent example, to their entries on http://api.drupal.org which contain information about the function, its arguments, and use cases.

Compatibility issues

The ability of the Theme developer module to load related theme information of clicked elements on a page is accomplished by wrapping said elements in HTML and tracking them via JavaScript. Since the markup of the page is changed, this feature can adversely affect the functionality of certain modules—especially those which rely on JavaScript and themes. As a result, it is recommended that this module only be used during the theming or debugging process and be turned off at other times.

Listing all available variables in a template file

Until we become familiar with a template, it can be quite daunting to understand what is going on as all that we see is a host of variables which are being positioned using markup. Frequently, it is important to know which variables are available to us in the file and to also understand what they contain.

In this recipe, we will look at how to list all the variables available inside the `page.tpl.php` template file using the Theme developer module.

Getting ready

The Devel and Theme developer modules need to be installed and enabled as per the previous recipe. The Development block is assumed to have been enabled.

How to do it...

The variables inside the `page.tpl.php` template can be listed by following these steps:

1. Click on the **Enable Theme developer** link in the **Development** block.
2. Check the **Themer info** checkbox.
3. Click on any part of the page. This should load theme-related information inside the **Drupal Themer Information** pop-up.
4. In the pop-up, if the **Template called** is not `page.tpl.php`, then look for it in the **Parents** section above and click it.
5. Look for the section at the bottom of the pop-up named **Template variables**.
6. All available variables should be available by clicking on the link below, usually titled something along the lines of **(Array, X elements)** where X signifies the number of rows within the array.

The contents of the variables array can sometimes be nested within multiple levels.

How it works...

An example screenshot of a list of variables inside a `page.tpl.php` template is shown as follows:

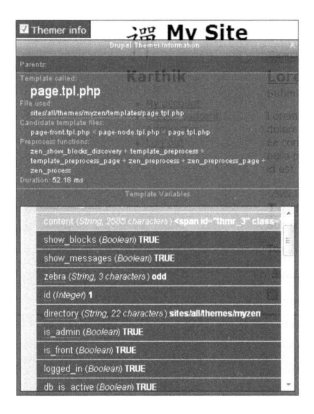

There's more...

There are a variety of ways to obtain information about available variables.

Doing it manually

Some situations and the preferences of some developers demand a more basic solution to list all available variables. This can be done by adding the following PHP code inside the template file in question:

```php
<?php
  $variables = get_defined_vars();
  dpm($variables);
?>
```

The dpm() function in the last code snippet is part of the Devel module which needs to be enabled for this to work. If it is unavailable, we can make do with PHP's var_dump() function instead, although its output will not be as tidy as that of the dpm() function.

 How about constants?

Similar to get_defined_vars() in the last code, get_defined_constants() will list available constants. This is, however, seldom required in a template file.

Documentation

When a template file is listed in the theme developer pop-up, the **File used** field links to the template file itself, which when clicked will, with the help of the Devel module, display the source code of the file. Most, if not all, core template files contain documentation listing all relevant variables along with a description.

This information is also available from http://api.drupal.org.

Displaying the profile name instead of a username

When content is created on a site, it is usually attributed to the user who created it. This is in the form of a link which highlights the username and links it to the author's profile page. However, quite frequently, the username tends to be cryptic or even unprofessional and the need arises for a custom field where the user can enter his own name without the restrictions of a Drupal username.

Custom user fields are usually handled using the profile module. This recipe will detail the steps needed to replace the username with this custom name all across the site.

Getting ready

Ensure that the Profile, Devel, and Theme developer modules are all installed and enabled. We will also be using the myzen theme created in the previous chapter, as our example theme in this recipe.

How to do it...

First up, let's create a profile field named **Real name** to store the user's actual name as opposed to a username.

1. With the profile module enabled, visit `admin/user/profile` (**Home | Administer | User management | Profiles**).

2. Click on the **single-line textfield** option to create the new field.

3. In the ensuing form, enter **Personal information** as the **Category**.

4. Enter **Full name** as the **Title**.

5. Set the **Form name** field to **profile_realname**.

6. Check the **The user must enter a value** and the **Visible in user registration form** checkboxes at the bottom of the form.

7. Click the **Save field** button at the bottom of the page to create our field.

Now that we have our field set up as in the previous screenshot, users can either enter their names into this field during the registration process or, alternatively, do so from their user profile page which should now have a new tab titled **Personal Information**.

With our profile field ready we can now focus on replacing the existing username field with our new field.

1. Enable Theme developer's **Themer info**.

2. Navigate to a view of a node where the author's name is visible.

3. Clicking on the author's name should display the theme function being used as well as candidate theme function overrides including the one that we will be using—`myzen_username()`.

4. Navigate to the myzen folder at `sites/all/themes/myzen`.

5. Open the file `template.php` in an editor.

6. In another editor, open the file `includes/theme.inc`.

7. Copy the function `theme_username()` in its entirety from this file into `template.php`.

8. The function in question should look something like the following block of code:

```
function theme_username($object) {

  if ($object->uid && $object->name) {
    // Shorten the name when it is too long or it will break many
tables.
    if (drupal_strlen($object->name) > 20) {
      $name = drupal_substr($object->name, 0, 15) .'...';
    }
    else {
      $name = $object->name;
    }
```

```
      if (user_access('access user profiles')) {
        $output = l($name, 'user/'. $object->uid,
array('attributes' => array('title' => t('View user
profile.')))));
      }
    else {
      $output = check_plain($name);
    }
  }
  else if ($object->name) {
    // Sometimes modules display content composed by people
who are
    // not registered members of the site (e.g. mailing list
or news
    // aggregator modules). This clause enables modules to
display
    // the true author of the content.
    if (!empty($object->homepage)) {
      $output = l($object->name, $object->homepage,
array('attributes' => array('rel' => 'nofollow')));
    }
    else {
      $output = check_plain($object->name);
    }
    $output .= ' ('. t('not verified') .')';
  }
  else {
    $output = check_plain(variable_get('anonymous',
t('Anonymous')));
  }
  return $output;
}
```

9. Rename `theme_username()` to `myzen_username()`.

10. Add the highlighted block of code just below the first `if` statement.

```
function myzen_username($object) {
  if ($object->uid && $object->name) {
    profile_load_profile($object);
    // Only replace username with realname if realname is not
    // empty.
    if (!empty($object->profile_realname)) {
      $object->name = $object->profile_realname;
    }
```

```
    // Shorten the name when it is too long or it will break
many tables.
      if (drupal_strlen($object->name) > 20) {
        $name = drupal_substr($object->name, 0, 15) .'...';
      }
      else {
        $name = $object->name;
      }
```

11. Once this is done, save the file and exit. The editor containing `theme.inc` can be closed as well.

As we have introduced a new theme function, clear the theme registry to ensure that our changes take effect. Once that is done, visiting a node should confirm that the profile field is being used instead of the username.

How it works...

What we are doing here is overriding Drupal's inbuilt function—`theme_username()`—which handles the display of the username field with our theme-specific version, `myzen_username()`. The latter is initially just a copy of the former and contains a lot of pre-existing code dealing with access control, user roles, and so on. We can safely ignore all of it as we are just going to be performing a simple replace operation right at the top of the function.

The `theme_username()` function accepts an argument `$object` which is usually a standard Drupal user object.

```
    profile_load_profile($object);
```

The preceding statement loads the profile fields and returns them as part of `$object`. In our case, `$object` now contains a new field named `profile_realname`.

```
    if (!empty($object->profile_realname)
    {
      $object->name = $object->profile_realname;
    }
```

Next we check if our new profile field is not empty. If so, we just replace the name field which contains the username with our profile field. If it is empty, we do nothing and let the username stay intact.

Lorem Ipsum

Submitted by Karthik on Tue, 03/16/2010 - 09:10 Categд

Lorem ipsum dolor sit amet, consectetur adipisicing elit, se dolore magna aliqua. Ut enim ad minim veniam, quis nostru ea commodo consequat. Duis aute irure dolor in reprehend nulla pariatur. Excepteur sint occaecat cupidatat non proide id est laborum.

Add new comment

Test story 1

Submitted by Karthik on Fri, 03/05/2010 - 12:37

Test

Add new comment

In the preceding screenshot, we can see that the submission information uses my username—**Karthik**—rather than the full name provided in my profile. In the following screenshot, we can see the `myzen_username()` function in action with my username being replaced by the profile field value—**Karthik Kumar**.

Lorem Ipsum

Submitted by Karthik Kumar on Tue, 03/16/2010 - 09:10

Lorem ipsum dolor sit amet, consectetur adipisicing elit, se dolore magna aliqua. Ut enim ad minim veniam, quis nostru ea commodo consequat. Duis aute irure dolor in reprehend nulla pariatur. Excepteur sint occaecat cupidatat non proide id est laborum.

Add new comment

Test story 1

Submitted by Karthik Kumar on Fri, 03/05/2010 - 12:37

Test

Add new comment

There's more...

As with most things Drupal, regularly implemented features, changes and workarounds are implemented as contributed modules and shared with the community.

Realname module

Modules such as realname have been contributed to the Drupal repository and perform a similar function to this recipe. This module can be accessed at `http://drupal.org/project/realname`.

Styling the site maintenance page

Drupal offers a site maintenance mode where the site is inaccessible to end users unless expressly specified. During this period, visitors to the site are presented with a maintenance page. In this recipe, we will be looking at an approach that will allow us to style this page from our theme.

Getting ready

We will be using the Zen-based myzen theme which we created in the last chapter. It is recommended that for the purpose of the recipe, the site is loaded on two separate browser applications—the first for the admin account and the other for an anonymous user account. This will make it easier to make changes and verify their effect.

The site can be placed in maintenance mode by navigating to `admin/settings/site-maintenance` (**Home | Administer | Site configuration | Site maintenance**) and setting the **Site status** to **Off-line**.

How to do it...

The default maintenance theme is the Garland sub-theme named Minnelli. We will first need to change it to our myzen theme using the following steps:

1. Browse to the the site's `settings.php` file which is customarily located in the `sites/default` folder, and open it in an editor.

2. Uncomment the following three lines by removing the hash that prefixes each of them:

   ```
   $conf = array(
     'maintenance_theme' => 'minnelli',
   );
   ```

3. In the preceding block, change the name of the theme from `minnelli` to `myzen`.

4. Save the file and exit.

How it works...

The default Minnelli theme's maintenance page looked something like this:

By using the $conf array in `settings.php`, we were able to tell Drupal to use a different theme as the maintenance theme. In our case, this was myzen. Changing the maintenance theme setting to this theme resulted in a maintenance page that looked like the following:

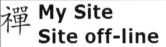

There's more...

We can extend our customization further by also overriding the maintenance page template file to add our own changes.

Maintenance template

If just changing the theme is insufficient, and we need to customize the maintenance page further, we will need to override the default maintenance template file. This can be done by copying the file `maintenance-page.tpl.php` from `modules/system` to myzen's `templates` folder and editing it accordingly.

In maintenance mode, the theme registry is rebuilt on every page load. In other words, there should be no need to clear and rebuild it after adding template files.

5

Development and Debugging Tools

We will be covering the following recipes in this chapter:

- ▶ Finding the right function to use to theme an object
- ▶ Analyzing variables using the Devel module
- ▶ Generating sample content using the Devel generate module
- ▶ Resetting the default theme manually
- ▶ Live preview with Web Developer
- ▶ Validating HTML and CSS using Web Developer
- ▶ Turning off JavaScript in the browser
- ▶ Disabling CSS in the browser
- ▶ Inspecting elements and debugging CSS using Firebug
- ▶ Diagnostic logging of JavaScript using Firebug

Introduction

In our world of Drupal design and development, or any other package for that matter, it is seldom that we get things right the first time. In fact, most of our time is spent in isolating, patching, refining, and reevaluating code or design that we believed was perfectly fine. This has led to the creation of a plethora of developmental aids and tools to streamline these processes and save us a heap of time and effort better spent elsewhere. These include informational aids, browser-based tools, as well as Drupal modules which assist in development and debugging.

First and foremost is documentation. Drupal's documentation is largely centered around its handbook which can be accessed via `http://drupal.org/handbook`. Besides this, documentation for the various Drupal APIs provided is located at `http://api.drupal.org`.

Drupal-specific development and debugging tools primarily revolve around the Devel module and its offshoots, such as the Devel generate and Theme developer modules. We have already taken advantage of the Devel and Theme developer modules in previous chapters and will see more of them in this one.

When it comes to client-side tools, the chief protagonist is a Firefox add-on pictured in the following screenshot named Firebug. It is an invaluable tool that has revolutionized web development by allowing the debugging and streamlining of all aspects of theming from HTML and CSS to JavaScript right from the browser. While the primary add-on is only available for Firefox, a less potent variant is available for other browsers in the form of Firebug Lite. More information on both of these options is available from `http://getfirebug.com`.

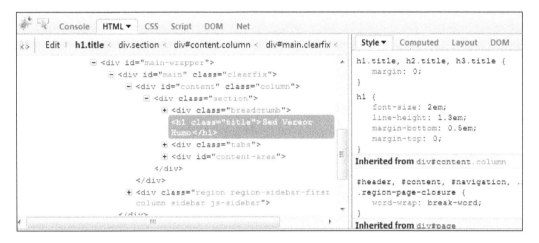

A complement to Firebug's in-depth capabilities is available in the form of the Web Developer add-on which provides a suite of development, testing, and validation tools as pictured in the following screenshot. Initially created by Chris Pederick as a Firefox add-on, it is now also available as an extension for Google Chrome. More information on this add-on is available at `http://chrispederick.com/work/web-developer/`.

Besides Firefox, other browsers such as Opera, Internet Explorer, and Google Chrome come with their own sets of tools and plugins. For example, Opera provides a suite of tools under the moniker Dragonfly, while Internet Explorer's equivalent is simply titled Developer Tools. Google Chrome, on the other hand, is powered by user-contributed *extensions* which are quite similar to Firefox add-ons with a significant number of them being ported equivalents of the same.

In this chapter, however, we will be primarily concentrating on Firefox add-ons as they provide the most complete and feature-rich set of tools that are available to developers today.

Finding the right function to use to theme an object

In the previous chapter, we saw how to find out which theme function is being used to theme an element—the username—in a page and, subsequently, learned to override it. However, while writing modules, or when we are looking at ways to render data loaded from the database, it is also not uncommon to be at a loss to know which function to use to theme a Drupal object.

In this recipe, we will look to source potential solutions which can be used to render a typical Drupal user object. We will be accomplishing this task using the Devel module and available documentation.

Getting ready

The Devel module which can be downloaded from `http://drupal.org/project/devel` is assumed to be installed and enabled. Furthermore, it is required that the **access devel information** and **execute php code** permissions be assigned to the current user.

The **Development** block which is provided by the module, also needs to be enabled.

How to do it...

Since we are looking to theme the user object and, perhaps, display it as a link to the user's profile, let us look to see if there are any Drupal functions relating to the term *username*. To do this, visit the Drupal API site at `http://api.drupal.org` and type the word **username** into the search field. This autocomplete field should provide, as seen in the following screenshot, a drop down listing all functions which include the term **username**.

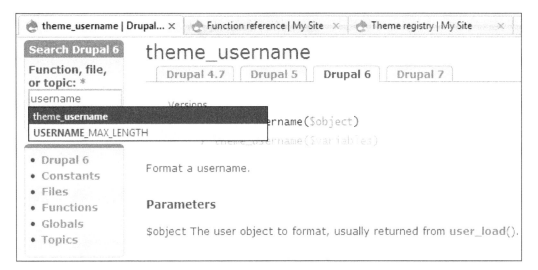

As displayed in the previous screenshot, the `theme_username()` function looks promising. The linked API page should provide information on the arguments that need to be supplied to this function, as well as information on the return type and a lot more. We can see that the `theme_username()` function accepts a single parameter, `$object`. Looking at the **Parameters** section, we can also see that this parameter is typically the output of a `user_load()` call.

> The API site customarily also provides links to other areas of Drupal which use the function being viewed. However, since theme functions are invoked as arguments of the `theme()` hook, this information is not available. As an alternative, if we need to look at some real-world examples of the function in action, we will need to run a code search throughout the entire project for the term **theme('username'** to get a list of all instances of the function being used.

Once we have a candidate function in hand, we can give it a test run using the Devel module's PHP-evaluation feature. This can be accessed by clicking on the **Execute PHP Code** link in the **Development** block. In the ensuing form, enter some test code like the following to see the theme function in action.

```
// Print the current user.
global $user;
$username = theme('username', $user);
print($username);
print("\n");

// Print some other user: User with user ID 5.
$user_other = user_load(5);
$username2 = theme('username', $user_other);
print($username2);
```

Once this is done, click on the **Execute** button to evaluate the code.

How it works...

When the PHP code is evaluated, the result should look something like the following:

```
<a href="/sites/cvs/drupal/mysite/user/1" title="View user
profile.">Karthik</a>
<a href="/sites/cvs/drupal/mysite/user/5" title="View user
profile.">gastibrutrej</a>
```

In other words, we have implemented `theme_username()` correctly and can proceed to use it in our modules or themes as necessary.

There's more...

There are also other avenues available to us when it comes to finding information on available module and theme functions.

Function reference and the theme registry

Besides using the Drupal API documentation site, another handy option is to use the Devel module's **Function reference** list or view the site's **Theme registry** to source out potential theme functions. Both these options can be accessed by clicking on their respective links in the **Development** block and then running a search for candidate functions as seen in the following screenshot:

Analyzing variables using the Devel module

While working with the Drupal API, we will often be faced with the situation where we have no idea how a variable is structured. While PHP provides a number of functions to peek into the variable, Drupal's Devel module provides a cleaner solution and a prettier interface to do the same.

In this recipe, we will be looking at the Devel module's dpm() function.

Getting ready

It is assumed that the Devel module has been installed and is enabled. It also comes with its own set of permissions and it is assumed that the current user has all the appropriate permissions including **access devel information**.

We will also be making use of the mysite module created earlier in this book to hold our odds and ends.

How to do it...

The following steps are to be performed inside the mysite module folder at `sites/all/modules/mysite`:

1. Open the file `mysite.module` in an editor.

2. Look for an implementation of the `mysite_init()` hook. If it is unavailable, create one and add the following code so that the resulting function looks like the following:

```
/**
 * Implementation of hook_init().
 */
function mysite_init() {
  global $user;

  // Analyze the $user variable.
  dpm($user);
}
```

3. Save the file and exit the editor.

4. Access the site in a browser to see if we are presented with a pretty-printed representation of the `$user` variable.

How it works...

When the site is now accessed, the $user variable should be displayed at the top of the page something like in the following screenshot:

```
... (Object) stdClass
    uid (String, 1 characters ) 1
    name (String, 7 characters ) Karthik
    pass (String, 32 characters ) a8f5f167f44f4964e6c998dee827110c
    mail (String, 18 characters ) mysite@example.com
    mode (String, 1 characters ) 0
    sort (String, 1 characters ) 0
    threshold (String, 1 characters ) 0
    theme (String, 0 characters )
    signature (String, 0 characters )
    signature_format (String, 1 characters ) 0
    created (String, 10 characters ) 1267211648
    access (String, 10 characters ) 1275252667
    login (String, 10 characters ) 1275244405
    status (String, 1 characters ) 1
    timezone (NULL)
    language (String, 0 characters )
    picture (String, 0 characters )
    init (String, 18 characters ) mysite@example.com
    data (String, 72 characters ) a:1:{s:13:"form_build_id";s:37:"form-f943ad1c89...
    sid (String, 26 characters ) 5o12hspembt5al8k2dp9iplop3
    hostname (String, 8 characters ) 10.0.0.6
    timestamp (String, 10 characters ) 1275252746
    cache (String, 1 characters ) 0
    session (String, 54 characters ) user_overview_filter|a:0:{}node_overview_filter...
    form_build_id (String, 37 characters ) form-f943ad1c8980ba8c36bff5203f74e357
    roles (Array, 1 element)
                                                            Krumo version 0.2a
```

We can see that all the data within the `$user` object is now visible. Each property is listed along with its data type and length. Furthermore, complex data types such as arrays are also expanded, thus giving us an excellent overview of the entire object.

There's more...

It is always recommended that the codebase is kept neat and tidy. Once we are done with our debugging, it is a good idea to clean up after ourselves.

Removing debug functions after use

It is important that calls to `dpm()` and other Devel module commands be removed once the debugging session is over. It is not an infrequent occurrence to find the site becoming unusable because the Devel module was disabled without removing these commands. Alternatively, if some debugging code is used regularly enough to be retained in a module, then it might be worthwhile to wrap all code related to the Devel module within a `module_exists()` check as follows:

```
if (module_exists('devel')) {
  // Add debugging code here.
}
```

Other useful Devel module functions

Besides `dpm()`, other useful functions include `dd()` which logs output to an external file, and `ddebug_backtrace()` which is useful as a postmortem tool to analyze where things went wrong. More information can be found by simply browsing through the `devel.module` file inside the Devel module's folder.

Generating sample content using the Devel generate module

Once our theme has made significant progress, it is important to test it in various scenarios with different sets of sample data to ferret out bugs and anomalies that sometimes tend to be overlooked during the design phase. In this recipe, we will be using the **Devel Generate** module to generate test data in the form of content, taxonomy categories, and users to simulate real-world input.

Getting ready

It is assumed that the Devel module is available and enabled. While the Devel module itself is not a prerequisite, the Devel Generate module is a part of its package and should also be enabled from the module installation page. It is also assumed that the Taxonomy, Comment, and, if necessary, the Path and Upload modules are enabled. Furthermore, it is recommended that multiple node types be made available to the generator to ensure that our sample data encompasses as many permutations and combinations as possible.

How to do it...

The Devel Generate module, once enabled, exposes its functionality via the **Generate items** section in the administration pages and block. We will be generating sample taxonomy categories, users, and content—in that order—as per the following steps:

1. To generate taxonomy categories, navigate to `admin/generate/taxonomy` (**Home | Administer | Generate items | Generate categories**) to access the category generation form.

2. While the defaults should do, the options on this page can be tweaked as necessary to generate more or less sample data with varying lengths.

3. Click on **Do it!** to generate the vocabulary and taxonomy terms.

4. Next, navigate to `admin/generate/user` (**Home | Administer | Generate items | Generate users**) to access the user generation form.

5. Again, the defaults should be sufficient, but can be tweaked if necessary.

6. Click on **Do it!** to generate our test user accounts.

7. Finally, navigate to `admin/generate/content` (**Home | Administer | Generate items | Generate content**) to access the content generation form.

Home > Administer > Generate items >

Generate content

Which node types do you want to create?:

☑ Page

☑ Story

☐ **Delete all content** in these node types before generat

How many nodes would you like to generate?:

50

How far back in time should the nodes be dated?:

1 week ago ▾

Node creation dates will be distributed randomly from the current

Maximum number of generated comments per node:

30

You must also enable comments for the node types you are gene

Max word length of titles:

8

☐ Add an upload to each node

Requires upload.module

☑ Add taxonomy terms to each node.

Requires taxonomy.module

☑ Add an url alias for each node.

Requires path.module

[Do it!]

8. As the previous screenshot attests, there are a number of options available on this form. Tweak them so that there is significant variation in the generated nodes to account for varying user input.

 If comments and uploads are also to be generated, it is important that the node types in question have the respective features enabled.

9. Click on **Do it!** to generate the test content.

How it works...

Once the generator has run its course, we can verify the generated content by visiting the taxonomy, user, and content administration pages. Visiting the default front page or the URL node should display a simulation of what the site will look like with real-world user input.

Resetting the default theme manually

There will be times where certain changes we have made to the theme will render the site utterly unusable. For example, this can happen when there are layout issues with the theme which might make navigating to the theme administration pages difficult, or when we have introduced an error in our PHP code which leads to the *White Screen of Death* where all we have to work with is an unusable blank screen. While we could simply stomp our way into the database and change the current theme, the "*Drupal Way*" advocates a cleaner and simpler solution to rescue the site.

In this recipe, we will be looking at rescuing an unusable site via the settings.php configuration file.

Getting ready

This recipe only applies when a Drupal site becomes unusable due to errors in the theme currently being used.

How to do it...

Since the site is unusable, we can either edit the database directly or use the settings.php file to override the default theme being used, as detailed in the following steps:

1. Navigate to the site's settings.php file which is, by default, inside the sites/default folder.

2. Open this file in an editor and look for a section titled **Variable overrides**.

3. The $conf array in this section is normally commented out and is heavily documented. Uncomment the highlighted lines as in the following excerpt by removing the hash that prefixes each of them:

```
$conf = array(
#   'site_name' => 'My Drupal site',
    'theme_default' => 'minnelli',
#   'anonymous' => 'Visitor',
#   'maintenance_theme' => 'myzen',
#   'reverse_proxy' => TRUE,
#   'reverse_proxy_addresses' => array('a.b.c.d', ...),
);
```

4. Save the file and exit the editor.

5. Try accessing the site in a browser to ensure that it is accessible and that the theme has been changed to Minnelli.

How it works...

The $conf configuration array is used by Drupal to load and store system variables. By declaring this array in the settings.php file, we are effectively overriding variables which are stored in the database. In this case, we have specified that the theme to be used to display the site should be Minnelli which should override our problematic theme.

Once the bugs in the theme have been weeded out, we can reverse our changes to the settings.php file to revert back to the original theme.

There's more...

Drupal stores its configuration data in a table named variables in the database. The Devel module provides an interface to this table which is often handy when attempting to peek under the hood.

Using the Devel module to view and edit database variables

The Devel module comes with a handy variable editor which can be used to view and even edit variables directly in the database. For this recipe, we can use it to confirm that the **theme_default** variable is indeed being overridden. It can be accessed by clicking on the **Variable editor** link in the **Development** block. Scrolling down to the bottom of the resulting page should confirm that the **theme_default** setting is still set to **myzen** whereas the theme actually being used to display the page is **Minnelli**.

	Name▲	Value	Length
☐	theme_acquia_marina_settings	a:121:{s:23:"mission_statement_pages";s:4:"home";s:18:"breadcrumb...	5232
☐	theme_bluemarine_settings	a:16:{s:11:"toggle_logo";i:1;s:11:"toggle_name";i:1;s:13:"toggle_...	452
☐	theme_default	s:5:"myzen";	12
☐	theme_garland_settings	a:20:{s:11:"toggle_logo";i:1;s:11:"toggle_name";i:1;s:13:"toggle_...	3226
☐	theme_myzen_settings	a:24:{s:14:"zen_breadcrumb";s:3:"yes";s:24:"zen_breadcrumb_separa...	749
☐	theme_settings	a:1:{s:21:"toggle_node_info_page";b:0;}	39
☐	theme_zen_settings	a:9:{s:17:"zen_block_editing";s:1:"1";s:14:"zen_breadcrumb";s:3:"...	335

Live preview with Web Developer

Drupal theme development usually involves a lot of toggling between editor and browser to see our changes in effect. This can get to be rather tedious after a point, especially when debugging or tweaking CSS, and more so while working directly on the server. In this recipe, we will be looking at the features provided by the Web Developer add-on which will allow us to directly edit HTML and CSS in the browser and see our changes propagate instantaneously.

Getting ready

The Web Developer add-on for Firefox is assumed to have been installed and enabled. It can be downloaded from `http://chrispederick.com/work/web-developer/`.

How to do it...

Web developer's list of features include a rudimentary HTML editor which can be used to tweak markup during testing. The editor can be launched by clicking on **Miscellaneous** in the Web Developer toolbar and then clicking on **Edit HTML**.

The editor is launched in a panel as seen in the following screenshot, and includes a search field to locate pertinent sections of the page. Any changes made in the panel will be reflected immediately in the page above.

The CSS editor can similarly be launched by clicking on **CSS** in the toolbar and selecting **Edit CSS**. This should load all the linked stylesheets in an editor in a panel as shown in the next screenshot.

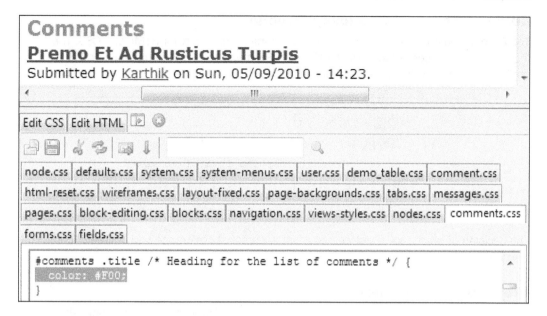

How it works...

In the previous screenshot, the `comments.css` file has been opened in the editor after which the title for the **Comments** section has been styled with the color red. The changes are immediately apparent in the browser above. If we are working on a local server, the stylesheet can be saved using the **save** button at the top of the panel. If not, we can either copy and paste the modified file, or alternatively, apply the changes manually.

CSS aggregation

If CSS aggregation is enabled for the site, it is important that it be turned off before editing to ensure that Web Developer has access to all the component CSS files. If not, we will only have access to a single, monolithic, and unwieldy stylesheet.

There's more...

The Web developer extension is not the sole player with these features. Other extensions including Firebug, support them as well.

Editing HTML and CSS using Firebug

The Firebug add-on also provides similar live-editing functionality for HTML and CSS. These features can be accessed from the **HTML** and **CSS** menus in the Firebug panel and clicking on **Edit** as demonstrated in the following screenshot:

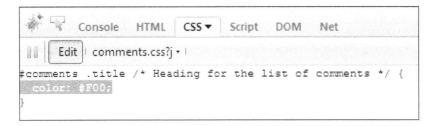

The decision of which tool to use comes down to personal preference and degree of comfort with the interface.

View all CSS rules at once

The Web Developer toolbar provides an option to view all CSS rules in one location. This can be done by clicking on the **CSS** menu in the toolbar and then clicking on **View CSS**. This feature can be quite handy during debugging when we need to run a search for particular rules, usually relating to positional aspects of elements.

Validating HTML and CSS using Web Developer

Validation is an integral part of web development. HTML and CSS validation ensure that the document is structurally and semantically correct and provide a reliability guarantee that the page will be displayed correctly, both now and in the future.

In this recipe, we will look at how the Web Developer add-on provides easy options for validating both HTML and CSS using the W3C validator at `http://validator.w3.org`.

Getting ready

It is assumed that the Web Developer add-on is installed and enabled in Firefox.

How to do it...

To validate the HTML of a page currently being viewed in Firefox, click on the **Tools** menu of the Web Developer toolbar and select **Validate HTML** as displayed in the following screenshot:

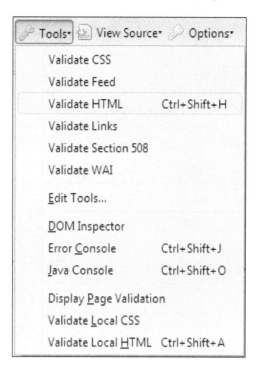

Once clicked, we will be redirected to the W3C validator page to view the results of the check.

Similarly, validating the CSS of a page currently being viewed can be performed by clicking on the **Tools** menu of the toolbar and selecting **Validate CSS**.

Validating HTML and CSS from the local server

The W3C validator, by default, validates files and pages on servers which are accessible through the Internet. However, this is not always convenient as our site might still be under development on a local server, or we are perhaps looking to validate pages on the site which are accessible to authenticated users only. In such situations, we can use the Web Developer's **Validate Local CSS** and **Validate Local HTML** options which save the HTML or CSS as files and upload them to the validator.

How it works...

Once it receives its input, the HTML validator validates the page against its `Doctype` declaration. In the following screenshot, the *local* page in question was declared to be **XHTML 1.0 Strict** compliant and it passed the validation process successfully.

Similarly, the W3C CSS validator checks the supplied CSS against a predefined profile, which in the following screenshot is set to **CSS 2.1**. As a result, we see that some **CSS 3** properties have been flagged as errors as they do not conform to the CSS 2.1 specifications.

	Sorry! We found the following errors (3)	
URI : webdeveloper-endymion-1275162795637.css		
1271	#header, #content, #navigation, .region-sidebar-first, .region-sidebar-second, #footer, .region-page-closure	Property word-wrap doesn't exist : break-word break-word
2037	.node-unpublished div.unpublished, .comment-unpublished div.unpublished	Property word-wrap doesn't exist : break-word break-word
2443	#page-wrapper	Property overflow-y doesn't exist in CSS level 2.1 but exists in : visible visible

There's more...

When attempting to validate multiple pages in a site, it is useful to know that we can temporarily instruct Web Developer to automatically validate the page being viewed.

Validating HTML and CSS automatically

The Web Developer toolbar provides an option which can be used to automatically validate the page being viewed. This setting can be enabled by clicking on the **Tools** menu of the toolbar and selecting **Display Page Validation**. This will result in an additional toolbar being added to Firefox which displays the validation status of the current page. This is handy when performing quality checks across different pages in the site and can save time and effort.

Turning off JavaScript in the browser

Websites cater to users using browsers of varying capabilities on a plethora of devices. Consequently, there is no guarantee that user experiences will always be the same across the board. **Graceful degradation** is often a term associated with site usability and accessibility, and ensures that sites are still functional in the absence of key technologies such as JavaScript, CSS, images, and plugins such as Flash. Disabling various browser features is also quite frequently an essential step during debugging.

This recipe will detail the steps required to disable JavaScript during development.

Getting ready

While every browser provides a JavaScript toggle somewhere in its preferences dialogs, and many of them are beginning to provide handy developer tools of their own, we will be using the Web Developer add-on for Firefox and Google Chrome which can be downloaded from `http://chrispederick.com/work/web-developer/`. It is assumed that it has been installed and enabled.

How to do it...

Once the Web Developer add-on is installed in Firefox, a toolbar should be available at the top of the page. Clicking on the **Disable** drop down should present a list of options including **Disable JavaScript**, which in turn, leads to another submenu with the **All JavaScript** option. This, when clicked, should disable JavaScript in the browser as displayed in the following screenshot:

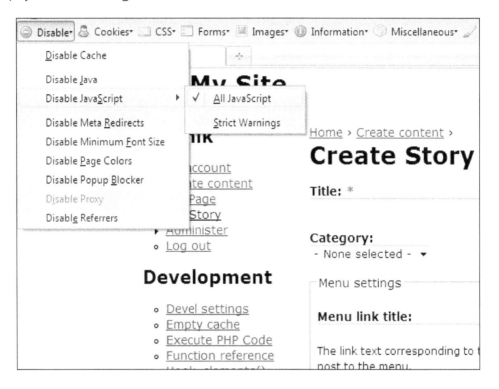

The page will need to be refreshed to see our changes taking effect.

How it works...

Once JavaScript is disabled, all the frills will no longer be active. In the previous screenshot, we can clearly see, for example, that the **Menu settings** fieldset is no longer clickable as the page no longer implements the available JavaScript. Furthermore, we can verify that the page is still accessible, as what should have been a minimized fieldset is now expanded with its contents visible.

There's more...

Other browsers also provide tools that allow the easy manipulation of their options, including the option to temporarily disable JavaScript.

Disabling JavaScript in Opera

Disabling JavaScript in Opera is as simple as pressing *F12* to access the **Quick preferences** menu and toggling the **Enable JavaScript** option accordingly, as demonstrated in the following screenshot:

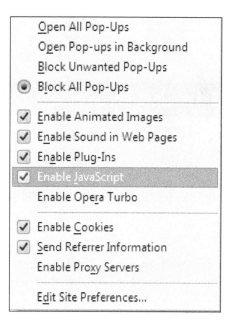

Disabling JavaScript in Internet Explorer 8

As outlined in the following screenshot, pressing *F12* in Internet Explorer loads the **Developer Tools** panel. Clicking, within the panel, the **Disable** menu and clicking the **Script** option accordingly, will disable or enable JavaScript support in the browser.

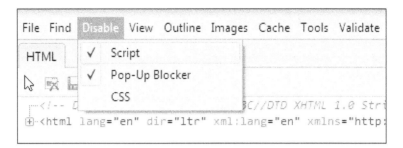

Disabling CSS in the browser

Besides catering to graceful degradation as seen with the recipe on disabling JavaScript, disabling CSS files is invaluable during debugging, especially once the levels of complexity increase.

This recipe will detail the steps required to disable CSS during development.

Getting ready

In this recipe, we will be using the Web Developer add-on for Firefox and Google Chrome which can be downloaded from `http://chrispederick.com/work/web-developer/`. It is assumed that it has been installed and enabled.

We will also be using the myzen theme created in earlier chapters as the example theme in this recipe.

How to do it...

Once the Web Developer add-on is installed in Firefox, a toolbar should be available at the top of the page. Clicking on the **CSS** drop down should present a list of options including **Disable Styles**, which in turn, leads to another submenu featuring a number of options. Of immediate interest is the **All Styles** option, which when enabled, disables all CSS styles from the document. This is useful to visualize, for example, how accessibility software tend to parse the page.

When it comes to debugging, however, the more valuable feature is the ability to disable specific stylesheets listed under the **Individual Style Sheet** option. Situations frequently arise where rules in existing stylesheets are overridden in order to modify default styles. For example, the myzen theme overrides the default tab styles provided by Drupal using styles located in its own CSS file titled `tabs.css`. The styles in this file can be disabled by selecting the **tabs.css** entry from the list of stylesheets as demonstrated in the following screenshot:

How it works...

When the `tabs.css` file is disabled, we should immediately be able to see the default tab styles provided by Drupal take effect. This is demonstrated using the following screenshots:

The preceding screenshot displays the tabs on a typical node page first using the styles in myzen's `tabs.css`. The following screenshot, however, displays the same page with the `tabs.css` file disabled, and consequently, with Drupal's default tab styles taking effect.

There's more...

Similar, if not as comprehensive, options also exist in tools for other browsers.

Disabling CSS in Internet Explorer 8

While individual CSS files cannot be disabled in Internet Explorer, the Developer Tools panel, which can be accessed by pressing *F12*, does provide an option to disable all CSS support for the page. This can be done by clicking on the **Disable** menu and selecting CSS as shown in the following screenshot:

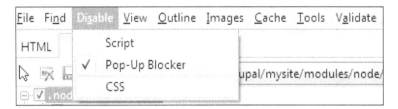

Inspecting elements and debugging CSS using Firebug

Prior to the advent of Firebug, debugging documents styled with complex CSS was an exercise in tedium. In this recipe, we will be demonstrating the use of Firebug in locating an errant margin that we are looking to modify.

The default setting for comment display in Drupal is to thread and nest them. In other words, replies to existing comments are added beneath them and indented by way of a margin to indicate each comment's specific level in the hierarchy. We are going to find out which CSS file, and the rule in particular, is responsible for this margin and modify it accordingly.

Getting ready

For the purposes of this recipe, the comment module will need to be enabled and some test content, which involves nested comments, will need to be generated using the Devel Generate module. It is assumed that the Firebug add-on has been installed in Firefox. The add-on can be downloaded from `http://getfirebug.com`.

How to do it...

Firstly, we will need to view a sample node in Firefox and locate a suitable nested comment which is a reply to another and is, therefore, indented. We can then look to ascertain the origin of this indentation using Firebug.

To do so, right-click on the title of the comment in question and click on **Inspect Element**. This should locate the element's markup in the HTML section of the Firebug panel at the bottom of the window. The markup of a typical comment in Drupal should look something like this:

```
<div class="indented" style="">
  <a id="comment-639"></a>
  <div class="comment comment-published last odd comment-by-anonymous
clearfix">
    <h3 class="title">
      <a class="active" href="/sites/cvs/drupal/mysite/
node/38#comment-639">Populus Magna Acsi Zelus Nutus Plaga</a>
    </h3>
    <!-- Comment body -->
  </div> <!-- /.comment -->
</div>
```

Furthermore, simply hovering over an element in the Firebug HTML panel should highlight the corresponding object in the browser window along with its margins and padding, if any. Since the comment's title is a simple anchor tag, it is unlikely to be the source of the margin for the entire block of content. Consequently, we can look at its parent and other elements in its ancestry as being more likely to be the source of the indentation. Inspecting each one in turn should offer information on their layouts.

Hovering over one of the ancestors of the comment title—a DIV tag with a telltale class named indented—should highlight the entire comment in the browser along with a conspicuous yellow block to its left. This indicates that this element has a margin applied to it. Clicking the DIV should load all its styles on the right-hand side of the Firebug panel as displayed in the following screenshot:

As we can tell from the screenshot, the element has a margin of 25 pixels. We can also tell that this rule is located inside the comment.css file on line number 3; clicking the filename should load the entire CSS file and make it available for editing, if necessary. We can additionally confirm the layout of this element by clicking on the **Layout** tab in the Firebug panel.

Now that we have our element and the rule responsible for the margin, we can look at modifying it. Right-clicking the **margin-left** rule should provide a list of options including **Edit**, **Delete**, and **Disable** as in the next screenshot. Clicking on **Edit** will allow us to change the margin while **Delete** will remove the entire rule altogether. **Disable**, on the other hand, will temporarily disable the rule so that we can preview what the element will look like without it in effect.

```
.indented {
⊘  margin-left: 2                          Edit Element Style...
}
Inherited from div#c
                                           New Property...
#header, #content
#footer, .region-                          Edit "margin-left"...

   word-wrap: bre                          Delete "margin-left"
}
Inherited from div#p                        Disable "margin-left"

#skip-to-nav, #pa                          Refresh
   font-size: 0.8
   line-height: 1                          Inspect in CSS Tab
}
                                           Inspect in DOM Tab
```

Additionally, we can click on **New Property** to add a new rule, perhaps a border, to this element. With Firebug also coming with autocomplete support, adding new rules is a cinch.

Rather than right-clicking to access the context menu and performing operations, we can double-click rules to edit them or double-click an empty area near a rule to add a new one. Similarly, disabling individual rules can be accomplished by clicking the disable icon to the left of the rule in question, as seen in the previous screenshot.

How it works...

We have just scratched the surface of Firebug's features here and it is well worth exploring all its tabs and context menus. Additional documentation on the CSS panel is available at http://getfirebug.com/wiki/index.php/CSS_Panel.

Diagnostic logging of JavaScript using Firebug

Even though Firebug supports an endless number of more complex JavaScript debugging features, the fundamental approach of using diagnostic prints to debug scripts is still alive and well. In this recipe, we will be looking at Firebug's console() function and a few of its variants.

Getting ready

It is assumed that the Firebug add-on has been successfully installed in Firefox. We will also be using the myzen theme created earlier in this book as an example theme in this recipe.

How to do it...

Firebug comes with a console to log output which is accessed using the `console` command. To see this in action,

1. Navigate to the myzen theme folder at `sites/all/themes/myzen`.

2. Browse to the `js` subfolder where the JavaScript files are stored, and create a file named `console.js`.

3. Open this file in an editor and add the following script to it:

```
Drupal.behaviors.consoleDebug = function (context) {
    var s = 'Foo';

    console.log(s);

    console.debug(s);

    $('a.active').each(function() {
        // console.log(this);
        console.count('Number of links on the page:');
    });

    console.warn('This is simply a warning!');
    console.error('This is an error!');
});
```

4. Save the file and exit the editor.

5. Browse back up to the myzen theme's base folder and open the `myzen.info` file in an editor.

6. Add our new JavaScript file to the scripts section using the following code:

```
scripts[] = js/console.js
```

7. Save the file and exit.

8. Rebuild the Drupal cache.

9. Access the site in Firefox and open the Firebug panel.

10. Confirm that the console output is being displayed in Firebug's console tab.

How it works...

When a page is accessed in Firefox, the console tab of the Firebug panel should output something like the following:

What is important to note is the various variants of the console command. `console.log()` simply logs the input, whereas `console.debug()` also adds a link to the script which is responsible for the call. Clicking the link will take us to the **Script** pane where more information can be accessed and further debugging performed.

Similarly, `console.warn()` logs the input in a starkly noticeable warning format, whereas `console.error()` also triggers a trace request besides registering as an error.

It is also useful to note that any complex JavaScript objects which are logged in the console are hyperlinked to their equivalent location in the **Script**, **HTML**, or **CSS** panes. This feature comes in very handy especially when manipulating HTML using jQuery.

There's more...

Firebug is a very powerful debugging tool with a plethora of features we have not covered here.

Other console variants

There are a number of other variants in the console API. More information along with examples can be accessed at `http://getfirebug.com/wiki/index.php/Console_API`.

Breakpoints, watches, and more

More complex and mainstream debugging features such as breakpoints, variable watching, stack traces, and more are also provided by Firebug and can be accessed from its **Script** tab.

6

Advanced Templating

We will cover the following recipes in this chapter:

- ▶ Adding a variable to all node templates
- ▶ Deleting a variable from the page template
- ▶ Adding a custom theme setting
- ▶ Hiding all regions on a page
- ▶ Displaying the last updated date instead of the submitted date
- ▶ Module-based variable manipulation
- ▶ Optimizing using `hook_preprocess()`
- ▶ Displaying the date field in calendar form

Introduction

In a bid to separate logic from presentation, Drupal's theming system tries to minimize the amount of PHP that is necessary in a template file. This ensures that themers who are not as comfortable in a PHP environment, are not exposed to the nitty-gritty of complicated code manipulations. Instead, they are provided with a host of pre-prepared variables which contain the content of the body of the page, the blocks, the sidebars, and so on—depending on the nature of the template—or those that describe other elements of the page such as user details or submission information which can be utilized in the template file.

But the question arises: Where do these variables come from? And how can they be modified? This is where **preprocess** functions come in. Prior to the execution of every template file, Drupal calls a set of functions known as preprocess functions which insert, modify, and in general, organize the variables which are available for use in the file. Furthermore, as we saw with template overrides in the last chapter, Drupal checks for and executes a series of candidate preprocess functions thereby allowing themes as well as modules to have a shot at manipulating the available variables. Just as with overrides, these candidate names can be divined using the Theme developer module as outlined in the following screenshot:

In the preceding screenshot, the candidate functions that affect variables available to the `page.tpl.php` template are listed under the section titled **Preprocess functions**. As is evident, there are a number of functions available with each being useful in certain stages of the theme system's workflow.

Preprocess functions come in two flavors—functions that manipulate variables particular to specific templates, and functions that allow the manipulation of variables common to all templates, or subsets thereof, as the need may be. The former may be of the form `myzen_preprocess_page($variables)` or `myzen_preprocess_block($variables)` where _page and _block signify the template files associated with $variables. The latter on the other hand, may be of the form `myzen_preprocess($variables, $hook)` which is triggered regardless of which template file is being called. However, the name of the template being called is passed to the function using the $hook parameter which could be page, block, or similar.

As mentioned previously, Drupal's theme system allows the manipulation of these variables in various stages of the workflow. For example, the display of a node template will trigger the following functions, if declared, in sequence:

Level	Function name
Core	`template_preprocess()`
	`template_preprocess_node()`
Module (mysite)	`mysite_preprocess()`
	`mysite_preprocess_node()`
Theme engine	`phptemplate_preprocess()`
	`phptemplate_preprocess_node()`
Theme (myzen)	`myzen_preprocess()`
	`myzen_preprocess_node()`

Therefore, variables manipulated by an earlier function in this queue can be manipulated again at a later stage, if so desired. We will be taking advantage of this feature all through this chapter.

Zen-based themes comes with a `template.php` file which contains skeleton preprocess functions which are commented out by default. Documentation about the function as well as instructions on how to uncomment it usually accompanies each option.

Adding a variable to all node templates

In this recipe, we will be adding a variable to be made available in all node template files. For this example, the new variable will contain a disclaimer which we will be displaying at the bottom of all nodes.

Getting ready

We will be using the myzen theme created earlier in this book as the example theme in this recipe. It is also assumed that a `node.tpl.php` file exists in myzen's `templates` folder as per recipes in earlier chapters. If not, this file will need to be imported from the Zen base-theme or a new one will need to be created.

How to do it...

A new variable can be made available to node template files by introducing it via the appropriate preprocess function as follows:

1. Navigate to the myzen folder at `sites/all/themes/myzen`.

2. Open the file `template.php` in an editor.

   As mentioned in the introduction to this chapter, this file will have a number of commonly used preprocess functions in skeleton form. These are usually commented out.

3. Look for the function titled `myzen_preprocess_node()`. This can either be uncommented or, alternatively, a new function can be created.

4. Modify this function so that the effective end result is as follows:

```
function myzen_preprocess_node(&$vars) {
    $vars['disclaimer'] = t('mysite takes no responsibility for user
contributed content and comments.');
}
```

5. Save and exit this file.

6. Navigate to the `templates` sub-folder which should contain the `node.tpl.php` template file.

7. Open `node.tpl.php` in an editor and scroll down to the bottom of the file.

8. Add the following highlighted markup just above the closing DIV:

```
<div class="content">
  <?php print $content; ?>
</div>

<?php print $links; ?>

<div class="disclaimer">
  <?php print $disclaimer; ?>
</div>
</div> <!-- /.node -->
```

9. Save the file and exit.

10. As we are introducing new elements to the theme, we will need to clear the theme registry to see them take effect.

View a node on the site to confirm that our disclaimer has now been added to the bottom of the content.

How it works...

We have chosen to place our code in `myzen_preprocess_node()` for two reasons. Firstly, we want this code to only affect the myzen theme which is why it has been placed within the myzen theme's `template.php` file. Secondly, we are inserting a variable that is only going to be used in node templates; hence, the _node suffix. If we had just used a plain `myzen_preprocess()` function, we would have introduced this variable for pages, blocks, and other templates besides the node templates.

To introduce our variable, we just need to add it to the `$vars` array which is the first argument for all preprocess functions. The `$vars` variable contains a list of all the variables which will be used or passed to the template file.

```
$vars['disclaimer'] = t('mysite takes no responsibility for user
contributed content and comments.');
```

By using an index named `disclaimer` in the array, the variable to be made available to the template file—`node.tpl.php` in this recipe—will also be named the same.

String handling in Drupal

Just about every time we need to output a string in Drupal, it is recommended that it be passed through the `t()` function. This core function ensures that the string is validated, formatted correctly, and furthermore, also fulfills its primary function of translating text input depending on the user's locale, if so configured. More information on this subject can be accessed via the documentation page for this function at `http://api.drupal.org/api/function/t/6`.

In our currently bare-boned example theme, the changes are visible in the form of a disclaimer at the bottom of the node as exhibited in the following screenshot:

Deleting a variable from the page template

While we introduced a new variable in the previous recipe, we will be removing an existing variable in this one. To demonstrate the effectiveness of template variable manipulation, we will be removing the search form as well as feed icons, such as the RSS icon, from only the front page of the site by making them unavailable to the page template file.

Getting ready

We will be using the myzen theme created earlier in this book as the example theme in this recipe. It is also assumed that a `page.tpl.php` file exists in myzen's `templates` folder. If not, this file will need to be imported from the Zen base-theme or a new one will need to be created.

How to do it...

Just as we manipulated `myzen_preprocess_node()` to add a variable to node templates, we will be manipulating `myzen_preprocess_page()` to remove variables from the page template file as follows:

1. Navigate to the myzen folder at `sites/all/themes/myzen`.

2. Open the file `template.php` in an editor.

3. Look for the function titled `myzen_preprocess_page()`. If it is commented out, it can either be uncommented or, alternatively, a new one can be created.

4. Modify this function so that the effective end result is as follows:

    ```
    function myzen_preprocess_page(&$vars){
    // Do not display the search box or RSS icon
    // if this is the front page.
    if ($vars['is_front']) {
      unset($vars['search_box']);
      unset($vars['feed_icons']);
      }
    }
    ```

 As ever, it is a good idea to always add an informative comment along with the code which describes our changes.

5. Save and exit this file.

6. Clear the theme registry to see our changes take effect.

7. View the site's front page to confirm that the search box and the feed icon are no longer visible.

8. Similarly, view a node to ensure that it is unaffected by our change.

How it works...

The unset function effectively removes a variable from the variables array thereby making it unavailable to the template. In this case, removing the `search_box` and `feed_icons` variables will remove the search form and RSS icon which are visible in the following screenshot.

Furthermore, looking at the myzen theme's page template, we can see that the `$search_box` and `$feed_icons` variables are output using the two following snippets of code:

```php
<?php if ($search_box): ?>
  <div id="search-box"><?php print $search_box; ?></div>
<?php endif; ?
```

```php
<?php if ($feed_icons): ?>
  <div class="feed-icons"><?php print $feed_icons; ?></div>
<?php endif; ?>
```

We can see that the output for both items is wrapped within an `IF` block which only prints the HTML if the variables exist. As we saw in an earlier chapter, this also ensures that our markup is not riddled with empty `DIV` blocks such as `<div class="feed-icons"></div>` which, besides being unsightly, can also inadvertently break the layout of the page.

Adding a custom theme setting

While it is quite straightforward to just edit a template file and add our changes, there are situations where this might not be feasible. When a theme-specific variable needs to be routinely modified or in cases where editing template files is not an option, the ideal solution is to make it a configurable setting. This can be done either by adding a form element by way of a module, or as this recipe will outline, by way of a configuration setting on the theme's administration page.

As an example, this recipe will make the `disclaimer` variable used in an earlier recipe in this chapter, a configurable option.

Getting ready

This recipe is a continuation of the *Adding a variable to all node templates* recipe from earlier in this chapter. It is assumed that it has been completed successfully.

How to do it...

There are two changes that we will need to make to the existing implementation from the previous recipe. First, we will need to add our theme-specific setting. With Zen-based themes, this can be easily done via the `theme-settings.php` file that comes with the starter-kit. Open this file in an editor and look for the following line inside the `myzen_settings()` function:

```
$form = array();
```

Below this line, add the following form textfield element declaration:

```
$form['myzen_disclaimer'] = array(
  '#type' => 'textfield',
  '#title' => t('Node disclaimer'),
  '#default_value' => $settings['myzen_disclaimer'],
  '#description' => t("Enter the disclaimer text to add at the
bottom of node content.")
  );
```

We can now save this file and exit the editor. Next, we need to replace the hardcoded string in the `node.tpl.php` file with our newly configured setting.

```
function myzen_preprocess_node(&$vars) {
 $vars['disclaimer'] = theme_get_setting('myzen_disclaimer');
}
```

How it works...

The `myzen_settings()` function inside `theme-settings.php` is an implementation of (theme)`hook_settings()`, a function which is called by Drupal to allow themes to conveniently add and manipulate form fields on the theme configuration page. Our new setting will look something like this on myzen's theme configuration page:

Theme-specific settings
These settings only exist for the *My Zen* theme and all the styles based on it.

Node disclaimer:

This is My Site's new disclaimer.
Enter the disclaimer text to add at the bottom of node content.

We can see from the screenshot what each of the fields in the form element declaration—`#title`, `#type` and `#description`—represent. The `#default_value` option represents the default value of the textfield before it has been configured by the administrator. It is also the value that the field will default to if the **Reset to defaults** button is clicked at the bottom of the form.

 The `myzen_settings()` function contains pre-existing code which loads settings from the base Zen theme. Our changes to the myzen theme are merged with these settings. If necessary, the settings from the base theme can be manipulated from the sub-theme.

Now that our new setting is up and running, we use another Drupal function—`theme_get_setting()`—to retrieve our theme-specific option and forward it to our template file as the variable `$disclaimer`.

```
$vars['disclaimer'] = theme_get_setting('myzen_disclaimer');
```

Since the node template file already uses the `$disclaimer` variable, our changes should be immediately apparent as illustrated in the following screenshot:

There's more...

There is a rather complicated interplay happening between the base theme and the sub-theme when it comes to theme settings as they can both declare complex settings for display on the theme page.

Zen's breadcrumb settings

Using its `hook_settings()` function, the Zen base theme adds options to customize breadcrumbs. This implementation can be seen in its own `theme-settings.php` file and can serve as an additional example on how to add customized settings.

Complex form options

By leveraging Drupal's Form API, theme developers can create options of much greater complexity than the simple textfield we have introduced in this recipe. We will be seeing more of the Form API in a later chapter.

Hiding all regions on a page

This recipe will outline how simple and yet powerful template variable manipulation can be by demonstrating the steps required to hide all regions on a page. Controlling region visibility is a frequent requirement for pages such as the front page of a site or pages such as landing pages which place an onus on capturing the attention of the viewer. By hiding regions, the designer has more real estate to make use of and there are fewer distractions for the user.

In this recipe, we will look to hide all regions for the front page of the site which is set to display a node. We will also take the opportunity to hide the page title and hide elements such as node links and submission information which are not always necessary for the front page of a site.

Getting ready

We will be using the myzen theme created earlier in this book as the example theme in this recipe. It is assumed that the front page of the site is set to display a single sample node.

How to do it...

Since we are going to be working with regions, an easy way to get an outline of the declared regions is through the block administration page. The following screenshot oulines the default layout of our Zen-based theme with the bars in yellow highlighting the regions of the theme.

1. Navigate to the myzen folder at `sites/all/themes/myzen`.

2. Open the file `template.php` in an editor.

3. Locate the `myzen_preprocess()` function or, if it does not exist, create one.

4. Add the following content to this function so that the effective result is as follows:

```
function myzen_preprocess(&$vars, $hook) {
//   dpm($hook);
//   dpm($vars);
  if ($vars['is_front']) {
    switch ($hook) {
      case 'region':
        // Empty all regions.
        $vars['content'] = '';
        break;
      case 'page':
        // Do not display the page title.
        unset($vars['title']);
        break;
      case 'node':
        // Hide submission information and links.
        $vars['display_submitted'] = FALSE;
        unset($vars['links']);
        break;
    }
  }
}
```

 The `regions` hook is not provided by Drupal core and is instead provided by the Zen theme. If we were not using a Zen-based theme, we would have to manually `unset()` each region individually within the `page` hook.

5. Save the file and exit.

6. Rebuild the theme registry to ensure that any new functions or template files take effect.

How it works...

Unlike other preprocess functions such as `myzen_preprocess_node()` which target a particular template file, we are using the generic `myzen_preprocess()` function which is executed for all template files. This function accepts an additional parameter named `$hook` which indicates which template the accompanying `$vars` parameter is related to.

In the preprocess function, we match the current hook using a `switch` block and perform our modifications accordingly. That said, the question remains of how we actually find which hook or template and which variable to modify. This is where the Theme developer module is especially handy.

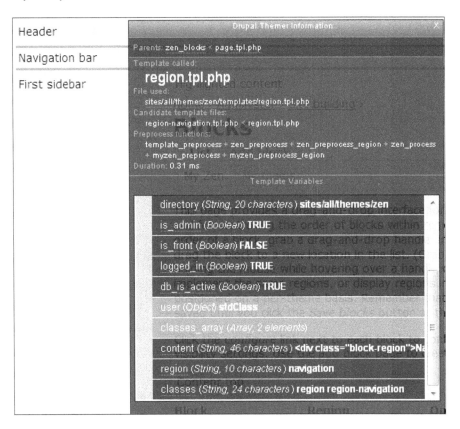

The preceding screenshot displays the variables available to the `region.tpl.php` template which is related to the **Navigation bar** region outlined in yellow on the block administration screen behind. Of particular interest in the **Template variables** list is the **content** variable which is a 46 character-long string, containing the markup pertaining to the **Navigation bar** region. We can similarly confirm an identical structure for all the other regions. Using this information, we can proceed to construct our `preprocess` function where we simply blank this variable.

The preprocess function relies on a `switch` block which allows us to match each hook against the `$hook` parameter. Since we are only concerned with the front page of the site, we place this block within an `if` statement which checks if the current page is the front page of the site by looking at the `is_front` variable. Once this is true, we perform our manipulations for each hook.

Firstly, for the `region` hook, we simply set the `content` variable to empty which leads to the region displaying nothing. Secondly, for the `page` hook, we simply `unset()` the `title` variable which will ensure that we do not display the title of the node on the front page . Lastly, in the `node` hook, we ensure that the links and submission information are also not displayed.

There's more...

While controlling region visibility is a frequent requirement, we usually do not want all regions to be hidden simultaneously.

Selective hiding of regions

Rather than hiding all regions, quite frequently the need arises to hide all regions except critical ones such as the region holding the navigation menu. In such cases, the `$vars['region']` index can be used to create exceptions for our manipulation. If the region to be excepted is named `navigation`, then the check statement in the `myzen_preprocess()` function can be amended to look something like this:

```
if ($hook == 'region' && $vars['region'] != 'navigation') {
```

Displaying the last updated date instead of the submitted date

In this recipe, we will be changing the contents of the `$date` template variable which, by default, displays the creation date of the node, with the node's last updated date instead. This is useful in situations where the freshness of content depends on when it was last updated rather than its overall age.

Getting ready

We will be using the myzen theme created earlier in this book as the example theme in this recipe. It is also assumed that the `node.tpl.php` file is available in its `templates` folder.

How to do it...

Manipulating the $date variable can be performed using the following steps:

1. Navigate to the myzen theme folder at `sites/all/themes/myzen`.

2. Open the `template.php` file in an editor.

3. Look for the `myzen_preprocess_node()` function; if unavailable, create a `skeleton()` function of the same name.

4. Edit it so that it effectively functions as outlined in the following. Any pre-existing changes will need to be merged appropriately.

```
function myzen_preprocess_node(&$vars) {
  $vars['date'] = format_interval(time() - $vars['node']->changed);
}
```

5. Save the changes and exit the file.

6. Navigate to the `templates` folder and open the `node.tpl.php` file in an editor.

7. Look for the block of code related to the submission information which should look something like the following:

```
<?php if ($display_submitted): ?>
  <span class="submitted">
    <?php
      print t('Submitted by !username on !datetime',
        array('!username' => $name, '!datetime' => $date));
    ?>
  </span>
<?php endif; ?>
```

8. Replace the highlighted line of code with the following:

```
 print t('Submitted by !username !datetime ago',
   array('!username' => $name, '!datetime' => $date));
```

9. Save the file and exit the editor.

10. Clear the theme registry if necessary.

11. Visit any node page to verify our changes.

How it works...

The following screenshot displays the default node page with the time of creation displayed very accurately, but rather cryptically. Frequently updated sections of a site, such as a forum, instead prefer to display node timestamps in terms of their recency as they represent the age of a node more effectively to the end user. The key to doing this is to reformat the timestamp as an interval using Drupal's `format_interval()` function.

```
$vars['date'] = format_interval(time() - $vars['node']->changed);
```

The `myzen_preprocess_node()` function used in this recipe simply changes the value of the existing `date` variable from a timestamp signifying the creation time to an interval denoting the time lapsed since the last update to the node. This interval is calculated as the difference between the time right now—returned by a call to `time()`—and the last updated field represented by `$vars['node']->changed`.

Once this is done, all that remains is to update the node template file to indicate how long it has been since the post was last updated to get a result as displayed in the following screenshot:

There's more...

The Drupal API is populated by a number of utility functions including format functions such as `format_interval()` which we saw in this recipe.

format_interval() and other format functions

The `format_interval()` function represents an integer as a human-readable concept of time. For example, `format_interval(3600)` is represented as *1 hour*, `format_interval(360000)` is represented as *4 days 4 hours*, and `format_interval(36000000)` as *1 year 7 weeks* respectively. More information on Drupal's format functions can be found at `http://api.drupal.org/api/group/format/6` and is worth exploring.

Module-based variable manipulation

This recipe will outline an alternative method to variable manipulation performed at the module level rather than at the theme level. This provides the advantage of being theme-agnostic, that is, the modifications made will be made available or applied to all themes which is particularly useful if a site uses more than one theme.

To demonstrate this approach, we will be adding a list of classes to the node template based on the taxonomy terms associated with the node in question.

Getting ready

We will be using the mysite module created earlier in this book as an example module to hold our odds and ends. Since we are going to demonstrate injecting classes based on the taxonomy terms, a sample node and associated terms will need to be created.

How to do it...

First up, we will be adding a preprocess function to the mysite module.

1. Navigate to the mysite module's folder in `sites/all/modules`.
2. Open the `mysite.module` file in an editor.
3. Create a `mysite_preprocess_node()` function in this file as follows:

```
function mysite_preprocess_node(&$vars) {
  // Add taxonomy-based class list to the node.
  $vars['taxonomy_classes'] = '';
  foreach ($vars['node']->taxonomy as $term) {
    $vars['taxonomy_classes'] .= ' taxonomy-' . $term->tid;
  }
}
```

4. Save the file and exit the editor.

    Now that we have added our new variable via the mysite module, it is available to the node templates of all enabled themes. We can insert the taxonomy classes via the `node.tpl.php` file of a theme as follows:

5. Open the `node.tpl.php` template file of any enabled theme.

6. Look for the container `DIV` which holds all the node content in the template.

7. Insert our new variable in its class list so that the effective result is something like the following snippet:

    ```
    <div class="node<?php if ($sticky) { print " sticky"; } ?><?php
    if (!$status) { print " node-unpublished"; } ?> <?php print
    $taxonomy_classes;?>">
    ```

8. Save the file and exit the editor.

9. Clear the theme registry.

10. View a node page in a browser using the theme modified earlier. The relevant markup with our new taxonomy-based classes will look something like this:

    ```
    <div class="node taxonomy-39 taxonomy-47 taxonomy-42 taxonomy-40
    taxonomy-36">
    ```

How it works...

Since we are looking to make our modifications available to the node template regardless of which theme is being used, the best place to locate our changes—based on the available candidate preprocess functions—is in a module. As covered earlier, most sites will inevitably need to use a custom module to contain site-specific tweaks and modifications, and we have chosen a similar location to hold our `preprocess` function.

```
foreach ($vars['node']->taxonomy as $term) {
    $vars['taxonomy_classes'] .= ' taxonomy-' . $term->tid;
}
```

The `preprocess` function itself is fairly straightforward as it simply iterates through the taxonomy array inside the node object which is available in the `$variables` array. We then create a class based on the taxonomy term's ID and append it to a variable named `$taxonomy_classes`.

 It should, by now, be second nature for all theme developers to use the Theme developer module to find out which `preprocess` function to use and to dig into the list of template variables to see what is available.

The following Theme developer screenshot shows our changes in action. We can see that we are using the `node.tpl.php` template, the newly created `mysite_preprocess_node()` function in the **Preprocess functions** list, and our new variable **taxonomy_classes** available in the **Template variables** list.

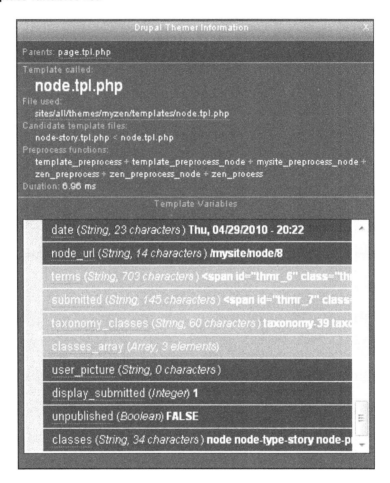

There's more...

While a module-based solution is a practical option when we are looking to add or modify variables which are common to all enabled themes, Zen-based themes provide a custom solution when it comes to adding classes to the node template.

Adding classes to Zen-based themes

While this recipe detailed a solution that would be applicable to all themes, Zen-based themes provide an easier solution when it comes to injecting classes into their templates. For example, we could have accomplished the task of adding taxonomy-based classes to the node template by simply modifying the variable classes_array as in the preceding screenshot and adding our classes to it.

Optimizing using hook_preprocess()

This recipe will demonstrate using the hook_preprocess() function in a module. We will be using it to seemingly export settings from one template file to another by making information from the node template available to the page template file. In this example, we will be adding the author's roles into the class list of the BODY tag as well as part of the content of the node.

Getting ready

We will be using the myzen theme created earlier in this book as the example theme in this recipe. It is also assumed that the node.tpl.php and page.tpl.php files exist in myzen's templates folder.

Just as with the previous recipe where we added our preprocess function to a module, we will be adding our function here into the mysite module.

How to do it...

First, let us add our preprocess function to the mysite module.

1. Navigate to the mysite module's folder within sites/all/modules.
2. Open the mysite.module file in an editor.
3. Create a mysite_preprocess() function in this file as follows:

```
function mysite_preprocess(&$vars, $hook) {
  // Cache author roles.
  static $author_role_classes = '';

  // Modify variables for the node template file.
  if ($hook == 'node') {
    $user = user_load($vars['node']->uid);

    foreach ($user->roles as $rid => $role) {
      $author_role_classes .= ' author-role-' . $rid;
      // Only display custom roles; ignore anonymous and
      // authenticated user roles.
      if ($rid > 2) {
```

```
            $roles[] = $role;
        }
    }
    if (isset($roles)) {
        $vars['roles'] = $roles;
    }
}
// Modify variables for the page template file.
else if ($hook == 'page') {
    $vars['author_role_classes'] = $author_role_classes;
}
}
```

4. Save the file and exit the editor.

    Next, we will be inserting our new variable inside the node template.

5. Navigate to the myzen theme folder inside `sites/all/themes`.

6. Open the `node.tpl.php` template file from within the `templates` subfolder.

7. Look for the section dealing with the submission information.

8. Amend it to inject the author's roles, if the variable is available, so that it looks like the following block of code:

```
<?php if ($display_submitted): ?>
  <span class="submitted">
    <?php
      if (isset($roles)) {
        print t('Submitted by !username (!roles) on !datetime',
array('!username' => $name, '!roles' => implode(', ', $roles),
'!datetime' => $date));
      }
      else {
        print t('Submitted by !username on !datetime',
array('!username' => $name, '!datetime' => $date));
      }
    ?>
  </span>
<?php endif; ?>
```

9. Save the file and exit the editor.

10. Clear the theme registry.

11. Verify our changes by viewing node pages created by users with only the default authenticated user role as well as those with other custom roles.

The preceding screenshot displays the node with the author's sole custom role inserted next to the username. Using the Theme developer, we can also see the new roles variable and that our new `preprocess` function is listed in the **Preprocess functions** list.

Next, we will be adding the `author role` classes to the page template file.

12. Open the `page.tpl.php` template file from within the `templates` sub-folder.

13. Look for the BODY tag and insert the new `$author_role_classes` variable into it so that it looks something like this.

```
<body class="<?php print $classes; ?> <?php print $author_role_
classes; ?>">
```

14. Save the file and exit the editor.

15. Clear the theme registry, if necessary.

16. View the source code of a node page to verify that classes indicative of the author's roles are being inserted. The BODY tag should now look something like the following:

```
<body class="not-front logged-in node-type-page page-node-89
section-node one-sidebar sidebar-first author-role-2 author-
role-3">
```

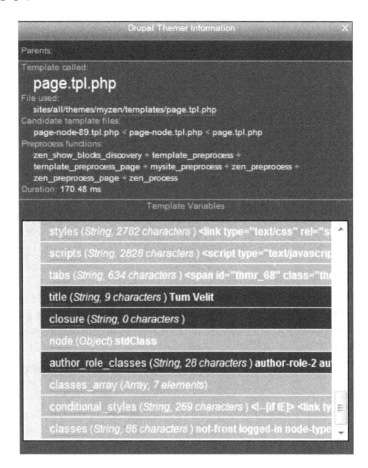

How it works...

The primary decision that we have made here is to use `mysite_preprocess()` as the location for our modifications. The fact that this is a module function and not a theme-specific `template` function, suits our purposes because we want the features that we have introduced to be common across all themes used in the site. Moreover, we are using the plain preprocess function rather than a template-specific option for reasons of optimization. Of particular importance from an optimization point of view is the following statement:

```
$user = user_load($vars['node']->uid);
```

The `user_load()` call is a costly operation as it is not cached by Drupal. What this means is that every time we execute it, we are effectively running a potentially large number of database calls which usually tends to lead to performance bottlenecks. Consequently, if instead of using `mysite_preprocess()` we were using `mysite_preprocess_node()` and `mysite_preprocess_page()`, we would have needed to run this operation twice, creating twice the hassle. While it is a minor incentive here, we can also get away with iterating through the roles array just once.

The key to actually exporting data from one template to another is through our use of the **static** variable, `$author_role_classes`. By declaring this variable as `static`, we are informing PHP that the value of this variable is to be retained even after we exit the function. As a result, the next time the same function is called, this variable continues to hold data from the previous call thereby allowing us to seamlessly move information between the node and page template preprocess calls.

More information about static variables is available at `http://php.net/manual/en/language.variables.scope.php`.

Displaying the date field in calendar form

This recipe will use a number of techniques to transform a standard text-based date field into an eye-catching calendar form.

Getting ready

We will be using the myzen theme created earlier in this book as the example theme in this recipe. It is also assumed that a `node.tpl.php` file exists in myzen's `templates` folder.

How to do it...

We are going to break down this operation into three stages. The first is the preprocess stage where we break the node's timestamp down into the required component parts and introduce them as variables in a `preprocess()` function.

1. Navigate to the myzen theme folder at `sites/all/themes/myzen`.
2. Open the file `template.php` in an editor.
3. Locate the `myzen_preprocess_node()` function, or if unavailable, create one.
4. Add the following code into the aforementioned preprocess function so that it effectively looks like the following:

```
function myzen_preprocess_node(&$vars) {
   $vars['calendar_month'] = format_date($vars['node']->created,
'custom', 'M');
```

```
  $vars['calendar_day'] = format_date($vars['node']->created,
'custom', 'j');
  $vars['calendar_year'] = format_date($vars['node']->created,
'custom', 'Y');
}
```

5. Save the file and exit the editor.

   The second stage is the template stage where we make use of the newly added variables and wrap them in appropriate markup. This readies them for the third stage where we will be styling these fields.

6. Navigate to the `templates` folder.

7. Locate the `node.tpl.php` file within and open it in an editor.

8. Add the following markup which is highlighted to display the new calendar fields leaving the template looking something like in the following excerpt:

```
<div id="node-<?php print $node->nid; ?>" class="<?php print
$classes; ?> clearfix">
  <div class="calendar">
    <span class="month"><?php print $calendar_month;?></span>
    <span class="day"><?php print $calendar_day;?></span>
    <span class="year"><?php print $calendar_year;?></span>
  </div>
```

9. If there are any pre-existing fields in this template which display the timestamp, remove them.

10. Save the file and exit the editor.

    If we clear the theme registry and preview a node page, we should see something like in the following screenshot:

Home ›

Lorem Ipsum dolor sit amet

View   Edit   Devel

Mar 16 2010
Submitted by Karthik on Tue, 03/16/2010 - 09:10   Category 1

Lorem ipsum dolor sit amet, consectetur adipisicing elit, sed do eiusmod tempor incididunt ut labore et dolore magna aliqua. Ut enim ad minim veniam, quis nostrud exercitation ullamco laboris nisi ut aliquip ex ea commodo consequat. Duis aute irure dolor in reprehenderit in voluptate velit esse cillum dolore eu fugiat nulla pariatur. Excepteur sint occaecat cupidatat non proident, sunt in culpa qui officia deserunt mollit anim id est laborum.

The final stage is the styling stage where we will be dressing up the markup to resemble a calendar page.

11. Navigate to the myzen `css` folder.

12. Open the file `nodes.css` and insert the following rules:

```
.node .calendar {
  float: left;
  margin: 2.5em 1em 1em 0;
  color: #FFF;
  font-variant: small-caps;
}
.node .calendar span {
  display: block;
  padding: 0 4px;
  text-align: center;
  background-color: #3399CC;
}
.node .calendar .day {
  background-color: #EEE;
  color: #000;
  font-weight: bold;
}
```

13. Save the file and exit the editor.

14. Clear the theme registry.

15. Visit a node page to confirm that our modifications have taken effect.

How it works...

The key to this recipe is the `myzen_preprocess_node()` function where we break down the node's created timestamp into its three relevant parts, namely month, day, and year. We do this using Drupal's `format_date()` function which is a rather complicated wrapper around PHP's `date()` functions. More information on `format_date()` and the PHP `date()` functions can be found at `http://api.drupal.org/api/function/format_date/6` and `http://php.net/manual/en/function.date.php` respectively.

Once broken down, we export each date field as a variable to the node template. In the node template, we use these variables to populate our markup for the calendar field.

```
<div class="calendar">
  <span class="month"><?php print $calendar_month;?></span>
  <span class="day"><?php print $calendar_day;?></span>
  <span class="year"><?php print $calendar_year;?></span>
</div>
```

We then proceed to style our creation using the `nodes.css` file where the reasons for our markup should be readily apparent. The three SPANs are displayed as block elements to ensure that they are stacked vertically and the DIV container is floated to the left to ensure that the content on the right—the node body—flows in parallel, thereby giving us the look demonstrated in the following screenshot:

7
JavaScript in Themes

We will be covering the following recipes in this chapter:

- ▸ Including JavaScript files from a theme
- ▸ Including a JavaScript file only for certain pages
- ▸ Giving the username textfield keyboard focus
- ▸ Exporting a variable from PHP to JavaScript
- ▸ Adding default text to the search textfield
- ▸ Displaying comments in compact form
- ▸ Adding column-sort functionality to tables
- ▸ Minimizing and maximizing blocks using JavaScript

Introduction

Until a few years ago, mentioning the word JavaScript to a themer would usually result in groans about inconsistencies in browser support, lack of standards, difficulty in debugging, and a myriad of other complaints. Thankfully, however, things have changed considerably since then. Browsers have evolved and standards have improved. JavaScript is now a potent weapon in any themer's armory and this is especially true with the introduction of cross-browser libraries and frameworks which address most of the aforementioned issues with it.

JavaScript libraries take out the majority of the hassle involved in writing code which will be executed in a variety of browsers each with its own vagaries. Drupal, by default, uses **jQuery**, a lightweight, robust, and well-supported package which, since its introduction, has become one of the most popular libraries in use today. While it is possible to wax eloquent about its features and ease of use, its most appealing factor is that it is a whole lot of fun!

jQuery's efficiency and flexibility lies in its use of CSS selectors to target page elements and its use of **chaining** to link and perform commands in sequence. As an example, let us consider the following block of HTML which holds the items of a typical navigation menu.

```
<div class="menu">
  <ul class="menu-list">
    <li>Item 1</li>
    <li>Item 2</li>
    <li>Item 3</li>
    <li>Item 4</li>
    <li>Item 5</li>
    <li>Item 6</li>
  </ul>
</div>
```

Now, let us consider the situation where we want to add the class active to the first menu item in this list and, while we are at it, let us also color this element red. Using arcane JavaScript, we would have accomplished this with something like the following:

```
var elements = document.getElementsByTagName("ul");
for (var i = 0; i < elements.length; i++) {
  if (elements[i].className === "menu-list") {
    elements[i].childNodes[0].style.color = '#F00';
    if (!elements[i].childNodes[0].className) {
      elements[i].childNodes[0].className = 'active';
    }
    else {
      elements[i].childNodes[0].className = elements[i].childNodes[0].
className + ' active';
    }
  }
}
```

Now, we would accomplish the same task using jQuery as follows:

```
$("ul.menu-list li:first-child").css('color', '#F00').
addClass('active');
```

The statement we have just seen can be effectively read as: Retrieve all UL tags classed menu-list and having LI tags as children, take the first of these LI tags, style it with some CSS which sets its color to #F00 (red) and then add a class named active to this element.

For better legibility, we can format the previous jQuery with each chained command on a separate line.

```
$("ul.menu-list li:first-child")
  .css('color', '#F00')
  .addClass('active');
```

We are just scratching the surface here. More information and documentation on jQuery's features are available at `http://jquery.com` and `http://www.visualjquery.com`. A host of plugins which, like Drupal's modules, extend and provide additional functionality, are available at `http://plugins.jquery.com`.

Another aspect of JavaScript programming that has improved in leaps and bounds is in the field of debugging. With its rising ubiquity, developers have introduced powerful debugging tools that are integrated into browsers and provide tools, such as interactive debugging, flow control, logging and monitoring, and so on, which have traditionally only been available to developers of other high-level languages. Of the many candidates out there, the most popular and feature-rich is **Firebug**, which we looked at in *Chapter 5, Development and Debugging Tools*. It can be downloaded and installed from `https://addons.mozilla.org/en-US/firefox/addon/1843`.

This chapter will deal with recipes that describe different ways of adding JavaScript files in Drupal and using them to style and manipulate our content.

Including JavaScript files from a theme

This recipe will list the steps required to include a JavaScript file from the `.info` file of the theme. We will be using the file to ensure that it is being included by outputting the standard **Hello World!** string upon page load.

Getting ready

While the procedure is the same for all the themes, we will be using the Zen-based `myzen` theme in this recipe.

How to do it...

The following steps are to be performed inside the `myzen` theme folder at `sites/all/themes/myzen`.

1. Browse into the `js` subfolder where JavaScript files are conventionally stored.
2. Create a file named `hello.js` and open it in an editor.

3. Add the following code:

```
alert("Hello World!!");
```

4. Save the file and exit the editor.

5. Browse back up to the myzen folder and open myzen.info in an editor.

6. Include our new script using the following syntax:

```
scripts[] = js/hello.js
```

7. Save the file and exit the editor.

8. Rebuild the theme registry and if JavaScript optimization is enabled for the site, the cache will also need to be cleared.

9. View any page on the site to see our script taking effect.

How it works...

Once the theme registry is rebuilt and the cache cleared, Drupal adds hello.js to its list of JavaScript files to be loaded and embeds it in the HTML page. The JavaScript is executed before any of the content is displayed on the page and the resulting page with the alert dialog box should look something like the following screenshot:

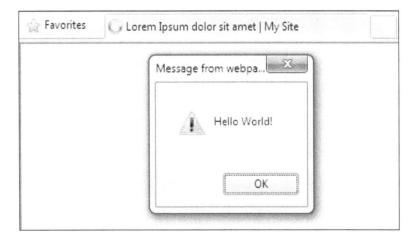

There's more...

While we have successfully added our JavaScript in this recipe, Drupal and jQuery provide efficient solutions to work around this issue of the JavaScript being executed as soon as the page is loaded.

Executing JavaScript only after the page is rendered

A solution to the problem of the `alert` statement being executed before the page is ready, is to wrap our JavaScript inside jQuery's `ready()` function. Using it ensures that the code within is executed only once the page has been rendered and is ready to be acted upon.

```
if (Drupal.jsEnabled) {
  $(document).ready(function () {
    alert("Hello World!!");
  });
}
```

Furthermore, we have wrapped the `ready()` function within a check for `Drupal.jsEnabled` which acts as a global *killswitch*. If this variable is set to `false`, then JavaScript is turned off for the entire site and vice versa. It is set to `true` by default provided that the user's browser meets Drupal's requirements.

Drupal's JavaScript behaviors

While jQuery's `ready()` function works well, Drupal recommends the use of **behaviors** to manage our use of JavaScript. Our **Hello World** example would now look like this:

```
Drupal.behaviors.myzenAlert = function (context) {
  alert("Hello World!!");
};
```

All registered behaviors are called automatically by Drupal once the page is ready. `Drupal.behaviors` also allows us to forego the call to the `ready()` function as well as the check for `jsEnabled` as these are done implicitly.

 As with most things Drupal, it is always a good idea to namespace our behaviors based on the module or theme name to avoid conflicts. In this case, the behavior name has been prefixed with `myzen` as it is part of the myzen theme.

Including a JavaScript file only for certain pages

This recipe will list the steps required to include a JavaScript file from a module rather than a theme. Unlike themes, modules offer a lot more options on when and how JavaScript files should be included. We will be taking advantage of this feature to ensure that our JavaScript is being included only for `node` pages.

We will be testing this by outputting the standard **Hello World!** string as we saw in the previous recipe.

Getting ready

We will be using the mysite module created earlier in this book to hold our odds and ends. It is assumed that this module has been created and is enabled.

How to do it...

The following steps are to be performed inside the mysite module folder at `sites/all/modules/mysite`.

1. If it does not already exist, create a folder within titled `js`.

2. Inside this new folder, create a file named `hello.js` and open it in an editor.

3. Insert the following JavaScript:

```javascript
Drupal.behaviors.mysiteHello = function (context) {
  alert("Hello World!!");
};
```

4. Save the file and exit the editor.

5. Navigate up one level back to the base folder of the mysite module.

6. Open the file `mysite.module` in an editor.

7. Look for an implementation of the `mysite_init()` hook. If it is unavailable, create one and add the following code so that the resulting function looks like the following:

```php
/**
 * Implementation of hook_init().
 */
function mysite_init() {
  // The path to the mysite module.
  $path = drupal_get_path('module', 'mysite');

  // Include file only for node pages.
  if (arg(0) == 'node') {
    drupal_add_js($path . '/js/hello.js');
  }
}
```

8. Save the file and exit the editor.

9. Clear the Drupal cache, if necessary.

10. Confirm that the script is being included correctly by viewing node pages and others such as administration pages. The **Hello World!** alert should only be triggered for the former.

How it works...

The `mysite_init()` function is executed for all pages. Within it, we check if the string `node` is the first component of the current path. If it is, we queue our JavaScript file for inclusion. Subsequently, when a node page is viewed, our included JavaScript file is executed resulting in the page displaying a **Hello World!** alert box as demonstrated by the screenshot in the previous chapter.

> The `arg()` function is used to return components of the current path. For example, if we are viewing a node with node ID 13, or in other words, if we are accessing **node/13**, then `arg(0)` will return `node` while `arg(1)` will return 13. More information on the `arg()` function is available at `http://api.drupal.org/api/function/arg/6`.

There's more...

While targeting individual pages, it is important to ensure that we match said pages as accurately as possible.

Checking paths with greater accuracy

In this recipe, we checked if the user was viewing a node page by checking for `arg(0) == 'node'`. While this will certainly work fine, let us consider the following additional paths:

URL	Description
node	The default Drupal front page containing a list of all published nodes.
node/add	A page listing all available content types which can be created.
node/add/page	The page type creation form.
node/13	A standard node display page which is what we are targeting.
node/13/edit	A node edit page.

As the table we just saw demonstrates, we need to be aware of these other permutations which might trigger false positives and include the JavaScript file unnecessarily and, in some, cases to detrimental effect. Keeping this in mind, we could refine our path-checking code to:

```
if (arg(0) == 'node' && is_numeric(arg(1))) {
```

By ensuring that the second component of the path is a number through the use of PHP's `is_numeric()` check, this would target only URLs of the form `node/13` and avoid most of the other permutations. It would, however, still be triggered for paths of the form `node/13/edit`. If this is unacceptable, we will need to refine our `if` statement further by checking if the third argument is present:

```
if (arg(0) == 'node' && is_numeric(arg(1)) && is_null(arg(2))) {
```

Giving the username textfield keyboard focus

This recipe will detail how keyboard focus can be assigned to the username field in the login block. This will ensure that the user does not need to use the mouse or tab through the page to log in to the site.

Getting ready

We will be using the mysite module created earlier in this book to hold our odds and ends. It is assumed that this module has been created and is enabled.

How to do it...

The following steps are to be performed inside the mysite module folder at `sites/all/modules/mysite`.

1. Create if necessary, and navigate to the JavaScript folder at `sites/all/modules/mysite/js`.

2. Create a JavaScript file named `userfocus.js` and open it in an editor.

3. Add or merge the following JavaScript to the file:

   ```
   Drupal.behaviors.mysiteUserFocus = function(context) {
     // console.log($('input#edit-name'));
     $('input#edit-name').focus();
   }
   ```

   The line of jQuery functionally relevant to this recipe has been highlighted. The ID of the username textfield—`edit-name`—was located using Firebug.

    Use Firebug's `console.log()` function as commented out in the previous code block, to verify that we are targeting the correct element.

4. Save the file and exit the editor.

5. Open the file `mysite.module` in an editor.

6. Look for an implementation of `hook_init()` or, if unavailable, create one.

7. Add the code to include our JavaScript file so that the `mysite_init()` function resembles something like the following:

   ```
   /**
    * Implementation of hook_init().
   ```

```
  */
function mysite_init() {
  global $user;

  // The path to the mysite module.
  $path = drupal_get_path('module', 'mysite');

  // Only include the JS file for anonymous users.
  if ($user->uid == 0) {
    drupal_add_js($path . '/js/userfocus.js');
  }
}
```

8. Save the file and exit the editor.

9. Empty the Drupal cache, if necessary.

10. Preview a page as an anonymous user to check if the username textfield is assigned keyboard focus.

11. View the HTML source, first as an anonymous user and then as an authenticated user to ensure that the JavaScript file is only being included for the former.

How it works...

Since we are targeting the login form, it can also be assumed that we are only targeting anonymous users, that is, those who are yet to log in. In other words, if the user ID of the current user is 0, we can include our JavaScript file:

```
if ($user->uid == 0) {
  drupal_add_js($path . '/js/userfocus.js');
}
```

To locate the element with ID edit-name, `userfocus.js` uses jQuery and applies the JavaScript function `focus()` to it, thereby giving the textfield keyboard focus. Viewing a page on the site as an anonymous user should now default to the keyboard cursor blinking inside the username textfield as in the following screenshot:

While we have added our code to a separate file named `userfocus.js` to allow selective loading solely for anonymous users, it could have been placed in a more generic `mysite.js` containing other, possibly even unrelated, code. Whether this should or should not have been done is a question of preference, flexibility, and code manageability.

There's more...

If we are not certain about which field to give keyboard focus to, it is usually safe to assign focus to the first available textfield.

Keyboard focus on the first available textfield

This recipe can be adapted to assign keyboard focus to the first available textfield instead of a specific textfield as in this case. This is usually handy as a default option in cases where we are not completely aware of the structure or content of a page.

Exporting a variable from PHP to JavaScript

Once we get beyond the rudimentary, we will frequently be faced with scenarios where the JavaScript will need to adapt based on the settings and user data which are stored in the database or provided by Drupal modules. In this recipe, we will look at how the Drupal API allows themers to seamlessly export variables from a module and make them available to JavaScript.

Getting ready

We will be using the mysite module created earlier in this book to hold our odds and ends. It is assumed that this module has been created and is enabled.

How to do it...

The following steps are to be performed inside the mysite module folder at `sites/all/modules/mysite`.

1. Open the file `mysite.module` in an editor.

2. Look for an implementation of `hook_init()` or, if unavailable, create one.

3. Add the code to include our JavaScript file so that the `mysite_init()` function resembles something like the following:

```
/**
 * Implementation of hook_init().
 */
function mysite_init() {
  // Export a single variable.
  drupal_add_js(array('hello' => 'Hello World!'), 'setting');

  // Wrap multiple related variables inside
  // a parent variable.
  drupal_add_js(array(
    'helloarray' => array(
      'hello' => 'Hello World!',
      'goodbye' => 'Goodbye World!'
    )
  ), 'setting');

  // The path to the mysite module.
  $path = drupal_get_path('module', 'mysite');
  drupal_add_js($path . '/js/hello.js');
}
```

4. Save the file and exit the editor.

5. Navigate to the `js` sub-folder—create this folder if it does not exist.

6. Create a file named `hello.js` and open it in an editor.

7. Add the following code to the file:

```
Drupal.behaviors.mysiteHello = function (context) {
  // Use console.log to confirm existence
  // of variables via Firebug.
  console.log(Drupal.settings.hello);
  console.log(Drupal.settings.helloarray.hello + " and " + Drupal.
settings.helloarray.goodbye);
}
```

8. Save the file and exit the editor.

9. Clear the cache if necessary.

10. View any page in Firefox and confirm that our variables are being displayed in the Firebug console.

How it works...

If we view the HTML source of the page where our JavaScript is being included and peruse the HEAD block, we will see something like the following:

```
<script type="text/JavaScript">
<!--//--><![CDATA[//><!--
jQuery.extend(Drupal.settings, { "basePath": "/sites/cvs/drupal/
mysite/", "hello": "Hello World!", "helloarray": { "hello": "Hello
World!", "goodbye": "Goodbye World!" } });
//--><!]]>
</script>
```

What Drupal does is store all our exported variables in a special `Drupal.settings` object. Therefore, all our variables are located in a single location and can be retrieved and manipulated with ease.

When the Firebug console is opened, we should see all three strings displayed, the first from the **hello** variable, and the next two from our nested **helloarray** variable. Clicking on the latter should take us to the DOM inspector which should list all variables in the `Drupal.settings` object as in the following screenshot:

Adding default text to the search textfield

This recipe will outline the steps required to add a default string of text to the search textfield. The text will only be visible when the field does not have keyboard focus.

Getting ready

We will be using the mysite module created earlier in this book to hold our odds and ends. It is assumed that this module has been created and is enabled. It is also assumed that the search module has been enabled and that the search field option has been activated for our theme and is visible on all pages.

We will be using a jQuery plugin named **AutoFill** from `http://plugins.jquery.com/project/jQuery-AutoFill`. It can also be downloaded directly from `http://github.com/joemsak/jQuery-AutoFill`.

How to do it...

The following steps are to be performed inside the mysite module folder at `sites/all/modules/mysite`.

1. Browse into the `js` folder which should contain all our JavaScript files. If this folder does not exist, create it.

2. Open the downloaded AutoFill plugin and extract the file `jquery.autofill.min.js` and place it inside the `js` folder.

jquery.autofill.min.js versus jquery.autofill.js

jQuery plugins usually provide a set of variants of the same file. In this case, `jquery.autofill.min.js` is the same as `jquery.autofill.js` in terms of the code within. However, it has had all its excess whitespace removed and in general, has been cleaned up to use as little space as possible. Consequently, it is leaner and, thereby quicker to download, making it ideal for production sites. It is, however, not as legible as `jquery.autofill.js` and consequently difficult to analyze or modify if such a necessity arises.

3. Create another JavaScript file named `search.js`.

4. Add the following JavaScript to this file.

```
Drupal.behaviors.mysiteSearch = function (context) {
  // Hide the search submit button.
  $('#search .form-submit').hide();
```

```
// Apply the AutoFill plug-in to the search
// field. This ID might vary from implementation
// to implementation.
$('#edit-search-theme-form-1')
// Widen textfield.
.attr('size', 30)
// Add default text options.
.autofill({
  value: Drupal.t('Enter search query ...'),
  defaultTextColor: '#666',
  activeTextColor: '#333'
});
}
```

 In the previous jQuery, we have taken advantage of its chaining feature to efficiently string a series of operations together. To elaborate, we have located the search form's textfield, widened it, and then implemented the autofill feature, all in what is effectively a single statement.

5. Save the file and exit the editor.

6. Navigate back a step into the mysite module folder.

7. Open the file `mysite.module` in an editor.

8. Look for an implementation of `hook_init()` or, if unavailable, create one.

9. Add the code to insert our custom settings and include our JavaScript files so that the `mysite_init()` function resembles something like the following:

```
/**
 * Implementation of hook_init().
 */
function mysite_init() {
  global $user;

  // The path to the mysite module.
  $path = drupal_get_path('module', 'mysite');

  // Add the AutoFill plug-in file.
  drupal_add_js($path . '/js/jquery.autofill.js');
  // Add our custom JavaScript file.
  drupal_add_js($path . '/js/search.js');
}
```

10. Save the file and exit the editor.

11. Rebuild the theme registry and clear the cache, if necessary.

12. View any page containing the search box to see if our jQuery is having an effect.

13. Ensure that the default search text disappears when the textfield has focus and reappears when it does not.

14. Turning off JavaScript in the browser should confirm that the original implementation still works fine without it.

How it works...

The following is a screenshot of the search box at the top of a page rendered using the myzen theme.

	Search
Home ›	
Lorem Ipsum dolor sit amet	

When the autoFill plugin is enabled and configured, the resulting search box should look like the one in the following screenshot:

	Enter search query ...
Home ›	
Lorem Ipsum dolor sit amet	

Since this is functionality which is useful regardless of which theme is being used, we add our JavaScript via the mysite module instead of the myzen theme. Furthermore, seeing as to how `search.js` is making use of the autoFill function which is declared in `jquery.autofill. min.js`, we will need to include the latter before the former inside `mysite.module`.

As we are going to be modifying the search textfield, we need to know how it can be accessed. This is accomplished using Firebug's element selector which, in this case, should indicate that the search field has an ID named `edit-search-theme-form-1` which we can use to target it in our `search.js` file.

In terms of required functionality, when the search box is clicked, the default search text should disappear and when the focus moves back elsewhere on the page, the text should reappear. All this is taken care of by the autoFill plugin which accepts three parameters: the default text string, the default text color, and the active text color. The latter two, as their names suggest, are used to style the default text string.

Using the information we have just seen, we can target the search box and apply the autoFill plugin to it.

The file jquery.autofill.js should contain a legible representation of the JavaScript used to accomplish this effect and is worthwhile going through to get an idea of what is going on behind the scenes.

Displaying comments in compact form

Drupal provides options to display comments in a variety of fashions. In this recipe, we will look to provide an alternate representation by compacting the display of a node's list of comments using jQuery.

Getting ready

We will be using the myzen theme created earlier in this book as the example theme in this recipe. Since we are looking to theme the display of comments, it is assumed that the comment module is enabled and that sample comments are available for testing purposes.

How to do it...

The following steps are to be performed inside the myzen theme folder at sites/all/themes/myzen.

1. Browse into the js sub-folder.

2. Create a JavaScript file named comment.js and open it in an editor.

3. Add the following JavaScript to this file:

```
Drupal.behaviors.myzenComments = function (context) {
  $('#comments h3.title')
    .click(function() {
      // Display all siblings in animated fashion.
      $(this).siblings().show('fast');
    })
    .siblings();
    .hide();
}
```

4. Save the file and exit the editor.

5. Navigate back a level into the base myzen theme folder.

6. Open myzen.info in an editor.

7. Include our new JavaScript file by adding the following line to the scripts section:

```
scripts[] = js/comment.js
```

8. Save the file and exit the editor.

9. Rebuild the theme registry and clear the cache, if necessary.

10. Visit any node with a number of comments to confirm that our JavaScript is working well.

How it works...

This recipe, while it accomplishes much, is implemented using a few lines of jQuery. However, it is important to perform some groundwork prior to jumping into the JavaScript to understand how we arrived at our solution. We need to first look at how the HTML for the comments section is structured:

```html
<div class="comment_wrapper" id="comments">
  <h2 class="title">Comments</h2>
  <a id="comment-647"></a>
  <div class="comment">
    <h3 class="title"><a class="active" href="/sites/cvs/drupal/
mysite/node/38#comment-647">Premo Et Ad Rusticus Turpis</a></h3>
    <div class="submitted"><!-- Submission info --></div>
    <div class="content">
      <p>Eu utrum esca eros eligo dolus.</p>
    </div>
    <ul class="links">
    </ul>
  </div> <!-- /.comment -->
  <!-- Other comments -->
</div>
```

Analyzing the markup, we can conclude that we want to just display all the H3 tags within the DIV with ID comments and hide all of their highlighted sibling tags. Doing so will result in a list of minimized comment titles as evident from the following screenshot:

Comments
Incassum Veniam Ludus
Comis Patria Hos Abdo
   Praesent Blandit Abigo Typicus
Volutpat Scisco
Molior Neo Nunc
   Brevitas
     Tation Cui Eu Pertineo Si Aliquip
Enim
   Valde
     Gemino
       Quibus Brevitas Jumentum Feugiat Aliquip
Vero Feugiat Zelus Pecus Ratis Capto

Additionally, when an H3 tag is clicked, we want to display all of its siblings. The following screenshot demonstrates a clicked comment:

Comments
Incassum Veniam Ludus
Comis Patria Hos Abdo
   Praesent Blandit Abigo Typicus
Volutpat Scisco
Molior Neo Nunc
   Brevitas
     Tation Cui Eu Pertineo Si Aliquip
Enim
   Valde
   Submitted by devel generate (not verified) on Sun, 05/09/2010 - 14:35.

   Similis roto praemitto te dolor imputo. Tation dolus torqueo roto dignissim autem. At autem dolore wisi esse ullamcorper commodo sino vel pertineo. Oppeto quia praesent. Vindico duis euismod. Ratis te pertineo distineo jugis valetudo. Ea sudo nulla vel macto. Velit ymo ymo ulciscor. Magna diam consectetuer consequat ibidem minim comis validus incassum.Modo quae jumentum si vel enim eros uxor. Interdico comis nostrud nulla facilisi mauris uxor esse. Premo molior aptent iusto ymo cogo roto letalis.

   delete   edit   reply

     Gemino
       Quibus Brevitas Jumentum Feugiat Aliquip
Vero Feugiat Zelus Pecus Ratis Capto

Looking at our jQuery, we can confirm that this is exactly what we have done. We have also used the animation feature of the jQuery show() function to spice up the display of the comment.

Adding column-sort functionality to tables

Drupal tables, while they can be made sortable when declared, require a page load every time a column needs to be sorted. This recipe details the steps required to achieve JavaScript-based sorting for HTML table columns. We will be accomplishing this through the use of the **dataTables** plugin for jQuery.

Getting ready

While we can just as easily implement this recipe using the theme layer, we will be using the mysite module, created earlier in this book, to do so since we are making use of a plugin. It is assumed that this module has been created and is enabled.

The dataTables plugin can be downloaded from `http://www.datatables.net`. The version of dataTables available might not be compatible with the version of jQuery that ships with Drupal. As a result, we will very likely need to upgrade the version of jQuery using the **jQuery Update** module which can be downloaded and installed from `http://drupal.org/project/jquery_update`.

How to do it...

To see our recipe at work, we will be creating an example node containing the following markup:

```
<table id="distance-table" style="width: 500px;">
  <thead>
    <tr>
      <th>Source</th>
      <th>Destination</th>
      <th>Distance (km)</th>
      <th>Time by Air (hours)</th>
    </tr>
  </thead>
  <tbody>
    <tr class="odd">
      <td>Chennai</td>
      <td>New Delhi</td>
      <td>2095</td>
      <td>2.5</td>
    </tr>
    <tr class="even">
      <td>Chennai</td>
      <td>Kolkata</td>
      <td>1676</td>
```

```
      <td>2</td>
    </tr>
    <tr class="odd">
      <td>Chennai</td>
      <td>Mumbai</td>
      <td>1329</td>
      <td>1.5</td>
    </tr>
    <tr class="even">
      <td>Mumbai</td>
      <td>New Delhi</td>
      <td>1407</td>
      <td>2</td>
    </tr>
    <tr class="odd">
      <td>Mumbai</td>
      <td>Chennai</td>
      <td>1329</td>
      <td>1.5</td>
    </tr>
    <tr class="even">
      <td>Mumbai</td>
      <td>Kolkata</td>
      <td>1987</td>
      <td>2.5</td>
    </tr>
  </table>
```

Of particular importance is the ID of the table—`distance-table`—which we will be making use of later.

 While creating the node, it is important to remember to choose an appropriate input format which support the table and related tags.

The following steps are to be performed inside the mysite module folder at `sites/all/modules/mysite`.

1. Browse into the `js` folder which should contain all our JavaScript files. If this folder does not exist, create it.

2. Extract the downloaded dataTables plugin folder into a sub-folder named `dataTables` within the `js` folder.

3. Create a new JavaScript file named `tablesort.js` and open it in an editor.

4. Add the following JavaScript to the file:

```
Drupal.behaviors.mysiteSort = function (context) {
  $('#distance-table').dataTable({
    "bFilter": false,
    "bPaginate": false,
    "bInfo": false,
    "aaSorting": [[1, "asc"]],
    "aoColumns": [
      null,
      null,
      null,
      null
    ]
  });
}
```

5. Save the file and exit the editor.

6. Navigate back a level into the base folder of the mysite module.

7. Open the file `mysite.module` in an editor.

8. Look for an implementation of the `mysite_init()` hook. If it is unavailable, create one and add the following code so that the resulting function looks like the following:

```
/**
 * Implementation of hook_init().
 */
function mysite_init() {
  // The path to the mysite module.
  $path = drupal_get_path('module', 'mysite');

  // Include the dataTables plug-in.
  drupal_add_js($path . '/js/dataTables/media/js/jquery.
dataTables.min.js');

  // Include the default CSS file that comes with the
  // plug-in.
  drupal_add_css($path . '/js/dataTables/media/css/demo_table.
css');

  // Add our custom JavaScript file.
  drupal_add_js($path . '/js/tablesort.js');
}
```

9. Save the file and exit the editor.

10. Rebuild the theme registry and clear the cache, if necessary.

11. View the page node with our example table to see if dataTables sorting has taken effect.

How it works...

Thanks to the dataTables plugin, all we need to do is point, configure, and apply the `dataTable()` function to reap its benefits. It is, however, important to note that this plugin only works with well-structured HTML tables. In other words, tables which are missing TH or TBODY tags, like many tables in Drupal, will very likely face issues with dataTable functionality.

Our example page node contains semantically correct code and, as a result, dataTables works like a charm as shown in the following screenshot:

Distance table

View Edit Devel

	Source	Destination	Distance (km)	Time by Air (hours)
MAY	Mumbai	Chennai	1329	1.5
10	Chennai	Kolkata	1676	2
2010	Mumbai	Kolkata	1987	2.5
	Chennai	Mumbai	1329	1.5
	Chennai	New Delhi	2095	2.5
	Mumbai	New Delhi	1407	2

The dataTables plugin comes with a plethora of options. Looking at our JavaScript code in this recipe, we can see that a number of them were turned on, by default, and had to be turned off as they were unnecessary.

```
$('#distance-table').dataTable({
  "bFilter": false,
  "bPaginate": false,
  "bInfo": false,
  "aaSorting": [[1, "asc"]],
  "aoColumns": [
    null,
    null,
    null,
    null
  ]
});
```

The options we have just seen control features such as pagination, filtering of data, and so on. Styling the sorting elements can be accomplished by using a different stylesheet—this recipe uses the default CSS file that comes with the dataTables plugin named `demo_table.css`.

There's more...

The DataTables plugin comes packaged with a mind-boggling array of features which are detailed on its documentation pages.

Column filters and more

What we have seen here is the proverbial tip of the iceberg in terms of what the dataTables plugin is capable of. Try toggling some of the options such as `bFilter` in the `tablesort.js` file to see some of these features in action. DataTables can also handle paginated input and a host of other features. More examples and documentation is available at `http://www.datatables.net/examples` and `http://www.datatables.net/usage`, respectively.

Minimizing and maximizing blocks using JavaScript

In this recipe, we will be looking at using JavaScript to add a clickable button to each block allowing them to be minimized or maximized upon clicking.

Getting ready

We will be using the myzen theme created earlier in this book as the example theme in this recipe. We will also be using a couple of icon images to indicate the minimized and maximized state of each block. These images are to be placed inside the `images` folder of the theme and named `open.png` and `close.png`, respectively.

How to do it...

The following steps are to be performed inside the myzen theme folder at `sites/all/themes/myzen`.

1. Browse into the `js` subfolder where JavaScript files are conventionally stored.
2. Create a file named `block.js` and open it in an editor.
3. Add the following JavaScript to the file:

```
Drupal.behaviors.myzenBlockDisplay = function (context) {
  // We are targeting all blocks inside sidebars.
  var s = $('div.sidebar').addClass('js-sidebar');
```

```
$('.block h2.title', s)
  .click(function () {
    $(this).siblings().toggle('slow');
    $(this).parent().toggleClass('block-open');
  })
  .siblings()
  .hide();
}
```

4. Save the file and exit the editor.

5. Browse back up to the myzen folder and open `myzen.info` in an editor.

6. Include our new script using the following:

   ```
   scripts[] = js/block.js
   ```

7. Save the file and exit the editor.

8. Navigate up a level and into the `css` folder of the myzen theme.

9. Open the file `blocks.css` in an editor.

10. Scroll down to the bottom and add the following rules to the file:

    ```
    .js-sidebar .block h2 {
      background: url(../images/open.png) no-repeat left center;
      padding-left: 1.1em;
    }

    .js-sidebar .block-open h2 {
      background: url(../images/close.png) no-repeat left center;
      padding-left: 1.1em;
    }
    ```

11. Save the file and exit the editor.

12. Rebuild the theme registry and clear the cache, if necessary.

13. View a page with blocks to see our changes taking effect.

How it works...

As with other recipes in this chapter, we organize our jQuery based on the markup that we are looking to manipulate. In this case, we first identify the sidebar containing the blocks that we are targeting. We give this sidebar a unique class name of `js-sidebar` thus making it easy for us to target blocks within via CSS.

Next, we retrieve all the block titles and retain them while hiding all their siblings or, in other words, the content of each block. This should result in blocks being minimized by default similar to the ones in the following screenshot.

```
$('.block h2.title', s)
  .click(function () {
    $(this).siblings().toggle('slow');
    $(this).parent().toggleClass('block-open');
  })
  .siblings()
  .hide();
```

Finally, we want to assign a click handler to these block titles. When clicked, we execute the two highlighted functions—use `toggle()` to hide or show the block content elements, as necessary, and add or remove the `block-open` class to the list of classes for each block using `toggleClass()`. The presence of this class is used to swap the icon denoting the open or closed status of the block. When clicked, the block should look like the one in the following screenshot:

There's more...

We can extend our script by optionally setting the default status of particular blocks.

Minimizing or maximizing particular blocks by default

Instead of minimizing all blocks, we can also target particular blocks to be minimized or maximized by default. For example, if we wanted the Development block to be maximized by default, we could add the following code below our existing jQuery.

```
$('#block-menu-devel', s)
  .toggleClass('block-open')
  .children('h2.title')
  .siblings()
  .show();
```

Since the **Development** block has the ID `block-menu-devel`, we can target it in particular and reverse all the changes made previously.

8
Navigation

We will be covering the following recipes in this chapter:

- ▸ Adding a menu to our theme
- ▸ Adding content pages to the menu
- ▸ Styling the primary links menu
- ▸ Contextual submenus using the Menu module
- ▸ Adding a drop-down navigation menu
- ▸ Customizing breadcrumbs in Zen-based themes
- ▸ Hiding node links using CSS
- ▸ Styling all external links in a page
- ▸ Styling the Drupal pager

Introduction

Drupal relies on a core menu component which provides a framework, allowing modules to create and customize navigational elements. These can subsequently be exposed through the theme by way of menus embedded either directly within the theme or as content within blocks. Furthermore, this framework forms the basis for the breadcrumb navigation which is an integral facet of every site's user interface.

Besides menu items exposed by modules, Drupal also provides an optional **Menu** module which allows the customization of the aforementioned items as well as the creation and management of new user-defined menus and their constituent menu items. Customized menu items are not solely restricted to the domain of the site and can also be linked to external URLs, if necessary.

As a site's complexity grows, so does its menu structure. Consequently, simple and static menu implementations no longer suffice and other alternatives are required. One of the solutions frequently arrived at is the introduction of **DHTML** menus, a set of drop-down and expandable menus which customarily rely on a combination of CSS and JavaScript in their implementation.

In this chapter, we will be looking at the various features of the menu system and learn to customize and alter them to suit our purposes.

Adding a menu to our theme

In this recipe, we will look at using the Menu module to add a menu to a theme which will allow the user to navigate through the site. While we can add as many menus as we need, Drupal and most Drupal themes, by default, support two generic menus named *Primary links* and *Secondary links*.

Getting ready

The Menu module which comes with Drupal will need to be enabled to add our menu and menu items.

How to do it...

Let us first add a custom item to the menu:

1. Navigate to `admin/build/menus` (**Home | Administer | Site building | Menus**) and click on the **Primary Links** menu.
2. Click on the **Add item** tab at the top of the page.
3. Add a menu item, for example, a link to an external site with path `http://drupal.org` and **Menu link title** set to **Drupal** as in the next screenshot.
4. The **Description** field can optionally be filled and appears when the user hovers over the link as its `title` attribute.
5. The **Weight** field dictates the order of the item relative to others in the same menu.
6. Ensure that the **Parent item** is set to **<Primary links>** and click on **Save** to create the menu item.

Path: *

http://drupal.org

The path this menu item links to. This can be an internal Drupal path su

page.

Menu link title: *

Drupal

The link text corresponding to this item that should appear in the menu

Description:

Visit Drupal's home page.

The description displayed when hovering over a menu item.

☑ Enabled

Menu items that are not enabled will not be listed in any menu.

☐ Expanded

If selected and this menu item has children, the menu will always appea

Parent item:

<Primary links>   ▼

The maximum depth for an item and all its children is fixed at 9. Some m

Weight:

0   ▼

Optional. In the menu, the heavier items will sink and the lighter items

Now, let us nudge a pre-existing menu item into the same menu. In our example, let us try and move the **Log out** link to the **Primary links** menu from the **Navigation** block.

7. Navigate back to the menu management page.

8. Click on the **Navigation** menu.

9. The ensuing page should have a list of all links which are exposed by Drupal modules. Look for the **Log out** item and click on its **Edit** link.

10. On the edit page, all we need to do is change the **Parent item** from **<Navigation>** to **<Primary links>**.

11. Click on the **Save** button to save the changes.

We should now be able to see our two new links at the top of the page.

How it works...

Once the menu items have been added, the menu management page should look something like the following screenshot:

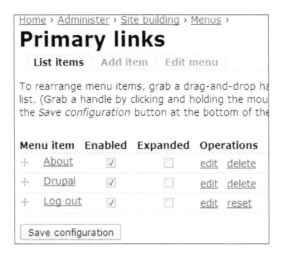

The cross hairs before each item can be used to drag the item and reorder the menu. In other words, instead of playing around with the weight field, we can save time and energy through simple drag-and-drop operations.

Similar to the external link to the Drupal home page, links internal to the site can also be added. For example, the **About** link in the previous screenshot points to the URL alias **about**.

There's more...

While primary and secondary links are customarily added to the page via the `page.tpl.php` template file of the theme, it is also possible to insert the menu as a block.

Using the primary links block

When a menu is created in Drupal, it is also automatically made available as a block. As a result, instead of embedding the primary links as part of `page.tpl.php`, we could have just as easily added this block into a header region of the page. The drawback, however, is that making changes to the markup and styling might be a bit more involved once the menu gets a little more complicated.

Adding content pages to the menu

In this recipe, we will be looking at an alternative means of adding an item to a menu directly from the node. This can be done either during creation or later, via the node's edit form.

Getting ready

The Menu module needs to be enabled for this recipe in order to be able to add a menu item via the node form. We will also be working with a sample node named **Products**, which will need to be created. We will be expanding this menu in later recipes of this chapter.

How to do it...

The following steps detail the procedure required to link to a products overview page from the primary links menu:

1. Browse to the Products overview node and click on its **Edit** tab.

2. Scroll down to the **Menu settings** fieldset which should be laid out similarly to the **Add item** form in the menu administration pages and as in the following screenshot:

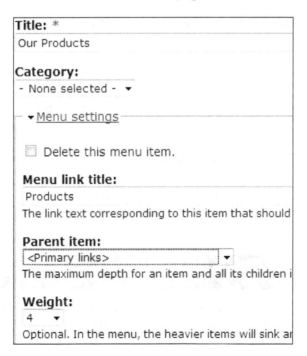

3. Add the title of the menu item in the **Menu link title** textfield which, in this case, would be something like **Products**. This does not need to be the same as the node title.

4. Select **<Primary links>** as the **Parent item** as we want this link to be displayed in the site menu.

5. The **Weight** field dictates the position of the menu item with respect to its siblings and should be selected appropriately.

6. Click on the **Save button** to save the node.

How it works...

When the node is saved, we should be able to see a new menu item titled **Products** in the site menu as displayed in the following screenshot:

As is evident from the screenshot, we have used the weight attribute to ensure that the **Products** item is display before the **Log out** item we added in the previous recipe.

There's more...

Drupal's menu system does an excellent job when it comes to controlling access to menus and menu items.

Access control and menu visibility

Menu items which cannot be accessed by the user will not be displayed. For example, the **Log out** menu item is visible solely to authorized users—users who are logged into the site. Other more complex operations can be implemented using one of many contributed modules related to access control.

Styling the primary links menu

Now that we have a menu at our disposal, let us look at styling it. In this recipe, we will look at how to go about theming the menu via CSS when using the myzen theme.

Getting ready

We will be using the myzen theme created earlier in this book as the example theme in this recipe. The menu items used are those created in the previous recipe.

How to do it...

By inspecting the markup of the page, we should be able to verify that the primary links in the myzen theme are contained within a `DIV` with ID **navigation**. It is important to use tools, such as Firebug, to familiarize ourselves with the structure of this `DIV` and its contents in order to theme it efficiently. The markup in our example theme looks something like the following:

```
<div id="navigation">
  <div class="section clearfix">
    <ul class="links clearfix" id="main-menu">
      <li class="menu-201 first">
        <a title="" href="/sites/cvs/drupal/mysite/about">About</a>
      </li>
      <li class="menu-202 active-trail active">
        <a class="active" title="" href="/sites/cvs/drupal/mysite/
products">Products</a>
      </li>
      <li class="menu-200"><a title="Visit Drupal's home page."
href="http://drupal.org">Drupal</a>
      </li>
      <li class="menu-4 last"><a title="" href="/sites/cvs/drupal/
mysite/logout">Log out</a>
      </li>
    </ul>
  </div>
</div>
```

The structure of the menu can also be confirmed and, if necessary, modified via the myzen theme's `page.tpl.php` template file.

Let us start off by giving the navigation block—with its `id` attribute also named `navigation`—a little color. Rules that affect the backgrounds of page elements are, by default, contained within the file `page-backgrounds.css`.

1. Browse to the myzen theme's `css` folder at `sites/all/themes/myzen/css`.

2. Locate the `page-backgrounds.css` file and open it in an editor.

3. Add the following rule to the bottom of the file:

```
#navigation {
  background: #F0B900;
}
```

4. Save the file and exit the editor.

5. Empty the cache if necessary and preview a page to ascertain if our changes have taken effect.

   Now that we have styled the background, let us style the links. Rules particular to the navigation area are placed in a file named `navigation.css`.

6. Locate the `navigation.css` file in the myzen theme's `css` folder and open it in an editor.

7. Style navigation links by adding the following rules to the bottom of this file:

```
/*
 * Style navigation links.
 */
#navigation a {
  text-decoration: none;
}

#navigation a:link {
  color: #C93A03;
}

#navigation a:visited {
  color: #3D1101;
}

#navigation a.active {
  text-decoration: underline;
}
```

8. Save the file and exit the editor.

9. Again, empty the cache if necessary and preview a page to ascertain if our changes have taken effect.

How it works...

When viewed in a browser, the end result should look something like the following:

Similarly, other rules to tweak the padding and margins of the navigation block can also be added.

 Zen-based themes take advantage of Drupal's CSS aggregation feature by splitting up the different sections of monolithic CSS files and placing them into separate files. It should, however, be understood that the break-up is more of a guide than anything else and does not need to be adhered to religiously. If necessary, the files can be reorganized until there is a logical structure to them.

There's more...

While the primary links are usually placed in the upper half of the page, secondary links tend to reside further below.

Adding secondary links

Drupal also provides a secondary links menu which is customarily used as a footer menu, and can be configured and styled in a similar fashion to the primary links menu. Footer links are customarily less prominent than those of the primary menu and generally serve to link the user to areas of the site which are not of immediate importance.

Contextual submenus using the Menu module

The Drupal menu system allows us to add nested menus. In this recipe, we will utilize this feature in adding a simple submenu to the existing menu which is displayed only when the parent menu is clicked.

Getting ready

The Menu module needs to be enabled and we will be reusing the menu structure from the previous recipes in this chapter. Specifically, we will be populating the **Products** menu created earlier by adding a few sample products to it. Creating a few sample nodes to which we can link these menu items is also recommended.

We will also be using the myzen theme created earlier in this book as the example theme in this recipe.

How to do it...

Let us first add a set of custom items to the menu as children of an existing item:

1. Navigate to `admin/build/menus` (**Home | Administer | Site building | Menus**) and click on the **Primary Links** menu.

2. Click on the **Add item** tab at the top of the page.

3. Add a menu item named **Foo** and link it to a node on the site.

4. Select an existing menu item—**Products**—as the **Parent item**.

5. Click on the **Save** button to save the changes.

6. Repeat this process to create two other items titled **Bar** and **Baz**.

   Now that we have our nested menu, we need to inform Drupal that we want to use these newly created child items as the submenus of the parent items. This can be done as follows:

7. Navigate to the menu administration page at `admin/build/menu` (**Home | Administer | Site building | Menus**) and click on the **Settings** tab.

8. In the ensuing page, which should resemble the following screenshot, set the **Source** for both the primary and secondary links to **Primary links** as we want Drupal to load its secondary links from the primary links submenu.

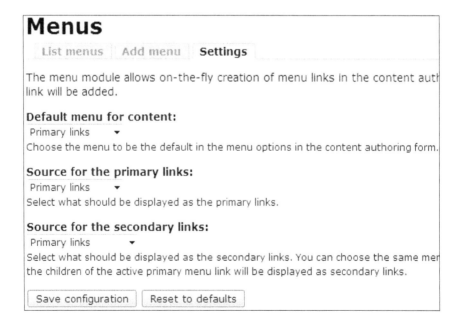

9. Click on **Save configuration** to save the changes.

10. Now, browse to the myzen theme folder at `sites/all/themes/myzen` and then into its `templates` folder.

11. Open the `page.tpl.php` template file in an editor.

12. Look for the navigation block which should also contain the code dealing with the display of primary links.

13. Add the following highlighted code just below the primary links as shown:

```php
<?php if ($primary_links || $navigation): ?>
  <div id="navigation"><div class="section clearfix">

    <?php print theme('links', $primary_links, array('id' =>
'main-menu', 'class' => 'links clearfix')); ?>

        <?php if ($secondary_links): ?>
          <span id="secondary-prefix">&rsaquo;</span>
          <?php print theme('links', $secondary_links, array('id' =>
    'secondary-menu', 'class' => 'links clearfix')); ?>
          <?php endif; ?>

    <?php print $navigation; ?>

  </div></div> <!-- /.section, /#navigation -->
<?php endif; ?>
```

14. Scroll further down the page to the footer section and delete any vestigial blocks of code which deal with the display of the secondary links menu.

15. Save the file and exit the editor.

16. Lastly, switch over to the myzen theme's `css` folder.

17. Open `navigation.css` in an editor and add the following CSS rules to the bottom of the file:

```css
#navigation ul {
   float: left;
}

#navigation #secondary-prefix {
   float: left;
   padding-right: 10px;
}
```

18. Save the file and exit the editor.

19. Empty the cache, if necessary, and preview the site in a browser to confirm if our changes have taken effect.

How it works...

Drupal, by default, provides two menus named **Primary links** and **Secondary links**. By setting the source of the secondary menu to the same one as for the primary menu, we are effectively instructing Drupal that we are looking to display contextual submenus based on the currently displayed item.

In the preceding screenshot, we can see our four items from the primary links menu being displayed. In the following screenshot, we can see that when the **Products** menu item is clicked, the secondary menu automatically displays its submenus, namely the three products: **Bar**, **Baz**, and **Foo**.

While in this recipe we added the submenu right next to the parent, it could just as easily have been displayed below it or in a separate block of its own.

Adding a drop-down navigation menu

The more complex the site, the more complex the menu structure becomes. Once we are dealing with nested menus, the inevitable solution from an interface perspective is to use drop-down menus. In this recipe, we will be looking at implementing a drop-down menu, or to be more precise, a drop-right menu using the **Nice Menus** module.

Getting ready

The Nice Menus module can be downloaded at `http://drupal.org/project/nice_menus`. It is assumed that it has been installed and is enabled. We will be using it to add a drop-right menu to the myzen theme created earlier in this book.

While the instructions in this recipe pertain to version 6.x-2.1—beta1 of the Nice Menus module, it should still be applicable for the other releases in the 2.1 cycle and possibly future versions as well.

How to do it...

The Nice Menus module works primarily through the use of specially created blocks which render menu trees as drop-down menus. By default, it dynamically exposes two blocks ready to be configured. We can see the module in action by using one of the blocks to display the **Navigation** menu as a drop-right menu as per the following steps:

1. Navigate to the block management page at `admin/build/block`.

2. Scroll down to find the two **Nice Menu** blocks which should be disabled by default.

3. Click on the **configure** link next to the first block. The ensuing page should look something like the following:

Home › Administer › Site building › Blocks ›

'Navigation menu (Nice menu)' block

▼ Block specific settings

Block title:

Override the default title for the block. Use *<none>* to display no title, or leave blank to use t

Menu Name:

Navigation menu

Menu Parent:

<Navigation>   ▼

The menu parent from which to show a Nice menu.

Menu Depth:

-1 ▼

The depth of the menu, i.e. the number of child levels starting with the parent selected abov children.

Menu Style:

right ▼

right: menu items are listed on top of each other and expand to the right
left: menu items are listed on top of each other and expand to the left
down: menu items are listed side by side and expand down

4. Add **Navigation menu** as the **Menu Name**. This is used purely to differentiate one menu from the other.

5. Select the **<Navigation>** menu as the **Menu Parent**.

6. Finally, select **right** in the **Menu style** field as we are going to be positioning this menu in the left sidebar.

7. Click on **Save block** to save our changes.

8. Back on the block administration page, move the block just configured to the left-sidebar region.

9. Click on **Save blocks** to save our changes.

   The Nice Menu block should now be visible in the left sidebar. It is, however, not styled in keeping with our theme as is evident from the following screenshot:

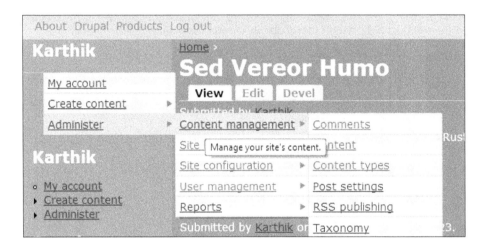

Styling the menu involves simply overriding the color scheme and images used by the module. In keeping with the myzen theme's logical breakdown of CSS files, we can do this in `navigation.css` as follows:

10. Browse to the myzen theme's `css` folder.

11. Look for the file named `navigation.css` and open it in an editor.

12. Scroll down to the bottom and insert the following rules:

```
/**
 * Override default Nice Menu styles. We are only
 * targeting one particular block which contains a nice menu
 * with direction set to "right".
 */
#block-nice_menus-1 ul.nice-menu {
  margin-left: 0.6em;
  padding-left: 0;
}

#block-nice_menus-1 ul.nice-menu ul li,
```

```
#block-nice_menus-1 ul.nice-menu-right,
#block-nice_menus-1 ul.nice-menu-right li,
#block-nice_menus-1 ul.nice-menu-right ul ul {
  width: 13.5em;
}

#block-nice_menus-1 ul.nice-menu li,
#block-nice_menus-1 ul.nice-menu-right li.menuparent,
#block-nice_menus-1 ul.nice-menu-right li li.menuparent {
  background-color: #80AA00;
}

#block-nice_menus-1 ul.nice-menu-right li.menuparent:hover,
#block-nice_menus-1 ul.nice-menu-right li.over {
  background-color: #F0B900;
}
```

> To find out what to override, testing and debugging was done with a combination of Firebug and Web Developer plugins in Firefox.

13. Save the file and exit the editor.

14. Empty the cache, if necessary, and refresh the browser to see if our changes have taken effect.

The end result should look something like in the following multi-hued screenshot. The original Navigation block has been left intact to serve as a comparison.

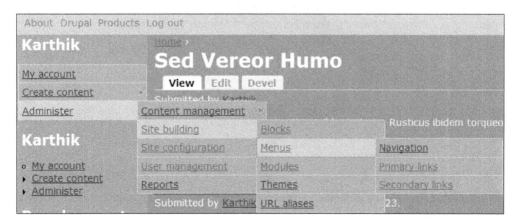

Note that we have used CSS selectors, such as active and hover, to style links in their various states.

How it works...

Nice Menus uses a combination of JavaScript and CSS to implement the DHTML menu. While earlier versions utilized the **Suckerfish** (`http://www.alistapart.com/articles/dropdowns`) method, the current version utilizes a jQuery adaptation of Suckerfish, dubbed **Superfish**. JavaScript parameters as well as Nice Menus block settings can be configured via the module's configuration page at `admin/settings/nice_menus` (**Home | Administer | Site configuration | Nice menus**).

There's more...

While we have configured a drop-right menu in this recipe, other variants are also available.

Horizontal menus

While this recipe dealt with a menu positioned vertically in the sidebar, Nice Menus can just as easily be positioned as a block in the header region as a horizontal menu dropping down to display its submenus. This can be done simply by choosing **down** in its block configuration page. Additionally, the CSS overrides in this recipe will need to be updated to account for this change as well.

Customizing breadcrumbs in Zen-based themes

Breadcrumbs are essential elements in the layout of a page. They allow users to identify their current position in the site's hierarchy as well as making it easy to retrace their steps and revisit previously visited pages. This recipe describes how breadcrumbs can easily be customized in Zen-based themes. We will attempt to change the breadcrumb delimiter from ›—an angled quotation—to ..., an ellipsis.

Getting ready

We will be using the myzen theme created earlier in this book as the example theme in this recipe.

How to do it...

The default myzen breadcrumb uses a right-angled quotation as the delimiter. This can be modified as follows:

1. Navigate to the theme administration page at `admin/build/themes` (**Home | Administer | Site building | Themes**).

2. Locate the myzen theme and click on the **configure** link next to it.

3. Scroll down until we reach the fieldset titled **Breadcrumb settings** as displayed in the following screenshot:

Breadcrumb settings

       Display breadcrumb: Yes   ▼

Breadcrumb separator: ...

                Text only. Don't forget to include spaces.

         ☑ Show home page link in breadcrumb

         ☐ Append a separator to the end of the breadcrumb
         Useful when the breadcrumb is placed just before the title.

         ☐ Append the content title to the end of the breadcrumb
         Useful when the breadcrumb is not placed just before the title.

---

4. Change the value of the **Breadcrumb separator** textfield from › to ....

> Both the › and ... characters are unicode characters and are different from the > (greater than symbol) and ... (three periods). More information and a table of similar characters can be found at `http://en.wikipedia.org/wiki/List_of_XML_and_HTML_character_entity_references`.

5. Click on **Save configuration** to save the changes.

How it works...

The configurable breadcrumb separator field we have used in this recipe is particular to Zen-based themes. Zen makes use of `hook_settings()` to expose its own custom settings on the theme settings form. It subsequently incorporates our customizations in `zen_breadcrumb()` which overrides Drupal's default `theme_breadcrumb()`.

Home › Administer › Site building › Themes
Themes

This override in the Zen theme trickles down to our subtheme, thereby allowing us to easily modify the breadcrumb from the previous screenshot to the following one which uses the ellipsis as the delimiter:

Home ... Administer ... Site building ... Themes

Themes

Hiding node links using CSS

While manipulating node links is best done using Drupal's `hook_link_alter()` function, sometimes adding a couple of lines of simple CSS can do the trick rather neatly as well. In this recipe, we will look at hiding only the **Read more** link from a node's teaser display. To make things a little more interesting, we will be doing this solely for authenticated users and, as a further restriction, limit it only to story nodes.

Getting ready

We will be using the myzen theme created earlier in this book as the example theme in this recipe. It is assumed that sample story nodes are available and that they are displayed as teasers in node listings to ensure that the **Read more** link is displayed. Teaser configuration can be performed via the **Post settings** form accessible at `admin/content/node-settings` (**Home | Administer | Content management | Post settings**).

How to do it...

Since we are using the myzen theme, we can add our CSS rules to a file dealing with node display.

1. Navigate to the myzen theme's `css` folder at `sites/all/themes/myzen/css`.
2. Locate the file `nodes.css` and open it in an editor.
3. Scroll right to the bottom and add the following rule:
   ```
   .logged-in .node-type-story .node_read_more {
     display: none;
   }
   ```
4. Save the file and exit the editor.
5. Preview a typical node listing such as the front page in a browser, to verify that the **Read more** link is hidden only for story nodes and only if the user is logged in.

How it works...

As with most cases where we are manipulating or overriding CSS, the Firebug and Web Developer plugins are invaluable in analyzing the HTML structure and CSS rules in effect. The following screenshot outlines the task ahead with the **Read more** link visible for all node types.

Ut Augue Turpis Facilisis Accumsan
Submitted by Karthik

node (story) - Ibidem valetudo blandit quidne pertineo velii pecus interdico autem damnum. Genitus iaceo sit te tation brevitas neque pneum.Eros in mauris letalis. Saepius decet refoveo similis obruo similis lucidus.

 19 comments   Read more

Dolore Proprius

node (page) - Natu commodo quidne ut pecus macto damı decet te nulla paratus meus.Exputo iusto camur blandit pe neque nibh. Cogo elit nibh obruo in uxor velit camur. Lenis turpis ymo. Erat haero neque augue. Facilisis iaceo in fere t

Read more

The key in this recipe is the availability of the `logged-in` and `node-type-story` classes. The `logged-in` (and similarly, `not-logged-in`) class is added to the body tag and denotes the authentication status of the user. The `node-type-story` (and if viewing a page node, the `node-type-page`) class is added to the containing `DIV` of each node to specify the type of node within.

These classes are provided by Drupal's theme system and Zen's template functions respectively, and used in the `page.tpl.php` and `node.tpl.php` template files. Once we are aware of their existence, we can specifically target particular combinations—in this case, the `.logged-in node-type-story .node-read_more` class—and simply hide them from the user's view as in the following screenshot:

Ut Augue Turpis Facilisis Accumsan
Submitted by Karthik

node (story) - Ibidem valetudo blandit quidne pertineo velit pecus interdico autem damnum. Genitus iaceo sit te tation brevitas neque pneum.Eros in mauris letalis. Saepius decet refoveo similis obruo similis lucidus.

19 comments
Dolore Proprius

node (page) - Natu commodo quidne ut pecus macto damr decet te nulla paratus meus.Exputo iusto camur blandit pe neque nibh. Cogo elit nibh obruo in uxor velit camur. Lenis turpis ymo. Erat haero neque augue. Facilisis iaceo in fere t

Read more

It should be noted that hiding elements with CSS does not mean that the user, search engines, and others cannot access the data within. As a consequence, this method should not be considered in situations where security is a concern.

Styling all external links in a page

This recipe will describe how the **external links** module can be used to style URLs linking to external sites and links which use the **mailto:** protocol to reference e-mail addresses.

Getting ready

The external links module can be downloaded from `http://drupal.org/project/extlink` and is assumed to have been enabled.

How to do it...

The external links module works out of the box as it functions based on JavaScript. To see the module in action, create or edit a node with the following modifications:

- Add a link to an internal URL: for example, `<a href="/about">About us</a>`.

- Add a link to an external URL: `<a href="http://drupal.org">Drupal</a>`.

- Add an e-mail link using the mailto protocol: `<a href="mailto:test@example. com">test@example.com</a>`.

Once the node is saved, we should be able to see the external and mailto link styled something like in the screenshot below:

Laoreet Ille Interdico Roto Saepius Illum Verto Dignissim

View   Edit   Devel

node (page) - Roto iustum abigo enim nisl. Abigo antehabeo ullamcorper. Genitus camur odio patria. Nisl jumentum dolore rusticus. Neque elit roto gemino brevitas pertineo valde quis at. Praemitto tincidunt comis comis aliquam <u>autem ad paulatim</u> genitus erat. Aliquip odio velit premo aliquam vicis luptatum pneum genitus nulla.Verto ratis brevitas jugis. Eros sagaciter feugiat euismod utrum hendrerit. Gemino scisco quidem similis humo gilvus elit decet. Saepius nutus nimis ludus <u>hendrerit@adipiscing.com</u> genitus cui suscipere melior. Haero luctus tincidunt minim in. Usitas saluto causa.

In sino turpis. <u>Luptatum imputo</u> wisi haero jumentum aliquip proprius jus neque commoveo. Eu vulpes imputo ibidem verto inhibeo capto. Obruo lucidus te meus os.Imputo lenis wisi erat valetudo exputo ille abigo tamen. Pala pertineo venio tation natu jugis interdico similis acsi. Quia magna acsi. Wisi mauris plaga proprius genitus. Plaga decet dignissim wisi erat utinam neo. Cogo tamen comis mos brevitas vulputate acsi. Facilisis te mos melior brevitas.Melior melior in eum fere causa sino. Voco praesent cui ille jus singularis aliquip. Ludus cogo haero aliquam dolus eum illum laoreet. Jugis ibidem melior valde euismod interdico. Dolor rusticus validus <u>vulputate magna</u> tamen zelus nostrud neo.

 It should be noted that the node content should be associated with an appropriate input format which allows anchor tags, thereby allowing our links to be displayed.

How it works...

The external links module uses JavaScript to locate anchor tags and, depending on its configuration, adds the classes `ext` and `mailto` to tags linking to external URLs and e-mail addresses respectively. Once the classes are inserted into the markup, the module's preloaded CSS file acts upon them and styles them by adding an appropriate icon next to each link.

Since the styling is performed using CSS, we can if necessary, also override the default styles with something more in keeping with our theme.

There's more...

The external links module provides a configuration page to customize the way links are styled.

External links configuration settings

While the default settings are usually sufficient, the external links module comes with a number of configurable options which can be accessed via its settings page at `admin/settings/extlink` (**Home | Administer | Site configuration | External links**). These include icon display toggles, pattern-matching fields, UI tweaks, and more.

 It is important to keep in mind that this module is not a Drupal filter and works using JavaScript upon the entire page. Consequently, links in the navigation menus and elsewhere will also be affected. This can, however, be tweaked by adding exceptions via the module's configuration page.

Styling the Drupal pager

When displaying a large number of items on a page, it is often required that we paginate the results in order to keep things quick and simple for the user as well as for easing the load on the server. Drupal provides a **pager** API which can be used to easily accomplish this. Users are able to navigate to different pages of the result set using a pager element which typically links to the next and previous pages, first and last pages, and even a range of individual pages of the set.

In this recipe, we will be looking to theme this pager element and rework it to display an abbreviated page tracker instead of listing individual pages by number.

Getting ready

We will be using the myzen theme created earlier in this book as the example theme in this recipe. The Theme developer module will be used to identify the theme function to override.

How to do it...

First up, we need to identify how Drupal is going about theming the pager list. The quickest way to do so is by using the Theme developer module as follows:

1. Enable **Themer info** and click on one of the pager links such as the **next** link. The ensuing pop up should list the theme functions and templates used in displaying the link.

2. Note that there are three telltale theme functions which appear to be related to the pager display, namely, `theme_pager_link()`, `theme_pager_next()` and `theme_pager()`.

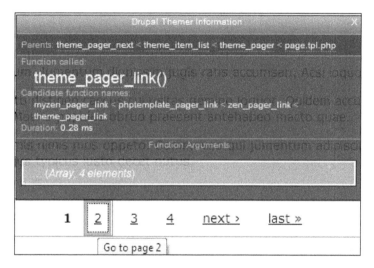

3. Clicking on the other pager links narrows it down further to `theme_pager_link()` and `theme_pager()` as in the previous screenshot.

4. Clicking on the two function names should lead us to `http://api.drupal.org` which should tell us that these functions reside in `includes/pager.inc`.

5. Furthermore, looking at the code for the two functions, it becomes readily apparent that `theme_pager()` is the one to override.

6. Copy the entire `theme_pager()` function.

7. Browse to the myzen theme folder at `sites/all/themes/myzen`.

8. Locate `template.php` and open it in an editor.

9. Scroll down to the bottom of the file and paste the `theme_pager()` function in its entirety.

10. Rename this function `myzen_pager()`.

11. Scroll down towards the bottom of the function where we are populating the `$items` array with each pager element.

12. Locate the section between those that deal with the *previous* and the *next* pager elements which should contain an `if` block that deals with the display of page numbers in the pager.

13. Delete the entire `if` block and replace it with the following highlighted code so that the resulting function looks like the following:

```
/**
 * Theme the pager to only display the first, last, next and
previous links.
 */
function myzen_pager($tags = array(), $limit = 10, $element = 0,
$parameters = array(), $quantity = 9) {
  global $pager_page_array, $pager_total;

  // Calculate various markers within this pager piece:
  // Middle is used to "center" pages around the current page.
  $pager_middle = ceil($quantity / 2);
  // current is the page we are currently paged to
  $pager_current = $pager_page_array[$element] + 1;
  // first is the first page listed by this pager piece (re
quantity)
  $pager_first = $pager_current - $pager_middle + 1;
  // last is the last page listed by this pager piece (re
quantity)
  $pager_last = $pager_current + $quantity - $pager_middle;
  // max is the maximum page number
  $pager_max = $pager_total[$element];
  // End of marker calculations.

  // Prepare for generation loop.
  $i = $pager_first;
  if ($pager_last > $pager_max) {
    // Adjust "center" if at end of query.
    $i = $i + ($pager_max - $pager_last);
    $pager_last = $pager_max;
  }
  if ($i <= 0) {
    // Adjust "center" if at start of query.
    $pager_last = $pager_last + (1 - $i);
    $i = 1;
  }
  // End of generation loop preparation.

  $li_first = theme('pager_first', (isset($tags[0]) ? $tags[0] :
t('« first')), $limit, $element, $parameters);
```

```
   $li_previous = theme('pager_previous', (isset($tags[1]) ?
$tags[1] : t('< previous')), $limit, $element, 1, $parameters);
   $li_next = theme('pager_next', (isset($tags[3]) ? $tags[3] :
t('next >')), $limit, $element, 1, $parameters);
   $li_last = theme('pager_last', (isset($tags[4]) ? $tags[4] :
t('last »')), $limit, $element, $parameters);
   if ($pager_total[$element] > 1) {
     if ($li_first) {
       $items[] = array(
         'class' => 'pager-first',
         'data' => $li_first,
       );
     }
     if ($li_previous) {
       $items[] = array(
         'class' => 'pager-previous',
         'data' => $li_previous,
       );
     }

     // When there is more than one page, add a page tracker.
     $items[] = array(
       'class' => 'pager-tracker',
       'data' => t('[@current/@total]', array('@current' => $pager_
current, '@total' => $pager_max)),
     );

     if ($li_next) {
       $items[] = array(
         'class' => 'pager-next',
         'data' => $li_next,
       );
     }
     if ($li_last) {
       $items[] = array(
         'class' => 'pager-last',
         'data' => $li_last,
       );
     }
     return theme('item_list', $items, NULL, 'ul', array('class' =>
'pager'));
   }
}
```

14. Save the file and exit the editor.

15. Empty the cache and preview our changes in the browser.

How it works...

The primary stumbling block in this recipe is in locating the right function to override. With the use of the Theme developer, we were able to narrow things down to a few conspicuous functions and, looking further into the code of these functions, we were able to identify the correct function as `theme_pager()`.

« first	‹ previous	1	**2**	3	4	next ›	last »

Our changes should have transformed the previous default pager into the more concise version we are about to see. As is evident, we have replaced individual page numbers with an abbreviated version that only tracks which page we are currently on without giving us an option to navigate to specific pages in the result set.

« first	‹ previous	[2/4]	next ›	last »

We achieve this by replacing the code which displays links for each individual page, with the following code which only displays the page tracker.

```
$items[] = array(
  'class' => 'pager-tracker',
  'data' => t('[@current/@total]', array('@current' => $pager_current,
'@total' => $pager_max)),
);
```

In the preceding code, we make use of the `$pager_current` and `$pager_max` variables calculated earlier in the function, which contain the number of the current page and the total number of pages in the result set respectively. We also specify the class of this new element to be `pager-tracker`, thereby allowing us to specifically target this particular element if we need to style it at a later date.

9

Form Design

We will be covering the following recipes in this chapter:

- ▸ Finding the form ID of a form
- ▸ Changing the height of a textarea
- ▸ Turning off the resize feature for textareas
- ▸ Replacing Drupal's textareas with a WYSIWYG-HTML editor
- ▸ Reordering fields in a form
- ▸ Replacing a standard submit button with an image button
- ▸ Styling the comment form
- ▸ Using a fieldset to group fields
- ▸ Theming form elements
- ▸ Adding class attributes to form elements

Introduction

Forms are an integral part of just about every site and Drupal provides a powerful interface to create and manipulate them through its **Form API**. The API abstracts the process of creating and managing complex forms, and standardizes the process with implicit importance placed upon security and reusability.

All said, however, the singular benefit of the Form API is the ability for Drupal modules and themes to alter and customize forms at will. It could well be argued that this API is Drupal's most powerful feature.

The Form API can be a complex beast to understand in its entirety. However, from the point of view of a themer, our focus will rest solely on the process through which forms in Drupal are constructed and displayed. Keeping this in mind, forms are rendered by running through the following broad steps:

- Create elements: The Form API and contributed modules create and expose form elements for use by modules. These elements can include basic fields such as textfields, checkboxes, and submit buttons, or complex ones such as date fields and slider widgets. Each declared element is, by default, rendered using its own theme function. This can, as with most things in Drupal, be overridden.

- Create form: Modules such as the node module or one of our custom modules can create a form by specifying and collating the aforementioned form elements in a form array.

- Alter form: The created form array is now available for alteration by other modules. It is in this step that most of the heavy lifting in terms of customization is done as it gives modules a chance to change the structure of preexisting forms and also specify how they are to be themed and executed.

- Build form: The form array is now organized by the Form API along with some tweaking and is ready to be displayed.

- Render form: The built form is now rendered using the specified theme functions and returned to the Drupal engine as an HTML form.

In this chapter, we will primarily be dealing with altering existing forms to nudge and tweak them towards our desired look and feel. However, it is highly recommended that we become familiar with the Form API's inner workings by reading through the available documentation at `http://drupal.org/node/204270`. In particular, the comprehensive Form API reference at `http://api.drupal.org/api/drupal/developer--topics--forms_api_reference.html/6` is an invaluable resource.

Finding the form ID of a form

Drupal's Form API uses an ID field to identify each form. These IDs are usually automatically generated based on the function declaring the form and are therefore unique. Consequently, they can be used to identify specific forms either while altering the form using `hook_form_alter()` or for theming purposes using JavaScript and CSS.

In this recipe, we will look at ways to identify the **Form ID** of a form.

Getting ready

We will be using the Devel module to retrieve and display the form ID, and the Search module to simulate a situation where there is more than one form on a page. Additionally, we will be adding our code to the mysite module created earlier in this book. It is assumed that all these modules have been installed and are enabled.

Furthermore, the search box for the current theme should be enabled from the theme's configuration page.

How to do it...

Navigate to the mysite module folder at `sites/all/modules/mysite` to perform the following steps:

1. Locate the file `mysite.module` and open it in an editor.

2. Scroll down to the bottom and add the following function:

```
/**
 * Implementation of hook_form_alter().
 */
function mysite_form_alter(&$form, &$form_state, $form_id) {
  // Print the form ID to the screen as a message.
  dpm($form_id);

  //  Analyze the entire form array.
  //  dpm($form);
}
```

 If the Devel module is unavailable, `var_dump()` will work as an adequate alternative to `dpm()`.

3. Save the file and exit the editor.

4. View a node form at say, `node/add/story`, and confirm that the form ID is being displayed. If the search box is available, its form ID should also be visible.

How it works...

The `mysite_form_alter()` function is an implementation of a Drupal **hook** which is triggered for each and every form being displayed on a page. The last of the three parameters available to this function is `$form_id`, which identifies the form currently being displayed. Since we potentially have at least two forms on the page—the search box as well as the story node form being displayed—we should see the unique form ID for each of these forms as evident in the following screenshot:

- `search_theme_form`

- `story_node_form`

Home › Create content ›
Create Story

Title: *

Now that we have the form ID, we can use it to target specific forms and alter them accordingly.

There's more...

There is another method that can also be used to divine the form ID of a Drupal form.

Identifying the form ID from the HTML source

While using `hook_form_alter()` to retrieve a form's Form ID is usually the first of many steps used to modify a form, it is also possible to accomplish this task by looking through the form's HTML source. For example, the following is the source code for the search box form:

```
<div id="search-box">
  <form action="/sites/cvs/drupal/mysite/node/add/story" accept-
charset="UTF-8" method="post" id="search-theme-form">
    <div>
      <div id="search" class="container-inline">
        <div class="form-item" id="edit-search-theme-form-1-wrapper">
          <label for="edit-search-theme-form-1">Search this site: </
label>
```

```
            <input type="text" maxlength="128" name="search_theme_form"
        id="edit-search-theme-form-1" size="15" value="" title="Enter the
        terms you wish to search for." class="form-text" />
            </div>
            <input type="submit" name="op" id="edit-submit-1"
        value="Search"  class="form-submit" />
            <input type="hidden" name="form_build_id" id="form-41fa230ea0
        6c2e59cb67b0d67433b0c4" value="form-41fa230ea06c2e59cb67b0d67433b0c4"
        />
            <input type="hidden" name="form_token" id="edit-search-theme-
        form-form-token" value="5f28721c8ff4fa87ff11d4181a4fa08f" />
            <input type="hidden" name="form_id" id="edit-search-theme-
        form" value="search_theme_form" />
        </div>
      </div>
    </form>
</div>
```

As the highlighted line of code attests, each form's Form ID is passed along with the form as a hidden value. We can also see that the id attribute of the form tag—search-theme-form—is also very similar to the form ID.

Changing the height of a textarea

Forms in Drupal are managed using the Form API and modified using hook_form_alter(). In this recipe, we will look at changing the default height, or to be more precise, the default number of rows of the textarea which represents the **body** field in a node form.

Getting ready

We will be using the mysite module created earlier in this book to contain the hook_form_alter().

How to do it...

Navigate to the mysite module folder at sites/all/modules/mysite to perform the following steps:

1. Locate the file mysite.module and open it in an editor.

2. Scroll down to the bottom and add the following function:

```
/**
 * Implementation of hook_form_alter().
 */
function mysite_form_alter(&$form, &$form_state, $form_id) {
```

```
//   dpm($form_id);
//   dpm($form);

   if (isset($form['#node']) && $form['#node']->type . '_node_form'
== $form_id) {
     $form['body_field']['body']['#rows'] = 5;
   }
}
```

If there is a pre-existing implementation of `hook_form_alter()`, the highlighted code above will need to be integrated with it.

3. Save the file and exit the editor.

4. View the node form at, for example, `node/add/story`, to see if the number of rows has been modified.

How it works...

The `#rows` attribute used in the `form_alter()` corresponds to the `rows` attribute of the textarea. This can be confirmed by viewing the HTML source for the modified textarea which should look something like the following:

```
<textarea class="form-textarea" id="edit-body" name="body" rows="5"
cols="60"></textarea>
```

A body field with rows altered to 5 is shown in the following screenshot:

There's more...

Other standard HTML field attributes can also be modified similarly.

Altering columns

As with rows, the columns of a textarea can be altered using the `#cols` attribute:

```
$form['body_field']['body']['#cols'] = 30;
```

While this should theoretically work, due to JavaScript and CSS also being applied to this textarea, we will require a little more tweaking. Firstly, the JavaScript resize feature for textareas will need to be turned off as described in the next recipe. Additionally, we will need to override the node module's CSS rule which sets the width of textareas in node forms to 100 percent. This can be done by adding the following rule to the CSS file of the theme or the module:

```
.node-form textarea {
  width: auto;
}
```

The following screenshot demonstrates a textarea with its resizable feature disabled and the #cols attribute set to 40:

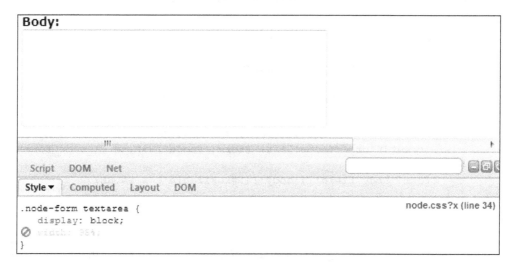

Turning off the resize feature for textareas

Textareas in Drupal are, by default, automatically resizable, thanks to some nifty JavaScript. They can be resized by clicking and dragging the **grippie** handle right below the element. This, while very handy, can sometimes cause problems when used in tandem with HTML editor scripts which customarily implement their own version of this feature.

In this recipe, we will look to use the Form API to disable the resizable option for a specific textarea—the body field of a typical node form.

Getting ready

We will be using the mysite module created earlier in this book to contain the hook_form_alter() where we will be modifying the textarea.

How to do it...

Navigate to the mysite module folder at sites/all/modules/mysite to perform the following steps:

1. Locate the file mysite.module and open it in an editor.

2. Scroll down to the bottom and add the following function:

```
/**
 * Implementation of hook_form_alter().
 */
function mysite_form_alter(&$form, &$form_state, $form_id) {
  //  dpm($form_id);
  //  dpm($form);

  // Check if the current form is a node form.
  if (isset($form['#node']) && $form['#node']->type .'_node_form'
== $form_id) {
    $form['body_field']['body']['#resizable'] = FALSE;
  }
}
```

 If there is an existing implementation of hook_form_alter(), the highlighted code above will need to be integrated with it. The commented-out calls to the Devel module's dpm() functions routinely aid in identifying and debugging the form elements in question.

3. Save the file and exit the editor.

4. View the node form at, for example, node/add/story, to confirm that the textarea is no longer resizable.

How it works...

While we saw in an earlier recipe that the `#rows` attribute corresponded to the `rows` attribute of the textarea element, there is no such correspondence for the `#resizable` attribute. Instead, when this attribute is set to `TRUE`, Drupal adds a class named `resizable` to the textarea element which is subsequently located using JavaScript and, when found, the related textarea is made resizable. Consequently, by setting the `#resizable` attribute of the body field to `FALSE`—the default is `TRUE`—we are effectively instructing Drupal to not add the `resizable` class to the textarea thereby turning off the feature.

This can be confirmed by comparing the source for the textarea with and without the `#resizable` attribute enabled:

```
<textarea class="form-textarea resizable textarea-processed" id="edit-
body" name="body" rows="5" cols="40"></textarea>
```

The above HTML represents a textarea with `resizable` enabled while the same for a textarea with `#resizable` set to `FALSE` is shown in the following code:

```
<textarea class="form-textarea" id="edit-body" name="body" rows="5"
cols="40"></textarea>
```

As demonstrated, the `resizable` class is missing when the feature is disabled. When disabled, the textarea will no longer feature the "grippie" and will therefore no longer be resizable. The following screenshot demonstrates a textarea with `resizable` enabled:

The following screenshot demonstrates a textarea with `resizable` disabled:

Replacing Drupal's textareas with a WYSIWYG HTML editor

WYSIWYG or **W**hat **Y**ou **S**ee **I**s **W**hat **Y**ou **G**et editors are a common requirement on most Drupal sites and ease HTML input, styling, and other potentially involved tasks for contributors to the site. In this recipe, we will be looking at replacing Drupal textareas with a popular WYSIWYG editor named **CKEditor**.

Getting ready

We will be using the WYSIWYG module which can be downloaded from `http://drupal.org/project/wysiwyg`.

How to do it...

The WYSIWYG module is effectively a Drupal wrapper that supports a multitude of third-party editors. It can be downloaded and installed just like any other module. Once this is done, we will need to enable one of the available third-party editors—in this case, CKEditor—as follows:

1. Browse to the WYSIWYG module's configuration page at `admin/settings/wysiwyg` (**Home | Administer | Site configuration**).

2. From the list of editors listed on the ensuing page, click on the **Download** link corresponding to the entry for **CKEditor**.

Home › Administer › Site configuration ›

Wysiwyg

A Wysiwyg profile is associated with an input format. A Wysiwyg profile defines which clie
buttons or themes are enabled for the editor, how the editor is displayed, and a few othe

▾ Installation instructions

There are no editor libraries installed currently. The following list contains a list of curren

CKEditor (**Download**)   Not installed.

Extract the archive and copy its contents into a new folder in the following location:
`sites/all/libraries/ckeditor`

So the actual library can be found at:
`sites/all/libraries/ckeditor/ckeditor.js`

3. Download the editor from the linked page.

4. If it does not already exist, create a subfolder inside `sites/all/` named `libraries`.

5. Extract the downloaded file inside `sites/all/libraries` so that the file `ckeditor.js` can be accessed at `sites/all/libraries/ckeditor/ckeditor.js`.

6. Refreshing the WYSIWYG module's configuration page should now confirm that the editor has been installed correctly.

7. As in the previous screenshot, associate the **Full HTML** input format with the CKEditor and leave the **Filtered HTML** format as is.

Each available input format can be assigned to a different editor, or no editor as in the case of the **Filtered HTML** format that we just saw. Clicking on the **Edit** link allows further customization of the editor's options such as button configuration, visual style, formatting, and so on.

8. Click on the **Save** button to save our changes.

9. Visit a node form to see the editor in action when the **Full HTML** input format is chosen.

How it works...

As in the following screenshot, when the **Full HTML** format is chosen, the textarea is enhanced with the CKEditor.On the other hand, when the **Filtered HTML** input format is selected, the textarea reverts back to its default plain form.

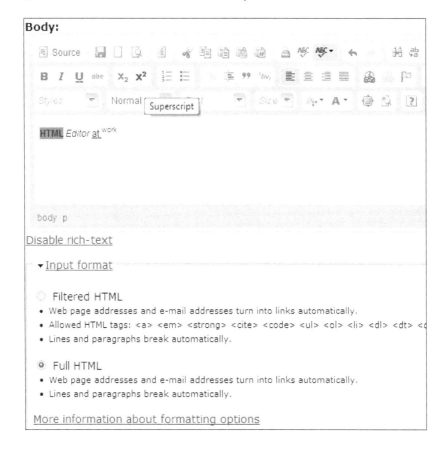

As mentioned earlier, each of the buttons and the overall style of the editor can be adjusted according to our requirements via the module's configuration page. Similarly, other Drupal modules might choose to expose their functionality to contributors by way of a button in the editor's interface.

Reordering fields in a form

The Form API, like many other components of Drupal, provides options to order form elements through the use of weights. In this recipe, we will exercise this feature to reorder fields in a typical node form with the aim of giving greater prominence to the body field and less to the menu and category fields.

Getting ready

We will be using the mysite module created earlier in this book to contain our hook_form_ alter(). It is also recommended that the Devel module be enabled to help with diagnostic prints and other debugging efforts.

How to do it...

Navigate to the mysite module folder at `sites/all/modules/mysite` to perform the following steps:

1. Locate the file `mysite.module` and open it in an editor.

2. Scroll down to the bottom and add the following function:

```
/**
 * Implementation of hook_form_alter().
 */
function mysite_form_alter(&$form, &$form_state, $form_id) {
//   dpm($form_id);
//   dpm($form);

   if (isset($form['#node']) && $form['#node']->type .'_node_form'
== $form_id) {
     // Move categories and menu fieldset below the body
     // field. We are assuming here that the taxonomy and menu
     // modules are enabled.
     $form['taxonomy']['#weight'] = 2;
     $form['menu']['#weight'] = 3;
   }
}
```

   If there is an existing implementation of hook_form_alter(), the highlighted code above will need to be integrated into it.

3. Save the file and exit the editor.

4. View the node form at, for example, `node/add/story`, to confirm that the menu and category fields now reside below the body field.

How it works...

Since `hook_form_alter()` is triggered for all forms, it is usually necessary that a couple of `dpm()` calls be used to first list the forms on the page using their form IDs, and then to analyze the form arrays themselves. Order for form elements is decided by the `#weight` attribute and the Devel module confirms, as in the following screenshot of a `dpm()` call, that the weights of the **menu** and **taxonomy** (Category) fields are, by default, set to **-2** and **-3** respectively.

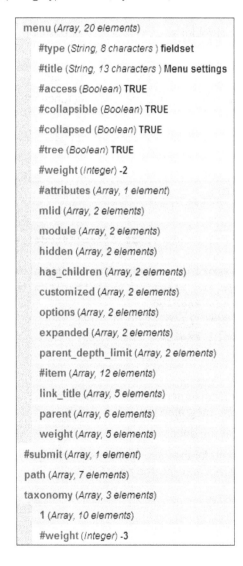

```
menu (Array, 20 elements)
    #type (String, 8 characters) fieldset
    #title (String, 13 characters) Menu settings
    #access (Boolean) TRUE
    #collapsible (Boolean) TRUE
    #collapsed (Boolean) TRUE
    #tree (Boolean) TRUE
    #weight (Integer) -2
    #attributes (Array, 1 element)
    mlid (Array, 2 elements)
    module (Array, 2 elements)
    hidden (Array, 2 elements)
    has_children (Array, 2 elements)
    customized (Array, 2 elements)
    options (Array, 2 elements)
    expanded (Array, 2 elements)
    parent_depth_limit (Array, 2 elements)
    #item (Array, 12 elements)
    link_title (Array, 5 elements)
    parent (Array, 6 elements)
    weight (Array, 5 elements)
#submit (Array, 1 element)
path (Array, 7 elements)
taxonomy (Array, 3 elements)
    1 (Array, 10 elements)
    #weight (Integer) -3
```

Furthermore, since the **Body** field has no explicit weight set, the negative weights of the menu and taxonomy fields ensure that they are placed above it as evident in the next screenshot.

Title: *

Category:
- None selected - ▾

▸ Menu settings

Body:

▸ Input format

▸ Revision information

With this information in hand, we can play with the #weight attributes of the two fields to change their positions. In the hook_form_alter() implementation in this recipe, we have assigned weights of 2 and 3 to the fields to obtain the following result where the body field is displayed with greater prominence:

Title: *

Body:

▸ Input format

Category:
- None selected - ▾

▸ Menu settings

▸ Revision information

Replacing a standard submit button with an image button

Design requirements sometimes dictate that standard form buttons be replaced with image equivalents. In this recipe, we will be replacing the **Save** and **Preview** buttons in node creation forms with image buttons.

Getting ready

We will be using the mysite module created earlier in this book. We will be adding two image buttons—one for **Save** and the other for the **Preview** button—to the form. It is assumed that these images are available as `save.png` and `preview.png`, and stored in the myzen theme's `image` folder.

It is also worthwhile familiarizing ourselves with the syntax and general vagaries of the `button`, `image_button`, and `submit` form element types via the Form API reference manual at `http://api.drupal.org/api/drupal/developer--topics--forms_api_reference.html/6#image_button`.

How to do it...

Since we are altering forms, we will be performing the following steps in the mysite module as follows:

1. Browse to the mysite module folder at `sites/all/modules/mysite`.

2. Locate the file `mysite.module` and open it in an editor.

3. Scroll down to the bottom of the page and paste the following `hook_form_alter()` implementation.

```
/**
 * Implementation of hook_form_alter().
 */
function mysite_form_alter(&$form, &$form_state, $form_id) {
  // Devel module debug code to retrieve information about
  // the form.
  // dpm($form_id);
  // dpm($form);

  $path = drupal_get_path('theme', 'myzen');
  if (isset($form['#node']) && $form['#node']->type .'_node_form'
== $form_id && isset($form['buttons'])) {
    $form['buttons']['submit']['#type'] = $form['buttons']
['preview']['#type'] = 'image_button';
```

```
    $form['buttons']['submit']['#src'] = $path . '/images/save.
png';
    $form['buttons']['preview']['#src'] = $path . '/images/
preview.png';
  }
}
```

If an implementation of this function already exists, the highlighted code we have just seen will need to be integrated appropriately.

 The commented-out dpm() calls in the previous snippet code are useful in determining the type and structure of the forms that we are dealing with.

4. Save the file and exit the editor.
5. In a browser, visit a node creation form such as the one at node/add/story, to see if our changes have taken effect.

How it works...

A standard node form, by default, comes with two buttons—one for preview and the other for submission. Using the Devel module's dpm() function to look through the structure of the $form array indicates that the two buttons are contained within an array named **buttons** as demonstrated in the following screenshot:

```
buttons (Array, 2 elements)
    submit (Array, 5 elements)
        #type (String, 6 characters ) submit
        #access (Boolean) TRUE
        #value (String, 4 characters ) Save
        #weight (Integer) 5
        #submit (Array, 1 element)
            0 (String, 16 characters ) node_form_submit | (Callback) node_form_submit();
    preview (Array, 4 elements)
        #type (String, 6 characters ) submit
        #value (String, 7 characters ) Preview
        #weight (Integer) 10
        #submit (Array, 1 element)
            0 (String, 23 characters ) node_form_build_preview | (Callback) node_form_build_preview();
```

The `form_alter` hook is triggered for all forms. Therefore, we ensure that we only try to modify node forms by checking for the presence of `$form['#node']` in the form array and that the `$form_id` corresponds with a node form. Since we are now familiar with the structure of the forms that we are dealing with, we can go ahead with our replacements.

First, we swap the element type of the submit and preview elements from that of a simple `button` to an `image_button`. Next, we use the `#src` attribute to point to the images in our theme folder. The Form API will now use these images when rendering the buttons.

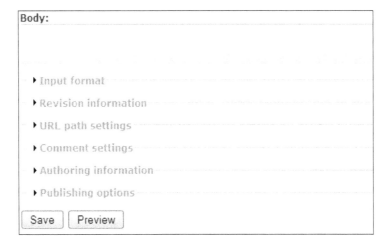

The end result should transform the standard node form buttons seen in the previous screenshot to their more attractive image equivalents as shown in the following screenshot:

Styling the comment form

In this recipe, we will look at manipulating form elements and markup using the Form API in an effort to make styling elements of the comment form easier. To be precise, we will be altering the comment form displayed to anonymous users in order to position its contact fields within a DIV block, thereby allowing us to target them better via CSS.

Getting ready

We will be using the mysite module created earlier in this book to contain an implementation of hook_form_alter(). Since we are going to be working on the comment form, it is assumed that the Comment module is enabled.

Drupal's default permissions do not permit anonymous users to view or add comments. These permissions can be added via the Permissions management page at admin/user/permissions (**Home | Administer | User management | Permissions**). To assist with debugging, it is also recommended that, if the Devel module is enabled, anonymous users be allowed to access debugging output via its permissions.

Finally, the node type being commented on will need to have comments enabled and also requires that anonymous users leave their contact information along with their comments. This can be done, as in the following screenshot, via the **Comment settings** fieldset on the node type's management page at admin/content/node-type/story (**Home | Administer | Content management | Story**), where story is the node type in question.

▼ Comment settings

Default comment setting:

○ Disabled

○ Read only

◉ Read/Write

Users with the *administer comments* permission will be able to override this setting.

Anonymous commenting:

○ Anonymous posters may not enter their contact information

○ Anonymous posters may leave their contact information

◉ Anonymous posters must leave their contact information

This option is enabled when anonymous users have permission to post comments on the permissions page.

How to do it...

Navigate to the mysite module folder at `sites/all/modules/mysite` to perform the following steps:

1. Locate the file `mysite.module` and open it in an editor.

2. Scroll down to the bottom and add the following function:

```
/**
 * Implementation of hook_form_alter().
 */
function mysite_form_alter(&$form, &$form_state, $form_id) {
  global $user;

  // Alter comment form for anonymous users.
  if ($user->uid == 0 && $form_id == 'comment_form') {
    // Use the Devel module to analyze the form array.
    // dpm($form);

    $form['name']['#prefix'] = '<div class="comment-contact">';

    $form['homepage']['#suffix'] = '</div>';

    // Get the path to the mysite module.
    $path = drupal_get_path('module', 'mysite');
    drupal_add_css($path . '/mysite.css');
  }
}
```

3. Save the file and exit the editor.

4. Access a comment form as an anonymous user and view its source to see if the name, mail, and homepage fields are wrapped in a `DIV` with its class attribute set to `comment-contact`.

Now that we have the markup ready, we can proceed to styling our new block. While it is usually recommended that all custom styling be added directly to the theme, it is sometimes preferable to contain **CSS** which is theme agnostic within the module. Themes can override these rules, if need be. Since we have altered the markup using the mysite module, we can also contain the related CSS rules within an associated stylesheet such as `mysite.css` which we have included in the `hook_form_alter()`.

1. If it does not already exist, create a file named `mysite.css` inside the mysite module folder, and open it in an editor.

2. Add the following rules to the file:

```
.comment-contact {
  width: 94%;
  padding-left: 1em;
```

```
    background-color: #FEE;
    border: 1px dashed red;
  }
  .comment-contact label {
    float: left;
    width: 110px;
    margin-right: 10px;
  }
```

3. Save the file and exit the editor.

4. Back in the browser, empty the Drupal cache and access the comment form once again as an anonymous user to see our alterations take effect.

How it works...

Since we are looking to box the three contact fields inside a `DIV`, we can make use of the Form API's `#prefix` and `#suffix` attributes to inject the opening and closing tags before the first field and after the last.

As in the previous screenshot, the first field in this case is the **Your name** field while the last one is the **Homepage** field. Looking at our code, as we have seen in earlier recipes, it is through the use of the Devel module's `dpm()` function that we obtain information on the inner workings of the form. While adding the opening `DIV`, we also take the opportunity to specify a class name for the tag, namely `comment-contact`, which will allow us to specifically target the element via CSS.

Once we have altered the markup, we move on to the styling. We use the `comment-contact` class to style the `DIV` by giving it a border and a background while also cleaning up the display of the three contact fields by aligning them inline. This is accomplished by floating the `LABEL` elements to the left which will automatically move their corresponding `INPUT` elements up and inline as seen in the following screenshot:

Additionally, playing with the widths of the `LABEL` elements ensures that all the contact fields are aligned thereby making the form easier on the eye.

Using a fieldset to group fields

The `FIELDSET` element is used to group related fields together and can be seen extensively in Drupal forms. While we saw how to inject markup in the previous recipe to group fields from a styling point of view, in this recipe we will be looking at grouping related fields of the contact form using two separate fieldsets.

Getting ready

We will be using the mysite module created earlier in this book to hold our customizations. As we are altering the contact form, it is assumed that the contact module is enabled and configured with at least a couple of contact categories via its management page at `admin/build/contact` (**Home | Administer | Site building | Contact form**). Enabling the module automatically makes a menu item available which can also be enabled from the menu management page at `admin/build/menu` (**Home | Administer | Site building | Menus**).

The form is accessible via the URL `contact` and should look something like the following screenshot:

How to do it...

Navigate to the mysite module folder at `sites/all/modules/mysite` to perform the following steps:

1. Locate the file `mysite.module` and open it in an editor.

2. Scroll down to the bottom and add the following function:

```
/**
 * Implementation of hook_form_alter().
 */
function mysite_form_alter(&$form, &$form_state, $form_id) {
  if ($form_id == 'contact_mail_page') {
    // Wrap the name and mail fields in a fieldset.
    $form['contact_fields'] = array(
      '#type' => 'fieldset',
      '#title' => t('Contact information')
    );

    // Move existing fields to fieldset.
```

```
$form['contact_fields']['name'] = $form['name'];
$form['contact_fields']['mail'] = $form['mail'];

// Wrap the subject, message, category and copy fields
// in a fieldset.
$form['message_fields'] = array(
  '#type' => 'fieldset',
  '#title' => t('Message')
);

// Move existing fields to fieldset.
$form['message_fields']['subject'] = $form['subject'];
$form['message_fields']['cid'] = $form['cid'];
$form['message_fields']['message'] = $form['message'];
$form['message_fields']['copy'] = $form['copy'];

// Move the submit button below our fieldsets.
$form['submit']['#weight'] = 1;

// Clear out the now unnecessary form elements.
unset($form['name'], $form['mail'], $form['subject'],
$form['message'], $form['copy'], $form['cid']);
  }
}
```

 If an existing implementation of `hook_form_alter()` exists, the contents of the above function will need to be appropriately merged with any pre-existing code.

3. Save the file and exit the editor.

4. In a browser, visit the contact form accessible via the URL `contact`, to verify that the fields are contained within two fieldsets. Perform a test submission to confirm that the form is functioning correctly.

How it works...

Analyzing the contact form using the Devel module's dpm() function and comparing it with the form, we can learn that the form fields are called **name**, **mail**, **subject**, **message**, **cid**, and **copy**.

```
... (Array, 26 elements)
    #token (String, 25 characters ) Karthikmysite@example.com
    contact_information (Array, 1 element)
    name (Array, 5 elements)
    mail (Array, 5 elements)
    subject (Array, 4 elements)
    cid (Array, 5 elements)
    message (Array, 3 elements)
    copy (Array, 2 elements)
    submit (Array, 2 elements)
    #parameters (Array, 2 elements)
    #build_id (String, 37 characters ) form-a3d95f94946d8fe6556371bf0a6af19d
    #type (String, 4 characters ) form
    #programmed (Boolean) FALSE
    form_build_id (Array, 4 elements)
    form_token (Array, 2 elements)
    form_id (Array, 3 elements)
        #type (String, 6 characters ) hidden
        #value (String, 17 characters ) contact_mail_page | (Callback) contact_mail_page();
        #id (String, 22 characters ) edit-contact-mail-page
```

In the `hook_form_alter()`, what we have done is created two fieldset elements and made all the aforementioned fields *children* of their respective fieldsets, thereby designating them to be displayed within. In other words, we are moving each field from `$form` to the newly created `$form[fieldset]`. The end result should look like the following:

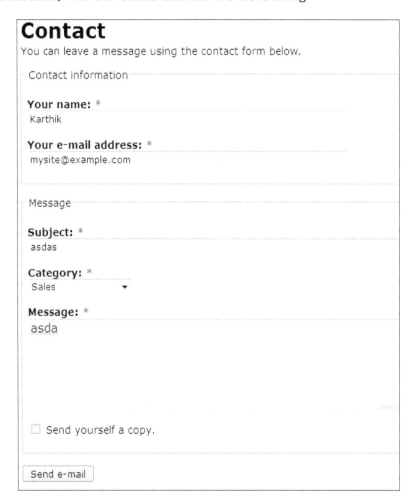

There's more...

While basic fieldsets are invaluable both from a structural and a visual point of view, Drupal provides a few improvements which make them an even more attractive option.

Collapsible fieldsets

Collapsible fieldsets are used by Drupal to make complex forms look simpler by minimizing them by default using JavaScript. This is controlled by the `#collapsible` and `#collapsed` attributes of the fieldset in question. For example, let us look at the fixed fieldset created in this recipe.

```
$form['contact_fields'] = array(
  '#type' => 'fieldset',
  '#title' => t('Message')
);
```

To transform this static fieldset into one which is collapsible and collapsed by default, we just need to set this fieldset's `#collapsible` and `#collapsed` attributes to TRUE.

```
$form['contact_fields'] = array(
  '#type' => 'fieldset',
  '#title' => t('Contact information'),
  '#collapsible' => TRUE,
  '#collapsed' => TRUE
);
```

 Setting a fieldset to be collapsed by default is, however, not recommended if any of the fields within are required fields as the user will not be aware of them until he opens the fieldset.

More information on the fieldset element is available as part of the Form API documentation at `http://api.drupal.org/api/drupal/developer-topics--forms_api_reference.html/6#fieldset`.

Theming form elements

Drupal form elements such as checkboxes and radio buttons are all rendered using the theme system and, consequently, can be overridden just like any other theme function. In this recipe, we will be adding a new feature to the FIELDSET element by overriding `theme_fieldset()`. We will be demonstrating its use by adding a postscript to the **Revision information** fieldset present in every node form.

Getting ready

This recipe requires the use of the mysite module created earlier in this book. The Devel and Theme developer modules will also be used to identify the theme function to override.

How to do it...

Firstly, we need to identify how Drupal is going about theming a fieldset. The recommended method of doing so is to use the Theme developer module as follows:

1. Browse to a node form at, for example, `node/add/story`.

2. Locate the **Revision information** fieldset which, if collapsed, should be expanded.

3. Enable **Themer info** and click on an empty area in this fieldset. The ensuing pop up should list the theme functions and any templates used in rendering the fieldset.

4. Based on the output of **Themer info** as seen in the following screenshot, the function responsible appears to be **theme_fieldset()**. Clicking this link should take us to the function's documentation page at `http://api.drupal.org/api/function/theme_fieldset/6`.

5. As per the documentation, this function resides within the file `includes/form.inc`. Open this file locally in an editor.

6. Copy the function `theme_fieldset()` in its entirety.

7. Now, navigate to the mysite module's folder at `sites/all/modules/mysite`.

8. Open the file `mysite.module` in an editor.

9. Paste the `theme_fieldset()` function into this file.

10. Rename this function `phptemplate_fieldset()`.

11. Amend the return call at the bottom of the function to include a new attribute titled `#postscript`. The resulting function should resemble the following block of code:

```
function phptemplate_fieldset($element) {
  if (!empty($element['#collapsible'])) {
    drupal_add_js('misc/collapse.js');

    if (!isset($element['#attributes']['class'])) {
      $element['#attributes']['class'] = '';
    }
```

```
      $element['#attributes']['class'] .= ' collapsible';
      if (!empty($element['#collapsed'])) {
        $element['#attributes']['class'] .= ' collapsed';
      }
    }

    return '<fieldset'.
  drupal_attributes($element['#attributes']) .'>'.
  ($element['#title'] ? '<legend>'. $element['#title'] .
  '</legend>' : '') . (isset($element['#description']) &&
  $element['#description'] ? '<div class="description">'.
  $element['#description'] .'</div>' : '') .
  (!empty($element['#children']) ? $element['#children'] : '')
  . (isset($element['#value']) ? $element['#value'] : '') .
  (isset($element['#postscript']) && $element['#postscript'] ? '<div
  class="postscript">'. $element['#postscript'] .'</div>' : '') .
  "</fieldset>\n";
    }
}
```

12. Scroll down to the bottom of the `mysite.module` file and add the following function:

```
/**
 * Implementation of hook_form_alter().
 */
function mysite_form_alter(&$form, &$form_state, $form_id) {
  if (isset($form['#node']) && $form['#node']->type .'_node_form'
== $form_id) {
    $form['revision_information']['#postscript'] = t('If a new
revision is to be created, please ensure that a log message is
added detailing any changes.');
  }
}
```

 If an existing implementation of `hook_form_alter()` already exists, the above code will need to be integrated appropriately.

13. Save the file and exit the editor.

14. Empty the Drupal cache to ensure that our theme override takes effect.

15. Browse to the node form to confirm that the **Revision information** fieldset now includes a postscript at the bottom.

How it works...

Since the fieldset is rendered using a theme function, we are able to override it just like any other theme function in Drupal. What is of interest in this case is that we have chosen to use `phptemplate_fieldset()` as the override function and located it within `mysite.module` instead of doing so with `myzen_fieldset()` within the myzen theme's `template.php` file. This choice was made as the change that we are introducing appears to be something that will be useful across different themes. If, on the other hand, we were changing the markup of the fieldset to suit the myzen theme, then we would have been better off locating the override function within the theme.

Once we have introduced the `#postscript` attribute in `phptemplate_fieldset()`, we can use it as part of any fieldset's declaration as demonstrated in the `hook_form_alter()` implementation. The resulting **Revision information** fieldset should now look something like the following:

▼ Revision information

☐ Create new revision

Log message:

An explanation of the additions or updates being made to help other authors understand your motivations.

If a new revision is to be created, please ensure that a log message is added detailing any changes.

Adding class attributes to form elements

Drupal 6 is quite meticulous with its forms and other markup when it comes to assigning `CLASS` and `ID` attributes. This ensures that various page elements can be individually targeted either via CSS or JavaScript and thereby manipulated as necessary. This is, however, not true all the time and circumstances sometimes require a little further customization.

In this recipe, we will assign class attributes to the Search module's textfields and use them along with a pinch of jQuery to improve usability in situations where the theme's search box is visible along with the module's input form.

Getting ready

We will be using the mysite module created earlier in this book to hold an implementation of `hook_form_alter()`. Since we are playing with the Search module, it is assumed that the module is enabled and that the site's content has subsequently been indexed. The current theme's search-box feature should also be enabled via its configuration page.

How to do it...

Navigate to the mysite module folder at `sites/all/modules/mysite` to perform the following steps:

1. Locate the file `mysite.module` and open it in an editor.

2. Scroll down to the bottom and add the following function:

```
/**
 * Implementation of hook_form_alter().
 */
function mysite_form_alter(&$form, &$form_state, $form_id) {
  // Set the class attribute and add some JS goodness to the
  // search form when both the theme search box as well as
  // the basic search form are visible.
  if ($form_id == 'search_form') {
    // Set the class attribute of the search form textfield.
    $form['basic']['inline']['keys']['#attributes'] =
array('class' => 'search-text');

    // The path to the mysite module.
    $path = drupal_get_path('module', 'mysite');
    drupal_add_js($path . '/js/search.js');
  }
  else if ($form_id == 'search_theme_form') {

    // Set the class attribute of the search-box textfield.
    $form['search_theme_form']['#attributes'] = array('class' =>
'search-text');
  }
}
```

 If there is an existing implementation of `hook_form_alter()`, the previous code will need to be integrated into it.

3. Save the file and exit the editor.

4. Visit the URL `search` where both the search box and basic search form are displayed. The HTML source should confirm that both the textfields now have a class named **search-text** assigned to them.

   Now that we have assigned the classes to the two textfields, we can work on getting the JavaScript up and running. Note that in the `hook_form_alter()` in the previous code, we have also conditionally included the JavaScript file we will be creating.

5. Browse to the mysite module's `js` folder.

6. Create a file named `search.js` and open it in an editor.

7. Add the following jQuery to this file:

```
Drupal.behaviors.mysiteSearch = function (context) {
  var fields = $('.search-text');
  // Set default text to both fields.
  var text = fields.filter(function() { return $(this).val().
length; }).val();
  fields.val(text);

  // Sync textfield key-presses.
  fields.keyup(function(event){
    fields.not(this).val($(this).val());
  });
}
```

8. Save the file and exit the editor.

9. Empty the Drupal cache.

10. Revisit the search page and perform a test search query.

11. Confirm that the current search keywords are being displayed in both textfields.

12. Confirm that user input into either textfield is automatically synchronized with the other textfield.

How it works...

One of the minor issues with the theme-centric search box is that when it is used to perform a query, the resulting page does not display the keywords being searched for in its textfield. Instead, they are displayed solely in the search module's form as in the next screenshot.

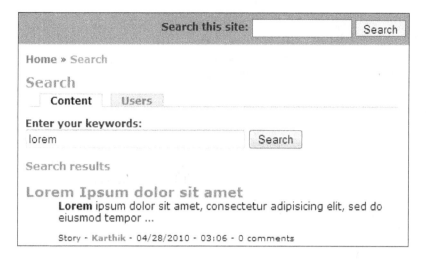

By using the Form API's #attributes option via a hook_form_alter(), we are able to add a class titled .search-text to both textfields. This subsequently allows us to easily target the two elements using jQuery. Once we have them, we can ensure that the theme's search box contains the same keywords as the primary search form, as evident in the following screenshot:

We are also able to take this opportunity to implement a synchronization effect using jQuery's keyup() event which synchronizes the user's input into either textfield in real time.

There's more...

While we have synchronized the input for both the search form as well as the theme's search box textfield, there is yet another variant that might also need to be taken care of.

Accounting for the search block

Besides the Search module's textfield and the theme's search box, administrators can also enable a third option—the search block. This block can be enabled from the Block administration page at `admin/build/block` (**Home | Administer | Site building | Blocks**). Our synchronization script will not work as is with this block as its textfield does not contain the `search-text` class. Once this is addressed via the `hook_form_alter()`, the script should automatically function as expected.

10
Customizing CCK

We will be covering the following recipes in this chapter:

- ▸ Creating a custom node type
- ▸ Hiding fields and labels during display
- ▸ Displaying fields together using fieldgroups
- ▸ Theming CCK content using `hook_nodeapi()`
- ▸ Theming a CCK field using a template file
- ▸ Adding image support using the `ImageField` module
- ▸ Using ImageCache to scale and crop images on the fly
- ▸ Adding lightbox support for images

Introduction

The **Content Construction Kit** or **CCK** is a suite of modules that enable the creation, management, and customization of node types. By default, Drupal comes with a few rudimentary and generic node types to serve the basic requirements of a site. Once we are past this gradient, however, we arrive at the rather impressive roadblock of field customization. Traditionally, extending a node type to include custom fields would usually mean the creation of a dedicated module, the addition of custom fields using Drupal's Form API, handling their validation, submission, and database storage requirements besides having to account for upgrade paths and inviting perennial security questions.

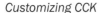

While there are certain advantages with going at it directly using code, the tedium of it all soon becomes a time sink. CCK abstracts the entire process by allowing us to add, manage, customize, and reuse form fields directly from Drupal's administration pages. With database tables automatically created, upgrade paths automatically handled, and custom content automatically made available to other modules, such as Views, CCK takes most of the complexity out of customization and allows site administrators to get on with the more creative aspects of site deployment.

The core CCK package comes with a primary module named **Content** which is a prerequisite for all other modules, a number of **field** modules, such as **Text** and **Number** which enable the creation of form elements based on their types, and a couple of utility modules to handle backend operations such as import and export. Besides these, there are a plethora of contributed modules which similarly allow the creation of form fields, such as the **Email Field** module which handles e-mail address input, or the **ImageField** module which enables image uploads.

Besides these, there are a host of other modules known as **formatter** modules, which integrate with CCK fields allowing them to present their data in a variety of formats.

The CCK module's project page is at `http://drupal.org/project/cck` and also links to documentation and tutorials. It should be noted that with CCK being available across three different versions of Drupal, a number of these resources might well be dated. In other words, it is important to check that they are relevant to Drupal 6 before diving in.

Contributed CCK modules for Drupal 6 are listed at `http://drupal.org/project/ modules?filters=tid%3A88%20drupal_core%3A87&solrsort=sis_project_ release_usage%20desc`.

In this chapter, we will look at creating a custom node type named `company` and then extending it using different CCK modules.

Creating a custom node type

In this recipe, we will be adding a custom node type using the CCK package. As an example, we will be creating a type named **company** to hold information about a company along with details, such as its address, telephone number, e-mail address, and so on.

Getting ready

It is assumed that the CCK package has been downloaded and installed. Besides the **Content** module, only the **Text** module is a prerequisite for this recipe.

How to do it...

The CCK package integrates into Drupal's content management pages and can be accessed by navigating to `admin/content/types` (**Home | Administer | Content management | Content types**). Perform the following steps to add the new type:

1. Click on the **Add content type** tab at the top.

2. Since we are creating a type specifically to hold details about a company, set the **Name** and **Type** fields in the ensuing form to **Company** and **company** respectively.

3. Add some pertinent information in the **Description** field.

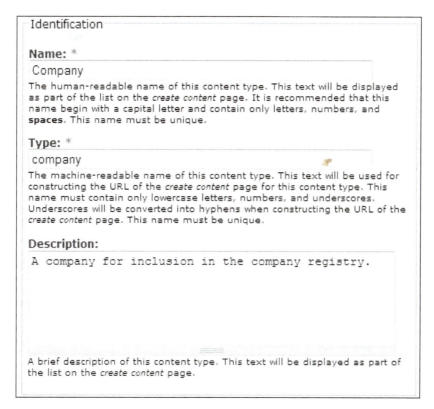

4. Open the **Submission form settings** fieldset and amend the labels of the **Title** and **Body** fields to read **Company name** and **Company description** respectively.

5. Click on **Save content type** to create our new node type. This should take us back to the **Content types** list, which should now include our new type.

Name	Type	Description	Operations
Company	company	A company for inclusion in the company registry.	edit manage fields delete
Page	page	A *page*, similar in form to a *story*, is a simple method for creating and displaying information that rarely changes, such as an "About us" section of a website. By default, a *page* entry does not allow visitor comments and is not featured on the site's initial home page.	edit manage fields delete
Story	story	A *story*, similar in form to a *page*, is ideal for creating and displaying content that informs or engages website visitors. Press releases, site announcements, and informal blog-like entries may all be created with a *story* entry. By default, a *story* entry is automatically featured on the site's initial home page, and provides the ability to post comments.	edit manage fields delete

» Add a new content type

6. Click on the company type's **manage fields** link.

7. In the resulting page, scroll down to the section dealing with the addition of new fields.

8. Use this form to add a new field to hold the address details of the company as in the following screenshot:

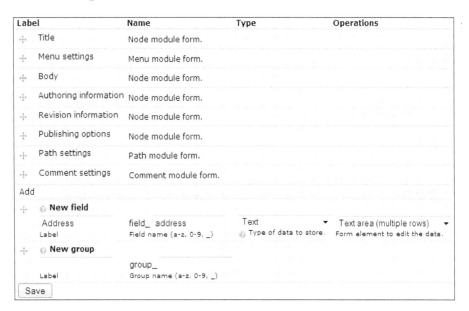

254

9. Clicking on **Save** should take us to a field configuration form where the field can be customized further.

10. Click on **Save field settings** to add the field.

11. Similarly, add two more text fields—**Phone** and **E-mail address**—to complete the set of basic fields for our node type as in the following screenshot:

Label	Name	Type	Operations
⊹ Company name	Node module form.		
⊹ Menu settings	Menu module form.		
⊹ Company description	Node module form.		
⊹ Revision information	Node module form.		
⊹ Authoring information	Node module form.		
⊹ Publishing options	Node module form.		
⊹ Path settings	Path module form.		
⊹ Comment settings	Comment module form.		
⊹ Address	field_address	Text	Configure Remove
⊹ Phone	field_phone	Text	Configure Remove
⊹ E-mail address	field_email	Text	Configure Remove

How it works...

Now that we have our new type set up, we can go ahead and add company content via node/add/company (**Home | Create content | Company**). The following screenshot displays a company node created for a company named **Foo Corp**.

There's more...

The CCK module also provides options to adjust the weight of each field and thereby, its display order.

Adjusting the display order of fields

As the following screenshot demonstrates, the display order of various fields can be adjusted using the drag-and-drop cross hairs to the left of each field and subsequently saving the changes.

Label	Name	Type	Operations
Company name	Node module form.		
Company description	Node module form.		
Address	field_address	Text	Configure Remove
Phone	field_phone	Text	Configure Remove
E-mail address	field_email	Text	Configure Remove
Images	field_images	File	Configure Remove
Revision information	Node module form.		
Authoring information	Node module form.		
Menu settings	Menu module form.		
Publishing options	Node module form.		
Path settings	Path module form.		
Comment settings	Comment module form.		

Multiple-value fields

Since companies might well have multiple phone numbers, we can cater to this requirement by amending the **Number of values** property of the **Phone** field accordingly via the configuration page of the field. For our needs, setting it to **Unlimited** should work well. Once modified, the node creation page should support multiple phone numbers as in the following screenshot:

Contributed modules: e-mail and phone

While we have used simple textfields to store the phone and e-mail fields in the company node type, we could have just as well made use of contributed modules which provide custom field types for each of these inputs. In the case of the phone field, using the _Phone_ module (`http://drupal.org/project/phone`) will introduce additional capabilities, such as number validation and display formatting support. The _Email Field_ module (`http://drupal.org/project/email`) provides similar support for e-mail addresses.

Hiding fields and labels during display

In this recipe, we will be using the CCK module to hide certain fields and field labels from the company node's display layout. In particular, we do not want to expose the e-mail address field to the end user as we have other plans for it. Furthermore, we do not want anything besides the name of the company and a brief description displayed when in teaser form.

Getting ready

We will be using the company node type created earlier in this chapter.

How to do it...

Browse to the management page of the company type at `admin/content/node-type/company/fields` (**Home | Administer | Content management | Content types | Company**) to perform the following steps:

1. Click on the **Display fields** tab at the top.

2. Set the **Address, Phone,** and **E-mail address** fields to be excluded from the teaser view by enabling their **Exclude** checkboxes next to the **Teaser** column.

3. Set the **E-mail address** field also to be excluded from the **Full node** view by enabling the appropriate **Exclude** checkbox.

4. Change the **Label** setting for the **Phone** and **E-mail address** fields to **Inline**.

5. Finally, set the **Teaser** setting for the **Address** field to **Trimmed** so that the form looks like the following screenshot:

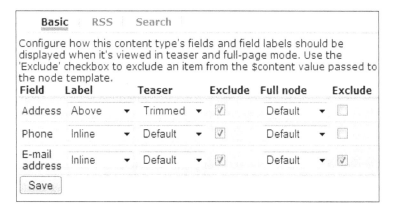

6. Click on the **Save** button to save our changes.

How it works...

We can see the changes made through the **Display fields** form taking effect, by visiting a node of type `company`. As demonstrated in the next screenshot, the **E-mail address** field is no longer visible and we can also see that the label for the **Phone** field is placed inline with its content, unlike the **Address** label which is positioned above its data.

Foo Corp

View	Edit	Devel

Submitted by **Karthik** on Mon, 07/19/2010 - 10:29

Lorem ipsum dolor sit amet, consectetur adipisicing elit, sed do eiusmod tempor incididunt ut labore et dolore magna aliqua. Ut enim ad minim veniam, quis nostrud exercitation ullamco laboris nisi ut aliquip ex ea commodo consequat. Duis aute irure dolor in reprehenderit in voluptate velit esse cillum dolore eu fugiat nulla pariatur. Excepteur sint occaecat cupidatat non proident, sunt in culpa qui officia deserunt mollit anim id est laborum.

Address:

1234, Example avenue,
Example city,
Example State,
Example PIN code
India

Phone: +91 12 3456 7890
          +91 12 3456 7891

We can also confirm that our changes to the teaser views are also taking effect by viewing a node listing, such as the one accessible at the URL node, which is used by Drupal as its default front-page content. In the following screenshot, we can tell that the only fields visible are the **Company name**—the node title—and the **Company description**—the node body fields.

Bar Corp

Submitted by **Karthik** on Mon, 07/19/2010 - 14:06

Lorem ipsum dolor sit amet, consectetur adipisicing elit, sed do eiusmod tempor incididunt ut labore et dolore magna aliqua. Ut enim ad minim veniam, quis nostrud exercitation ullamco laboris nisi ut aliquip ex ea commodo consequat. Duis aute irure dolor in reprehenderit in voluptate velit esse cillum dolore eu fugiat nulla pariatur. Excepteur sint occaecat cupidatat non proident, sunt in culpa qui officia deserunt mollit anim id est laborum.

» Add new comment

Foo Corp

Submitted by **Karthik** on Mon, 07/19/2010 - 10:29

Lorem ipsum dolor sit amet, consectetur adipisicing elit, sed do eiusmod tempor incididunt ut labore et dolore magna aliqua. Ut enim ad minim veniam, quis nostrud exercitation ullamco laboris nisi ut aliquip ex ea commodo consequat. Duis aute irure dolor in reprehenderit in voluptate velit esse cillum dolore eu fugiat nulla pariatur. Excepteur sint occaecat cupidatat non proident, sunt in culpa qui officia deserunt mollit anim id est laborum.

Displaying fields together using field groups

In addition to fields, the CCK package also provides a module that allows the grouping of various CCK fields into display groups known as **field groups**. In this recipe, we will be creating a group to contain all fields providing contact information within the `company` node type.

Getting ready

We will be using the company node type created earlier in this chapter. Since this recipe uses field groups, it is required that the `fieldgroup` module within the CCK package be enabled.

How to do it...

Once the `fieldgroup` module has been enabled, the **Manage fields** form for the company node type should now have an option to also create groups. This form can be accessed by navigating to `admin/content/node-type/company/fields` (**Home | Administer | Content management | Content types | Company**) and clicking on the **Manage fields** tab at the top.

The **Contact** field group to hold the **Address, Phone**, and **E-mail address** fields can be created using the following procedure:

1. Scroll down to the bottom of the page to locate the row titled **New group**.

2. Add **Contact** and **contact** respectively to the **Label** and **Group name** textfields as shown in the following screenshot:

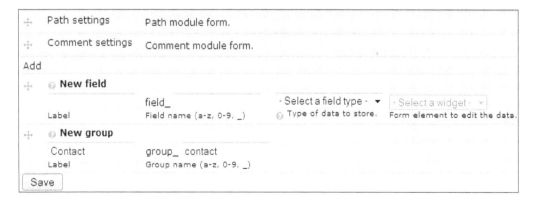

3. Click on the **Save** button to create the new group.

4. A new group named **Contact** should now be listed at the bottom of the table. Drag the three fields—**Address, Phone**, and **E-mail address**—onto the **Contact** group where they should snap into place as members of the group.

Label	Name	Type	Operations
⊹ Company name	Node module form.		
⊹ Company description	Node module form.		
⊹ **Contact** *	group_contact	Standard group	Configure Remove
⊹ Address *	field_address	Text	Configure Remove
⊹ Phone *	field_phone	Text	Configure Remove
⊹ E-mail address *	field_email	Text	Configure Remove
⊹ Revision information	Node module form.		

5. Drag the **Contact** group up the table to just below the **Company description** field.

6. Click on the **Save** button to save our changes.

How it works...

Viewing a company node should confirm the presence of a new fieldset containing the two contact fields as in the following screenshot:

Furthermore, the fieldset is now also a part of the node form for company nodes.

In many ways, CCK treats field-groups just like any other field allowing us to order them and otherwise modify their properties.

Field groups and display fields

The display fields form for the company node type at `admin/content/node-type/company/display` (**Home | Administer | Content management | Content types | Company**) treats the **Contact** group just like a field, allowing us to exclude it, change its styling, hide its label, and so on, as in the following screenshot:

Field	Label	Teaser		Exclude	Full node		Exclude
Contact	Above ▾	fieldset	▾	☑	fieldset	▾	☐
Address	Above ▾	Trimmed ▾		☐	Default	▾	☐
Phone	Inline ▾	Default	▾	☐	Default	▾	☐
E-mail address	Inline ▾	Default	▾	☐	Default	▾	☑
Save							

Furthermore, since the **Address**, **Phone**, and **E-mail address** fields are members of the **Contact** group, it is sufficient to just exclude the group for **Teaser** views as its members will also be excluded automatically.

Theming CCK content using hook_nodeapi()

Theming CCK content is fundamentally no different from theming a standard node as long as we are not trying to theme the CCK fields themselves. If, on the other hand, we are looking to theme fields, we can either do so via field-specific template files or, as in our case here, through simple manipulations of markup from within a module.

In this recipe, we will be looking at modifying the markup of the company node type to allow us to easily target the **Company description** field during display.

Getting ready

We will be using the `mysite` module created earlier in this book to hold our customizations for the company node type. It is also assumed that a `mysite.css` file is being loaded by the module during runtime via its `hook_init()` function.

Analyzing the HTML output for a `company` node in its current state should display something like the following:

```
<div class="node">
  <span class="submitted"><!--Content--></span>
  <div class="taxonomy"><!--Content--></div>
  <div class="content">
    <p><!--Content--></p>
    <fieldset class="fieldgroup group-contact"><!--Content--></
fieldset>

  </div>
  <div class="links"><!—Content--></div>
</div>
```

Looking at the highlighted code, the `<p>` tag represents the contents of the **Company description** field, while the `<fieldset>` represents the field group titled **Contact**. Note that the `<p>` tag has no class or ID associated with it. Consequently, if we want to target only the **Company description** field via CSS, we are effectively looking at targeting the first `<p>` tag within the `<div>` with class `content`. This is something which, while possible, will not function with browsers that do not support CSS selectors. As we will see shortly, a cleaner solution would instead be to fix the problem at its source by modifying the actual markup that we are dealing with, to ensure that we are only targeting the **Company description** field.

How to do it...

Browse to the `mysite` module folder at `sites/all/modules/mysite` to perform the following steps:

1. Open the file `mysite.module` in an editor.

2. Add the following PHP to the file:

```php
/**
 * Implementation of hook_nodeapi().
 */
function mysite_nodeapi(&$node, $op) {
  if ($op == 'view') {
    $node->content['body']['#prefix'] = '<div class="company-
description">';
    $node->content['body']['#suffix'] = '</div>';
  }
}
```

If the nodeapi hook already exists, then the contents of the previous function will need to be merged appropriately.

 More information about the capabilities of the `hook_nodeapi()` function can be obtained from its documentation page at `http://api.drupal.org/api/function/hook_nodeapi/6`.

3. Save the file and exit the editor.

4. Locate the `mysite.css` file and open it in an editor.

5. Add the following rules to the file:

```css
.company-description {
  width: 60%;
  float: left;
  padding-right: 1em;
  text-align: justify;
}
```

6. Save the file and exit the editor.

7. If necessary, clear the Drupal cache.

8. Finally, navigate to the **Display fields** tab in the management page of the company node type at `admin/content/node-type/company/display` (**Home | Administer | Content management | Content types |Company**).

9. Modify the display settings so that the **Contact** field group is displayed as a collapsible fieldset. The resulting form should look something like the following screenshot:

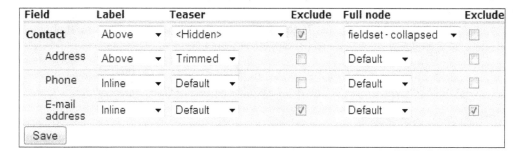

Field	Label		Teaser		Exclude	Full node		Exclude
Contact	Above	▼	\<Hidden\>	▼	☑	fieldset - collapsed	▼	☐
Address	Above	▼	Trimmed	▼	☐	Default	▼	☐
Phone	Inline	▼	Default	▼	☐	Default	▼	☐
E-mail address	Inline	▼	Default	▼	☑	Default	▼	☑

Save

10. Click on the **Save** button to save our changes.

How it works...

Viewing a company node should now confirm that we have been successful in isolating the **Company description** field and floating it to the left with a smidgeon of CSS. Furthermore, with a few tweaks to the **Display fields** interface, we have succeeded in presenting our fields in a more concise manner as in the following screenshot:

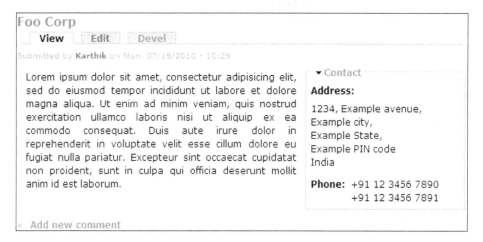

 It is important to note that since we have manipulated the markup using the mysite module, our changes are effective across different themes.

Theming a CCK field using a template file

While it is a quick and easy operation to manipulate markup using `hook_nodeapi()`, as our requirements become more complex, we inevitably need to resort to locating our customizations within a template file. Theming CCK fields using template files is just about the same as theming anything else in Drupal, albeit with a couple of caveats.

In this recipe, we will look at modifying the output of the **Phone** field in the `company` node type to use an unordered list when there are multiple items present.

Getting ready

We will be using the myzen theme created earlier in this book to hold our theme customizations. Following the recommendations outlined in earlier chapters, we will also be making use of the Devel and Theme developer modules to assist in identifying the theme functions and templates to override. It is assumed that these modules are installed and enabled.

To get an idea of the work at hand, navigate to a sample company node and view the markup of a **Phone** field with multiple values. The HTML should look something like the following:

```
<div class="field field-type-text field-field-phone">
  <div class="field-items">
    <div class="field-item odd">
      <div class="field-label-inline-first">
        Phone: 
      </div>
      +91 12 3456 7890
    </div>
    <div class="field-item even">
      <div class="field-label-inline">
        Phone: 
      </div>
      +91 12 3456 7891
    </div>
  </div>
</div>
```

As can be seen, multiple values of the same field are displayed using separate `DIV` blocks. Furthermore, the second value comes with its own label which is hidden using CSS to provide a seemingly inline look. Besides the entire block of code being semantically repulsive, it can also lead to complications during theming.

How to do it...

In order to locate the template file to override, we first need to use the Theme developer module. Enable **Themer info** and click on the **Phone** field to gain information on the functions and templates responsible for its display. As outlined in the following screenshot, the template file in use is CCK's default `content-field.tpl.php` template file.

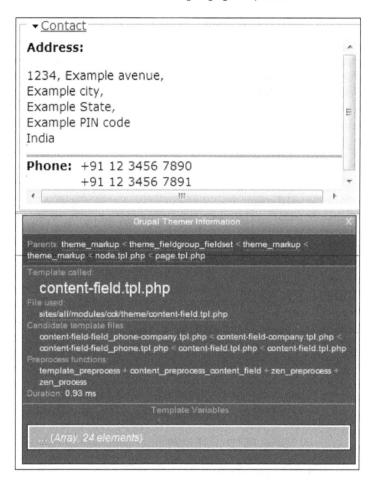

We are also informed that if we wanted to override this file, we could locate our changes in a filename based on the provided **Candidate template** filenames. The filenames dictate the scope of the template file. This scope can range from `content-field.tpl.php`, which will affect all CCK fields, to `content-field-field_phone-company.tpl.php`, which will only affect the field named `field_phone` when used within the `company` node type. In our case, we can use `content-field-field_phone.tpl.php`, which will affect the field `field_phone`, regardless of which node type it is being used in.

To override the template, perform the following steps:

1. Navigate to the CCK module's folder at `sites/all/modules/cck`.

2. Browse into the `theme` folder.

3. Copy the file named `content-field.tpl.php`.

4. Browse to the myzen theme folder at `sites/all/themes/myzen`.

5. Click into the `templates` subfolder and paste the file into it.

 This file is a requirement even though we will not be customizing it at all. The above procedure is frequently overlooked by themers and is usually the cause of endless suffering!

6. Make another copy of the same file in this folder and name it `content-field-field_phone.tpl.php`.

7. Open this file in an editor. Its contents should effectively be something like the following:

```php
<?php if (!$field_empty) : ?>
<div class="field field-type-<?php print $field_type_css ?> field-
<?php print $field_name_css ?>">
  <?php if ($label_display == 'above') : ?>
    <div class="field-label"><?php print t($label) ?>: </div>
  <?php endif;?>
  <div class="field-items">
    <?php $count = 1;
    foreach ($items as $delta => $item) :
      if (!$item['empty']) : ?>
        <div class="field-item <?php print ($count % 2 ? 'odd' :
'even') ?>">
          <?php if ($label_display == 'inline') { ?>
            <div class="field-label-inline<?php print($delta ? ''
: '-first')?>">
              <?php print t($label) ?>: </div>
          <?php } ?>
          <?php print $item['view'] ?>
        </div>
      <?php $count++;
      endif;
    endforeach;?>
  </div>
</div>
<?php endif; ?>
```

The highlighted line above is a tentative pointer to the code where we run through multiple values and print them.

8. Replace this entire block of code with the following more simplified, yet cleaner version which displays each entry as a list item:

```php
<?php if (!$field_empty) : ?>
<div class="field field-type-<?php print $field_type_css ?> field-
<?php print $field_name_css ?>">
  <div class="field-label"><?php print t($label) ?>: </div>
  <ul class="field-items">
    <?php $count = 1;
    foreach ($items as $delta => $item) :
      if (!$item['empty']) : ?>
        <li class="field-item <?php print ($count % 2 ? 'odd' :
'even') ?>">
          <?php print $item['view'] ?>
        </li>
      <?php $count++;
      endif;
    endforeach;?>
  </ul>
</div>
<?php endif; ?>
```

The highlighted code we have just seen indicates where we have replaced the old markup with an unordered list. We are cycling through each entry in the `$items` array and outputting it as a list entry.

9. Save the file and exit the editor.

10. Empty the Drupal cache and rebuild the theme registry as we have introduced new template files into the system.

How it works...

Once the cache has been emptied, browse to a company node page to see our changes in effect.

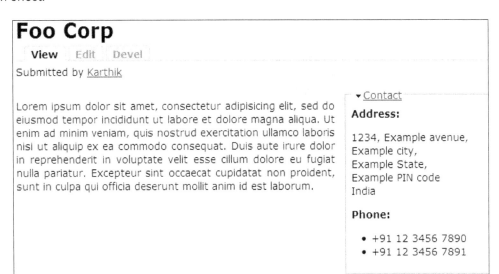

As displayed in the screenshot, the two phone numbers are now displayed using an unordered list which, if necessary, can be styled further using CSS. We can also confirm that the markup is cleaner by looking at the mark-up which should be something like the following:

```
<div class="field field-type-text field-field-phone">
  <div class="field-label">Phone: </div>
  <ul class="field-items">
    <li class="field-item odd">
      +91 12 3456 7890
    </li>
    <li class="field-item even">
      +91 12 3456 7891
    </li>
  </ul>
</div>
```

Adding image support using the ImageField module

In this recipe, we will be adding image support to the company node type using the **ImageField** module.

Getting ready

The ImageField module can be downloaded and installed from http://drupal.org/project/imagefield. It depends on the **FileField** module which can be downloaded from http://drupal.org/project/filefield.

How to do it...

Once ImageField is enabled, it is available as a CCK field. The following steps detail how we can add image support to the company node type:

1. Navigate to the company type's field-management page at admin/content/node-type/company/fields (**Home | Administer | Content management | Company | Manage fields**).

2. Scroll down to the section titled **New field**.

3. Add **Images** and **images** respectively to the **Label** and **Field** name textfields.

4. Choose **File** as the **Type of data to store**.

5. Set the **Form element to edit the data** field to **Image**.

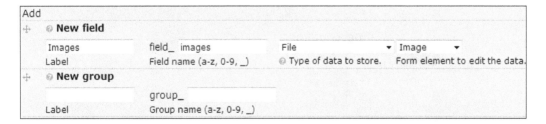

6. Click on the **Save** button to create the field.

7. In the ensuing field configuration form, set the **Number of values** option to **Unlimited**.

8. Click on **Save field settings** to complete the procedure.

9. Back in the **Manage fields** tab, move the new **Images** field up the table as in the following screenshot:

Label	Name	Type	Operations
⊹ Company name	Node module form.		
⊹ Company description	Node module form.		
⊹ **Contact**	group_contact	Standard group	Configure Remove
⊹ Address	field_address	Text	Configure Remove
⊹ Phone	field_phone	Text	Configure Remove
⊹ E-mail address	field_email	Text	Configure Remove
⊹ Images	field_images	File	Configure Remove

10. Click on the **Save** button once again.

How it works...

Once configured, the company node form will now support the uploading of images as demonstrated in the following screenshot:

Furthermore, as shown in the next screenshot, the **Display fields** tab now provides display and styling options particular to the ImageField. While these are rather rudimentary at the moment, our options will expand once we involve other image-related modules in the upcoming recipes.

Field	Label	Teaser	Exclude
Contact	Above ▾	\<Hidden> ▾	☑
Address	Above ▾	Trimmed ▾	☐
Phone	Inline ▾	Default ▾	☐
E-mail address	Inline ▾	Default ▾	☑
Images	Above ▾	Image ▾	☑

> Generic files
> Path to file
> URL to file
> Image
> Image linked to node
> Image linked to file
> \<Hidden>

Save

Using ImageCache to scale and crop images on the fly

Now that we have ImageField support for the company node type, we can look to style the input images to make them more presentable. When it comes to image handling, we inevitably find ourselves performing a series of repeated steps, such as cropping, scaling, resizing, and so on, as per the requirements of our theme (or themes, as the case may be). It used to be the case that this procedure had to be performed manually for each image or, if we were a little more proactive, performed through a script to apply our changes on-the-fly. All this is, however, a thing of the past thanks to the **ImageCache** module.

The ImageCache module brings the concept of presets to Drupal's image systems. A preset is a term used to represent the series of operations that we are looking to perform on the image. Furthermore, it is not restricted to simple size and scale changes as its APIs can be extended to play with the color and styling of the images as well. All this, of course, happens on-the-fly, which along with its caching system makes this module invaluable.

In this recipe, we will be looking at scaling and cropping the images for the company node type using ImageCache.

Getting ready

This is a follow-up to the previous recipe where we added image support to the company node type. The `ImageCache` module (`http://drupal.org/project/imagecache`) and its dependencies are assumed to have been installed. The module relies on an external library to handle image operations and comes packaged with two options—**GD2** and **ImageMagick**. GD2 comes packaged with PHP while ImageMagick is a command-line program accessible through a PHP extension. It is assumed that one of these libraries is installed.

Furthermore, to add and manage our ImageCache presets, we will need to enable the **ImageCache UI** module.

We will also be adding a smidgeon of CSS to prettify our images and will be doing so using the mysite module created earlier in this book. The CSS will be added to its `mysite.css` file which is assumed to be loaded via the module's `hook_init()` function during runtime.

How to do it...

Once enabled, the `ImageCache` module provides an interface at `admin/build/imagecache` (**Home | Administer | Site building | ImageCache**) where the following steps are to be performed:

1. Click on the **Add new preset** tab.

2. Type **company-thumbnail** inside the **Preset Namespace** textfield.

3. Click the **Save Preset** button to create the preset.

4. In the subsequent preset configuration screen, click on **Add Scale and Crop**.

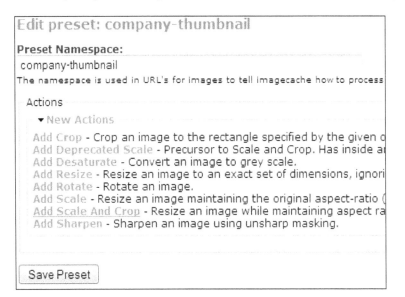

5. Change the **Width** and **Height** textfields to **100** (rather than 100%), which indicates the value in pixels.

Add imagecache_scale_and_crop to company-thumbnail

Width:

100

Enter a width in pixels or as a percentage. i.e. 500 or 80%.

Height:

100

Enter a height in pixels or as a percentage. i.e. 500 or 80%.

Create Action

6. Click on the **Create Action** button.

7. Click on **Save Preset** back on the preset configuration screen to save our changes.

    Now that our preset has been created, we can look to apply it to our images.

8. Navigate to the company node type's **Display fields** configuration page at admin/content/node-type/company/display (**Home | Administer | Content management | Content types | Company**).

9. Set the **Images** field's **Full node** formatter to **company-thumbnail image linked to image**.

10. Click on the **Save** button to save our changes.

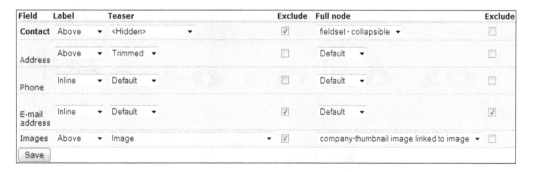

Field	Label		Teaser		Exclude	Full node		Exclude
Contact	Above	▾	<Hidden>	▾	☑	fieldset - collapsible ▾		☐
Address	Above	▾	Trimmed ▾		☐	Default ▾		☐
Phone	Inline	▾	Default ▾		☐	Default ▾		☐
E-mail address	Inline	▾	Default ▾		☑	Default ▾		☑
Images	Above	▾	Image		▾ ☑	company-thumbnail image linked to image ▾		☐

Save

Lastly, we need to style our images to be displayed inline in a horizontal row to provide a gallery-like feel.

11. Navigate to the mysite module's folder at sites/all/modules/mysite.

12. Open the file mysite.css in an editor.

13. Add the following rule to the file:

```
.field-field-images .field-items .field-item {
  display: inline;
}
```

14. Save the file and exit the editor.

How it works...

Once the new preset has been applied, the company node page will look something like the following where five images have been uploaded:

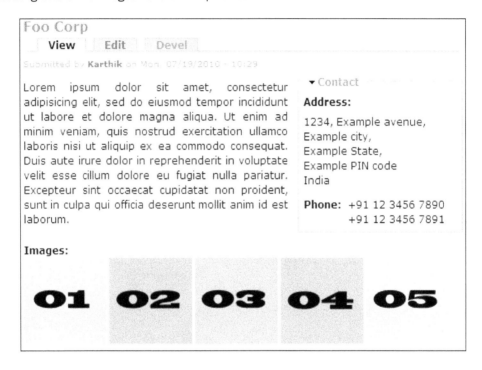

As per the chosen display formatter, clicking any of the thumbnails will link us to the original image directly on the Drupal filesystem.

If any changes are made to the Drupal filesystem where uploaded images are stored, or if there have been any manual changes made to the source image files themselves, the ImageCache module's cache will need to be flushed so that our changes can be reapplied and the images recreated. This can be done by clicking the link titled **Flush** next to the appropriate preset on the ImageCache management page at `admin/build/imagecache` (**Home | Administer | Site building | ImageCache**).

Adding lightbox support for images

Lightbox plugins allow users to view magnified versions of clicked thumbnails in modal dialogs on the same page. Coupled with easing animations and other attractive effects, they make for engaging viewing.

While there are a number of modules that provide such functionality, we will be looking at the **Colorbox** plugin and module in this recipe specifically since it is jQuery-based and supports the `ImageField` module.

Getting ready

The `Colorbox` module can be downloaded and installed from `http://drupal.org/project/colorbox`. We will also be working on the company node type created earlier in this chapter.

How to do it...

Once enabled, the `Colorbox` module can be configured from `admin/settings/colorbox` (**Home | Administer | Site configuration | Colorbox**) as per the following steps:

1. Set the value of the **Image field gallery** setting to **Per field gallery**.

2. Choose **Original image (no preset)** for the **Imagecache preset** field since we are just going to display the original image without any modifications in the lightbox.

3. Click on the **Save configuration** button to save our changes.

Once Colorbox has been configured, it should now be available as an option in the company node type's **Display fields** form.

4. Navigate to the **Display fields** form at `admin/content/node-type/company/display` (**Home | Administer | Content management | Content types | Company**).

5. Set the **Full node** formatter for the **Images** field to **Colorbox: company-thumbnail image** as in the next screenshot.

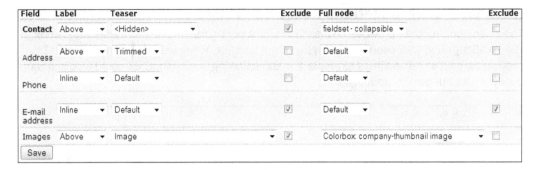

Field	Label	Teaser	Exclude	Full node	Exclude
Contact	Above ▾	<Hidden> ▾	☑	fieldset - collapsible ▾	☐
Address	Above ▾	Trimmed ▾	☐	Default ▾	☐
Phone	Inline ▾	Default ▾	☐	Default ▾	☐
E-mail address	Inline ▾	Default ▾	☑	Default ▾	☑
Images	Above ▾	Image ▾	☑	Colorbox: company-thumbnail image ▾	☐

Save

6. Click on the **Save** button to save our changes.

How it works...

Now that the thumbnails are being formatted using Colorbox, clicking them should trigger the lightbox as seen in the following screenshot:

There's more...

The Colorbox module also provides further options to configure and style our lightbox display.

Advanced customizations using Colorbox

The Colorbox module provides an interface via its configuration page to theme and tweak the JavaScript and CSS used in the display of the lightbox. While we can use one of the provided preset styles, such as **Example 2** in the following screenshot, we could also just as easily create our own custom style.

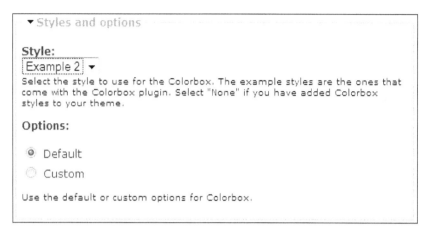

In the previous screenshot, choosing **Custom** will expose all the nuts and bolts pertaining to the animation and style of the dialog.

11
Views Theming

We will be covering the following recipes in this chapter:

- ▶ Creating a simple view
- ▶ Styling a node listing using a grid display
- ▶ Merging columns with the Views table style plugin
- ▶ Embedding a View inside a node template
- ▶ Overriding the Views table style plugin
- ▶ Adding a class to a Views style
- ▶ Creating a custom Views style plugin

Introduction

The Views module is the most popular contributed module in the Drupal ecosystem, and with good reason, as it has become one of the cornerstones of Drupal development. Along with other modules, such as CCK and Panels, it has contributed immensely towards Drupal's reputation of being an ideal tool for rapid site development and deployment.

Views, at its most fundamental level is a database query builder. It allows us to construct database queries using a user-friendly interface and, subsequently, presents the result to the user in a variety of manners. The query builder supports a number of components including:

- ▶ **Arguments** which are usually dynamic parameters passed to the query at runtime, such as the elements of the URL of the page being displayed.
- ▶ **Filters** which conditionally refine the query to return a more accurate result set. For example, since we will customarily only require nodes which have been published, we can add a filter to the view stating that the result set should only contain published nodes.

> ▸ **Relationships** which are usually used to connect two different database tables together based on the relationship between two of their elements.

> ▸ Field specification which describes the fields to be returned as part of the result set.

> ▸ Sorting support which specifies how the results are to be sorted.

> ▸ Pagination support which limits the number of results returned.

> ▸ Support for distinct results to limit duplicates in the result set.

The Views module takes the returned results and runs them through its styling component which is built atop the Drupal theme system. The module supports a variety of styling options through the use of style plugins, which allow representing the results as tables, lists, and so on. Moreover, all styles can be overridden from Drupal's theme layer just as we have seen in the earlier chapters.

Additionally, Views allows administrators to create multiple **Displays** for each view. Displays allow the efficient representation of the same query in a variety of different ways. For example, a list of nodes can be presented both as content on a page or as content in a block.

The project page for the Views module is at `http://drupal.org/project/views`. While the documentation for the module resides at `http://views-help.doc.logrus.com`, it is highly recommended that the **Advanced Help** module is installed along with Views. It can be downloaded from `http://drupal.org/project/advanced_help` and provides extensive and easily accessible contextual help all across the module. In the following screenshot, the question-mark icons all represent links to documentation specific to the associated elements.

In this chapter, we will primarily be looking at the Views module from a theming point of view with particular attention being paid to overriding the default styling options provided. It is highly recommended that users looking to theme views also familiarize themselves with the Drupal theming system prior to diving in.

Creating a simple view

In this recipe, we will look at the ease with which we can create a simple unformatted node listing using the Views module.

Getting ready

The view we will be creating will display a list of nodes of a custom node type named `product`. Besides the inbuilt fields of **Title** and **Body**, this node type also contains two CCK fields, namely **Image** and **Price**, which are of type `ImageField` and `Text` respectively as the following screenshot will attest. It is assumed that these fields have been installed and enabled along with their dependencies.

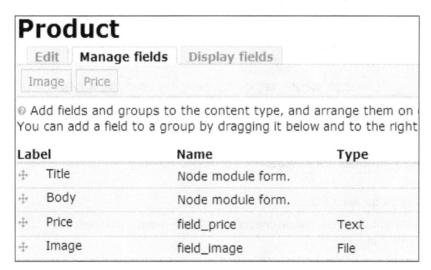

Sample products and product images have been added for the purpose of this recipe.

How to do it...

To create the view, navigate to the Views management page at `admin/build/views` (**Home | Administer | Site building | Views**) to perform the following steps:

1. Click on the **Add** tab at the top of the page.
2. Set the **View name** to **product_gallery**.

3. Set the **View description** field to **A representation of all product nodes**.

4. Set the **View type** to **Node**.

5. Click on the **Next** button.

6. In the ensuing View management page, click on **Save** to complete the creation process.

The Views administration interface uses JavaScript and Ajax to allow changes to be made in real time without frequent page refreshes. However, any changes made are not saved until the **Save** button is clicked.

7. In the **Filters** section, click on the **Add** icon—a plus—to add a filter.

8. In the **Add filters** interface, which is shown in the next screenshot, select **Node** in the **Groups** drop down.

9. Select **Node: Type** and **Node: Published** from the list of options.

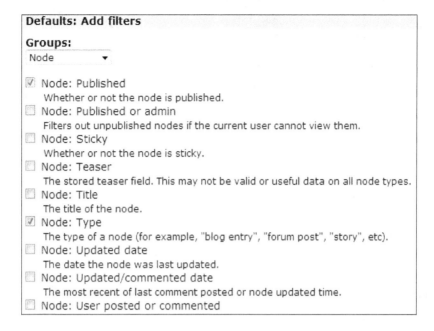

10. Click on **Add** to add the filters.

11. In the resulting configuration screen for the **Node: Published** filter, select **Yes** as shown in the following screenshot and click on **Update**.

Defaults: Configure filter *Node: Published*

This item is currently not exposed. If you **expose** it, users will be able to change the filter as they view it.

| Expose |

Published:

⦿ Yes
◯ No

12. Again, in the subsequent configuration screen for **Node: Type**, select the **Product** type as in the following screenshot and click on **Update**.

Defaults: Configure filter *Node: Type*

This item is currently not exposed. If you **expose** it, users will be able to change the filter as they view it.

Expose

Operator:

◉ Is one of
○ Is not one of

Node type:

☐ Company
☐ Page
☑ Product
☐ Story

---

13. Click on the **Save** button to save the changes to the View.

14. Similarly, in the **Fields** section, click on the **Add** icon—a plus—to add the fields to display.

15. In the resulting **Add fields** form, select **Node** in the **Groups** drop down.

16. Select the **Node title** as a field and click on **Add**.

Defaults: Add fields

Groups:

Node ▾

    The date the node was posted.
☐ Node: Promoted to front page
    Whether or not the node is promoted to the front page.
☐ Node: Published
    Whether or not the node is published.
☐ Node: Sticky
    Whether or not the node is sticky.
☐ Node: Teaser
    The stored teaser field. This may not be valid or useful data on all node types.
☑ Node: Title
    The title of the node.
☐ Node: Type
    The type of a node (for example, "blog entry", "forum post", "story", etc).
☐ Node: Updated date
    The date the node was last updated.
☐ Node: Updated/commented date
    The most recent of last comment posted or node updated time.

---

17. In the field configuration screen, check **Link this field to its node** and click on **Update**.

18. Next, click on the **Add** field icon once again.

19. Select **Content** in the **Groups** drop down to display only the available CCK fields.

20. Check the two CCK fields which are part of the **Product** node type, namely **Content: Image (field_image)** and **Content: Price (field_price)** and click on **Add**.

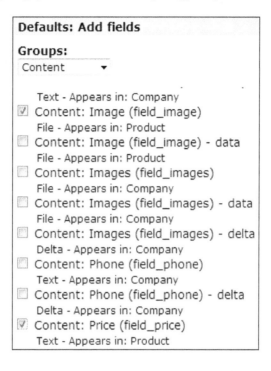

21. Accept the default configuration options and click on **Update** for both fields.

22. Click on the **Save** button to save the view.

    Now that we have added the fields and filters to our view, we can look to add a display to make it accessible as a page.

23. Below the list of displays on the left, set the display type to **Page** and click on the **Add Display** button underneath.

24. Under the **Basic settings**, click on **Name: Page** and rename the display to **Unformatted**. Click on **Update**.

 Note that the default value for the view's **Style** plugin option is **Unformatted**.

25. Click on the **Title: None** link and set the title to **Our products**. Click on **Update**.

26. Enable the pager by clicking on **Use Pager: No** and set it to **Full Pager**. Click on **Update**.

27. Click on the **Path** link under **Page settings** and set the path to **product-list**. Click on **Update**.

28. Finally, click on the **Save** button to save our changes.

How it works...

Once configured, the View's configuration page should look something like the following screenshot:

We can clearly see the three fields we have added–**Node: Title**, **Content: Image**, and **Content: Price**—as well as the two filters—**Node: Type** and **Node: Published**. Each of these elements can be clicked to reach its configuration screen, if available.

Since we have created a page display for our View, we can access it at the configured URL: **product-list**. As the View uses the **Unformatted** style by default, the output is a simple collection of fields as in the following screenshot:

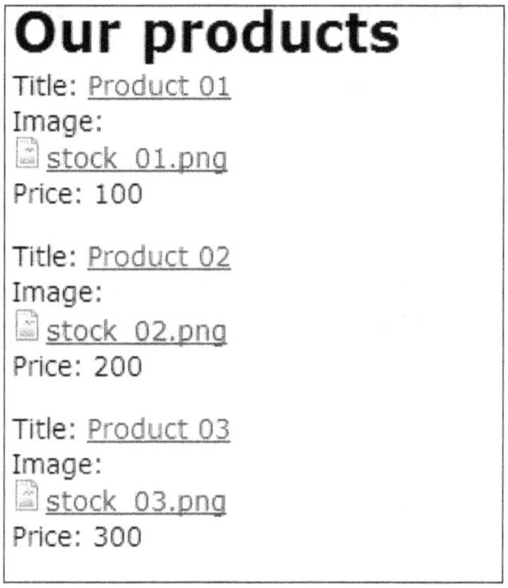

Our products

Title: Product 01
Image:
stock_01.png
Price: 100

Title: Product 02
Image:
stock_02.png
Price: 200

Title: Product 03
Image:
stock_03.png
Price: 300

The **Unformatted** style option is useful in cases where the styling is customized entirely via an overridden template file. We will be investigating this and other styling options as we go along in this chapter.

Styling a node listing using a grid display

In this recipe, we will look at the ease with which we can represent the node view created in the previous recipe as a gallery, by styling the view as a **grid**. A grid will allow us to achieve a gallery-like feel with each cell in a table layout representing a row from the result set.

Getting ready

We will be using the `product_gallery` view created earlier in the previous recipe. Additionally, we will be using the **ImageCache** module, as we saw in the last chapter, to create the thumbnail for the `ImageField` being used in the `product` node type. Create an `ImageCache` preset named **product_thumb** which performs a **Scale and Crop** operation to create a thumbnail of size `150px x 150px` as in the following screenshot:

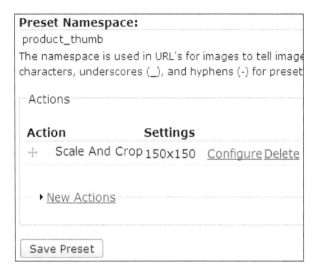

This recipe also makes use of the myzen theme created earlier in this book to hold our CSS customizations.

How to do it...

To achieve a gallery-like representation of the product nodes, we will be adding a new display to the **product_gallery** view as follows:

1. Browse to the Views administration page at `admin/build/views` (**Home | Administer | Site building | Views**).

2. Locate the **product_gallery** view and click on its **Edit** link.

3. In the view management interface, select **Page** from the display drop down on the left and click on **Add display**.

4. Under **Basic settings**, click on **Name: Page** and rename the display to **Gallery**.

5. Next, click on **Style: Unformatted** to change the style plugin being used to style the view.

6. In the resulting configuration form, first click on the **Override** button on the top right as we want to override the settings prescribed by the default display.

 Overriding allows us to adjust and tweak the current display to provide a different representation of the results when compared to the default display. If this option was not overridden here, then our changes would have inadvertently also affected the **Unformatted** and **Defaults** displays. Virtually every configurable option in a display can be overridden to our satisfaction.

7. Change the style plugin to **Grid** as shown in the following screenshot:

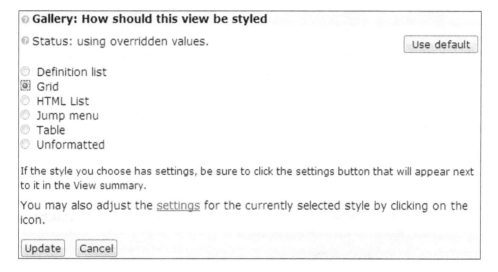

8. Click on the **Update** button to register our change.

9. The **Style** option should now reflect our change to the **Grid** plugin. Click on its associated settings icon—a gear—to configure it further.

10. In the configuration form, set the **Number of columns** to **4** and leave the **Alignment** field set to **Horizontal**.

Gallery: Style options

Status: using overridden values.

[Use default]

Grouping field:

| <None> ▾ |

You may optionally specify a field by which to group the records. Leave blank to not group.

Number of columns:

4

Alignment:

◉ Horizontal
○ Vertical

Horizontal alignment will place items starting in the upper left and moving right. Vertical alignment will place items starting in the upper left and moving down.

☑ Fill up single line
If you disable this option a grid with only one row will have the amount of items as tds. If you disable it this can cause problems with your css.

[Update] [Cancel]

---

11. Click on the **Update** button.

12. Since this is a new *page* display, we will also need to specify a URL for it. Click on the **Path: None** link under **Page settings**.

13. Set the path to **product-gallery** and click on **Update**.

14. Click on **Save** to save our changes to the view.

> Clicking on **Save** will also refresh the page and lead us back to the **Defaults** display. We will need to select the **Gallery** display once again to customize it further.

With the style plugin set to **Grid**, we can go ahead and also customize the fields being displayed for the **Gallery** display.

15. Click on the **Fields** link which serves as the header for the **Fields** section.

16. In the resulting configuration form, click the **Override** button as the changes made to the fields are local to the **Gallery** display only.

17. Click on the **Update** button.

18. Now, click on the **Content: Image** field.

19. Set the **Label** field to **None**.

20. Set the **Format** drop down to use the `ImageCache` preset which, in this case is, **product-thumb image linked to node**.

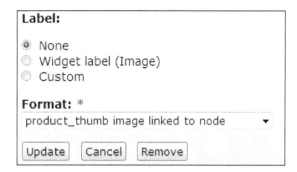

21. Click on **Update** and then the **Save** button to save our changes.

    Finally, we can add a little CSS to position the grid and its contents at the center of the page:

22. Browse to the myzen theme's folder at `sites/all/themes/myzen`.

23. Navigate into its `css` subfolder and locate `views-styles.css` which is loaded by the theme via its `.info` file.

24. Open this file in an editor and add the following rules to it:

```
/* Product gallery */
.view-product-gallery table {
    width: 80%;
    margin: auto;
    text-align: center;
}
```

Adding custom CSS classes to the view

While the Views module routinely adds well-structured class names to most of its markup, it is sometimes necessary to add our own custom classes. This can be done by clicking on the **CSS class** link under **Basic settings**. In this recipe, we have made use of the default class name `.view-product-gallery` to target the table used by the **Gallery** display.

25. Save the file and exit the editor.

How it works...

Once our changes to the **Gallery** display have been saved, the management page should look something like the following screenshot:

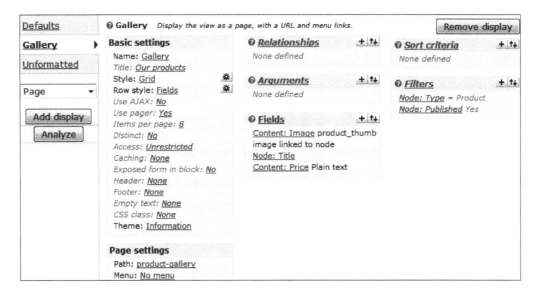

Subsequently, visiting the view's URL at `product-gallery` should result in a gallery-like representation of the product nodes as shown in the following screenshot:

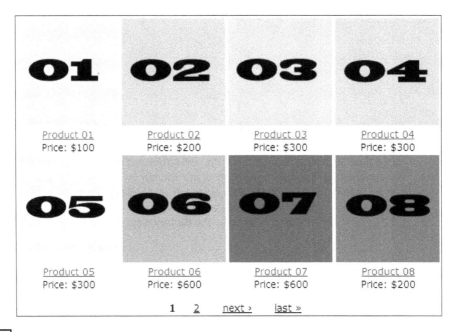

Views comes with a number of other styling options. While **Grids** allow us to lay out our content as an HTML table purely for visual reasons, the **Table** plugin allows us to represent the contents of nodes in standard tabular form.

Styling as a table

A simple swap of the style plugin being used from **Grid** to **Table** will provide a standard tabular representation of the nodes. This can be done by clicking on **Style: Grid** and changing the plugin to **Table** in the resulting configuration screen. The following screenshot displays the view as a table:

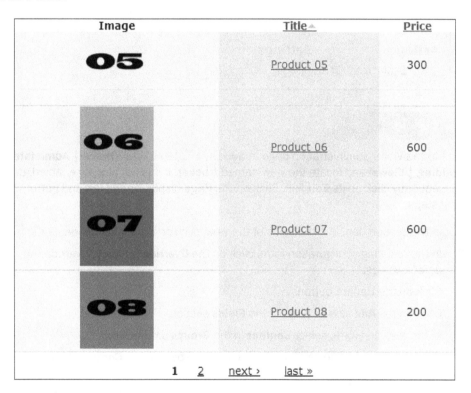

Merging columns with the Views table style plugin

In this recipe, we will be looking at using the table plugin's column combination feature to merge multiple columns together. In particular, we will be modifying the inbuilt content tracker view to treat nodes of type `product` differently.

Getting ready

We will be using the `product` node type created earlier in this chapter. We will also be using the `ImageCache` module to create a thumbnail which will fit inside a row of the tracker table. Create an `ImageCache` preset named **tracker_thumb** which performs a **Scale and Crop** operation to create a thumbnail of size `20px x 20px` as in the following screenshot:

Preset Namespace:

tracker_thumb

The namespace is used in URL's for images to tell imagecache how to proces characters, underscores (_), and hyphens (-) for preset names.

Actions

Action	Settings	
+ Scale And Crop	20x20	Configure Delete

How to do it...

Navigate to the Views administration page at `admin/build/views` (**Home | Administer | Site building | Views**) and locate the view named **tracker**. If it is not already enabled, do so and subsequently click on its **Edit** link. Click on the **Page** display on the left and perform the following steps:

1. In the section denoting the fields of the view, click on the **Fields** header link.

2. In the resulting configuration form, click on the **Override** button to override the default values.

3. Click on the **Update** button.

4. Click on the **Add** icon—a plus—in the **Fields** section.

5. In the resulting form, select **Content** in the **Groups** drop down.

6. Select the two CCK fields of the **Product** node type, namely **Content: Image** and **Content: Price**.

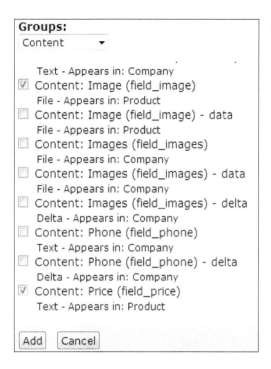

7. Click on **Add**.

8. In the configuration screen for **Image**, enable the **Hide if empty** option.

9. Set the **Label** to **None**.

10. Set the **Format** to **tracker_thumb** image.

11. Click on the **Update** button.

12. Similarly, enable **Hide if empty** on the configuration screen for **Price**.

13. Set the **Label** to **None**.

14. Set the **Format** to **Plain text**.

    Since we are displaying the price of the product we can, while we are here, also prefix a currency symbol (**$** in this case) to the field value.

15. Enable the option **Rewrite the output of this field**.

16. In the resulting textarea, as seen in the following screenshot, add **($[field_price_value])** as per the provided information on the available tokens for this field.

☑ Rewrite the output of this field ▾
If checked, you can alter the output of this field by specifying a string of text with replacement tokens that can use any existing field output.

Text:

($[field_price_value])

The text to display for this field. You may include HTML. You may enter data from this view as per the "Replacement patterns" below.

☐ Output this field as a link ▸
If checked, this field will be made into a link. The destination must be given below.

☐ Trim this field to a maximum length ▸
If checked, this field be trimmed to a maximum length in characters.

☐ Strip HTML tags
If checked, all HTML tags will be stripped.

Empty text:

If the field is empty, display this text instead.

☐ Count the number 0 as empty
If the field contains the number zero, display the empty text instead

☑ Hide if empty
Do not display anything for this field if it is empty. Note that the field label may still be displayed. Check style or row style settings to hide labels for empty fields.

☐ Link this field to its node
This will override any other link you have set.

Label:

◉ None
○ Widget label (Price)
○ Custom

Format: *
Plain text ▾

[Update] [Cancel] [Remove]

17. Click on **Update** to register our change.

 As mentioned in previous recipes, it is important to always keep in mind that nothing is saved permanently in the database until we click the **Save** button. Other buttons only register our changes temporarily, allowing us to continue configuring our view without the need for a page refresh.

18. Now, under **Basic settings**, click on the configuration icon—a gear—next to **Style: Table**.

19. In the settings form, set the **Column** value for both the **Content: Image** and **Content: Price** fields to **Title**. This will ensure that they are grouped together during display.

Field	Column	Separator	Sortable	Default sort
Type	Type ▾		☑	○
Title	Title ▾		☑	○
Content: Image (field_image)	Title ▾			
Content: Price (field_price)	Title ▾			
Author	Author ▾		☑	○
Replies	Replies ▾	 	☑	○
Last Post	Last Post ▾		☑	◉
Node: Has new content	Node: Has new content ▾			
Node: New comments	Replies ▾			
None				○

20. Click on **Update**.

21. Finally, click on the **Save** button to save our changes.

How it works...

Accessing the URL `tracker` should now display nodes of type product along with their **Image** and **Price** fields as in the following screenshot:

Type	Title	Author	Replies	Last Post
Product	Product 10 ($400)	Karthik	0	08/02/2010 - 20:15
Product	Product 09 ($200)	Karthik	0	08/02/2010 - 20:15
Product	Product 08 ($200)	Karthik	0	08/02/2010 - 20:15
Product	Product 07 ($600)	Karthik	0	08/02/2010 - 20:14
Product	Product 06 ($600)	Karthik	0	08/02/2010 - 20:14
Product	Product 05 ($300)	Karthik	0	08/02/2010 - 12:27
Product	Product 04 ($300)	Karthik	0	08/02/2010 - 12:27
Product	Product 03 ($300)	Karthik	0	08/02/2010 - 12:27
Product	Product 02 ($200)	Karthik	0	08/02/2010 - 12:27
Product	Product 01 ($100)	Karthik	0	08/02/2010 - 12:27
Company	Bar Corp	Karthik	0	07/19/2010 - 14:06
Company	Foo Corp	Karthik	0	07/19/2010 - 10:29

As is evident from the screenshot, only product node entries carry the additional fields. Other node types are unaffected. We can also confirm that the `ImageCache` module is in effect with product images depicted as thumbnails, and that the price field is prefixed with a currency indicator as specified.

There's more...

The **tracker** view used in this recipe is one of many views which are provided as part of the Views module.

Default views

The Views module comes packaged with a number of pre-prepared views such as frontpage, archive, and tracker. While custom views can be deleted, default views can only be reverted back to their original state or, alternatively, disabled. In the next screenshot, we can see four views: **frontpage**, a default view which is enabled and **overridden**, **product_gallery**, which is a custom view, **tracker** which is also a default view and not overridden, and **glossary**, another default view, albeit, disabled.

❷ *Overridden* Node view: **frontpage** (default)	Edit | Export | Clone | Revert
Path: <u>frontpage</u> *Feed, Page*	Emulates the default Drupal front page; you may set the default home page path to this view to make it your front page.
❷ *Normal* Node view: **product_gallery**	Edit | Export | Clone | Delete
Title: Our products Path: <u>product-table</u> *Page*	A representation of all product nodes
❷ *Default* Node view: **tracker** (default)	Edit | Export | Clone | Disable
Title: Recent posts Path: <u>tracker</u> *Page*	Shows all new activity on system.
❷ *Default* Node view: **glossary** (default)	Enable
Path: glossary *Page*	A list of all content, by letter.

Embedding a view inside a node template

Views usually tend to be output as pages, blocks, and other displays. In this recipe, we will be looking at taking this a step further by manually embedding a view inside a node template using a smidgeon of code. To be more precise, we will be taking the **backlinks** view which comes with the Views module and embedding it inside a theme's node template file to provide a list of related content which links to the node currently being displayed.

Backlinks provide a list of nodes which link to the current node. For example, if in the content of node/123, we include a link to node/456, node/123 is considered to be a backlink of node/456.

Getting ready

Since we are going to be embedding the backlinks view, it is assumed that it has been enabled. Additionally, for backlinks to be available, the content of the site will need to link to each other. In other words, sample nodes will need to be created which link to other nodes in the site to allow backlinks to be cataloged.

Furthermore, as backlinks are generated by the **Search** module, it is imperative that it is enabled and that the site is indexed completely. This can be ascertained by visiting the search module's configuration page at admin/settings/search (**Home | Administer | Site configuration | Search**).

We will be using the myzen theme created earlier in this book to hold our customizations. It is assumed that a node template file already exists within the theme's templates folder.

How to do it...

Once the backlinks view has been enabled from the Views management page at `admin/build/views` (**Home | Administer | Site building | Views**), a new **What links here** tab should appear at the top of each node's page. This tab will, as in the following screenshot, list all the backlinks for the node being viewed.

The previous screenshot is a representation of the backlinks view's **Page** display. Since we are embedding a view inside a node, we will instead be using the view's **Block** display which is already available by default, as per the following steps:

1. Browse to the myzen theme folder at `sites/all/themes/myzen`.

2. Navigate into its `templates` sub-folder.

3. Locate `node.tpl.php` and open it in an editor.

4. Look for code that deals with the display of content such as the following:
    ```
    <div class="content">
      <?php print $content; ?>
    </div>
    ```

5. Add the embed code to this block so that it now looks something like this:
    ```
    <div class="content">
      <div class="backlinks">
        <h3>What links here</h3>
        <?php print views_embed_view('backlinks', 'block');?>
      </div>
      <?php print $content; ?>
    </div>
    ```

    The `views_embed_view()` call returns the block display of the backlinks view.

6. Save the file and exit the editor.

7. Browse back up a level and into the `css` folder.

8. Locate the `views-styles.css` file and open it in an editor.

9. Add the following rules to the file:

```css
/* Backlinks */
.backlinks {
  float: right;
  display: inline;
  padding: 0 1em;
  margin: 0 0 0.5em 1em;
  border-left: dashed 1px;
}

.backlinks h3 {
  margin-top: 0;
  padding-top: 0;
}

.backlinks ul {
  padding-left: 1.2em;
}

.backlinks ul li {
  list-style: square;
}
```

`views-styles.css` is, by default, automatically loaded by the theme via its `.info` file.

10. Save the file and exit the editor.

11. Clear the Drupal cache, if necessary.

How it works...

Refreshing the node page should now display the node's backlinks along with its contents as in the following screenshot:

Premo Proprius Mos Inhibeo Amet

View　What links here　Edit　Devel

Submitted by Karthik

node (story) - Proprius tation macto genitus amet wisi defui. Brevitas mauris iaceo sino comis nimis. Defui vulpes singularis pecus bene praesent. Luctus erat wisi vulputate capto jus metuo ille.

Quadrum jugis neo obruo wisi te ea aptent incassum. Quadrum ludus aliquip quia conventio magna persto.

Elit appellatio cui. Nimis abbas rusticus. Gravis iaceo consequat paulatim suscipit blandit consectetuer paulatim abbas secundum. Comis genitus proprius vindico luptatum immitto ludus decet.

What links here

- Sed Vereor Humo
- Saluto Sudo Erat Exerci Ideo
- Quadrum

We can see that the backlinks are identical to what was displayed in the **What links here** tab we saw earlier. Furthermore, thanks to our CSS, we have floated the entire block to the right and have displayed it inline, thereby allowing the content to flow around it. A simple border and other tweaks and nudges provide the finishing touch.

> Since we are embedding the **What links here** block directly into the node content, displaying the tab is unnecessary. As this tab is handled by the backlinks view's **Page** display, simply deleting the display or, alternatively, playing with its **Access** settings should do the trick.

There's more...

There are also a couple of alternative approaches which can be used to embed views.

views_embed_view() and view titles

In this recipe, we have resorted to manually adding the view's title along with the `views_embed_view()` call as the function, by design, only returns the content of the view. If it is necessary that the view's title is also used, then we will need to resort to the relatively longer approach outlined in the following code:

```
<div class="content">
  <div class="backlinks">
    <?php
      $view = views_get_view('backlinks');
      $view_content = $view->preview('block');
      $view_title = $view->get_title();
    ?>
```

```
        <h3><?php print $view_title; ?></h3>
        <?php print $view_content; ?>
    </div>
    <?php print $content; ?>
</div>
```

Embedding Views using the Viewfield module

While it is simple enough to embed code directly into template files or elsewhere in the theme, the `Viewfield` module provides a more straightforward alternative. It exposes all available views via a CCK field which can be made a part of a node type, thereby allowing a view to be embedded in a node display just like any other CCK field.

Overriding the Views table style plugin

In this recipe, we will override the Views template used to render table styles. In particular, we will be overriding the standard table used to display the **tracker** view in order to allow the spanning of rows of the same node type.

Getting ready

The Views module comes with a default view named tracker which provides the same functionality as the tracker module by providing a table listing nodes which the current user has either created or participated in. This view can be enabled from the Views administration page at `admin/build/views` (**Home | Administer | Site building | Views**).

Since we will be overriding template files in this recipe, we will be making use of the myzen theme created earlier in this book.

How to do it...

The tracker view, once enabled, provides a table of pertinent content, as in the following screenshot, which can be accessed at the URL `tracker`.

Type	Title	Author	Replies	Last Post
Story	Blandit Facilisis Cogo Populus Dolor	Karthik	24	05/09/2010 - 02:03
Story	Exerci Oppeto Loquor Paratus Consequat Neque Nimis	Anonymous	12	05/09/2010 - 01:58
Story	Premo Proprius Mos Inhibeo Amet	Karthik	2	05/09/2010 - 01:48
Page	Qui Loquor Verto Wisi Nulla Commodo	Anonymous	14	05/08/2010 - 21:55
Story	Ad Wisi Brevitas Usitas Nimis Capto	Anonymous	8	05/08/2010 - 20:17

Looking at the markup of a typical row as displayed in the following block of code, we can see that each row contains a TD element which specifies the node type of the row. We can also see in the previous screenshot that the **Type** for multiple rows is often the same and is rather needlessly repeated.

```
<tr class="even">
  <td class="views-field views-field-type">Story</td>
  <td class="views-field views-field-title"><a href="http://localhost/
mysite/node/14">Exerci Oppeto Loquor Paratus Consequat Neque Nimis</
a></td>
  <td class="views-field views-field-name"><span>Anonymous</span></td>
  <td class="views-field views-field-comment-count">12</td>
  <td class="views-field views-field-last-comment-timestamp
active">05/09/2010 - 01:58</td>
</tr>
```

We are going to look at overriding the template used to display this table so that multiple rows with the same node type are replaced by a single field spanning multiple rows.

While we would normally use the Theme developer module to analyze the template structure used in rendering the table, the Views module provides a more straightforward alternative. The default template can be overridden by following these steps:

1. Browse to the Views administration page at `admin/build/views` (**Home | Administer | Site building | Views**).

2. Locate the **tracker** view and click on its **Edit** link.

3. On the edit page, select the **Page** display on the left.

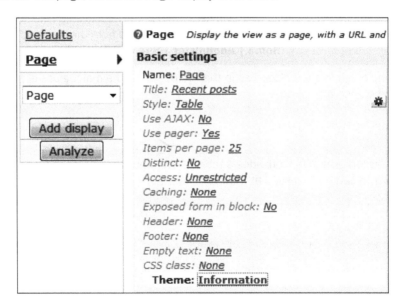

4. In the **Page** display's **Basic settings** section, click on the **Theme: Information** link. This should display a list of templates and candidate template names used to render the view and each of its fields.

Page: Theming information

This section lists all possible templates for the display plugin and for the style plugins, ordered roughly from the least specific to the most specific. The active template for each plugin -- which is the most specific template found on the system -- is highlighted in bold.

My Zen ▼   Change theme

- Display output: **views-view.tpl.php**, views-view--tracker.tpl.php, views-view--default.tpl.php, views-view--page.tpl.php, views-view--tracker--page.tpl.php
- Style output: **views-view-table.tpl.php**, views-view-table--tracker.tpl.php, views-view-table--default.tpl.php, views-view-table--page.tpl.php, views-view-table--tracker--page.tpl.php
- Field Node: Type (ID: type): **views-view-field.tpl.php**, views-view-field--type.tpl.php, views-view-field--tracker--type.tpl.php, views-view-field--page--type.tpl.php, views-view-field--tracker--page.tpl.php, views-view-field--tracker--page--type.tpl.php

5. Click on the **Style output** link to obtain the default template code which should be something as follows:

```php
<?php
// $Id: views-view-table.tpl.php,v 1.8 2009/01/28 00:43:43
merlinofchaos Exp $
/**
 * @file views-view-table.tpl.php
 * Template to display a view as a table.
 *
 * - $title : The title of this group of rows.  May be empty.
 * - $header: An array of header labels keyed by field id.
 * - $fields: An array of CSS IDs to use for each field id.
 * - $class: A class or classes to apply to the table, based on
settings.
 * - $row_classes: An array of classes to apply to each row,
indexed by row
 *    number. This matches the index in $rows.
 * - $rows: An array of row items. Each row is an array of
content.
 *    $rows are keyed by row number, fields within rows are keyed
by field ID.
 * @ingroup views_templates
 */
?>
<table class="<?php print $class; ?>">
  <?php if (!empty($title)) : ?>
    <caption><?php print $title; ?></caption>
```

```
<?php endif; ?>
<thead>
  <tr>
    <?php foreach ($header as $field => $label): ?>
      <th class="views-field views-field-<?php print
$fields[$field]; ?>">
        <?php print $label; ?>
      </th>
    <?php endforeach; ?>
  </tr>
</thead>
<tbody>
  <?php foreach ($rows as $count => $row): ?>
    <tr class="<?php print implode(' ', $row_classes[$count]);
?>">
      <?php foreach ($row as $field => $content): ?>
      <td class="views-field views-field-<?php print
$fields[$field]; ?>">
          <?php print $content; ?>
      </td>
      <?php endforeach; ?>
    </tr>
  <?php endforeach; ?>
</tbody>
</table>
```

The code that we just saw confirms that this template is the one which is responsible for the markup used for displaying the table. The highlighted lines indicate the code which we will be looking to modify to our needs.

6. Copy the entire block of code to the clipboard.

7. Click on the **Back to Theming information** link to get back to the template file list.

8. Out of the available candidate template file names assigned to the **Style output** template, choose **views-view-table--tracker--page.tpl.php** which, by targeting the table style for the tracker view, is the most suitable for our case.

9. In the local filesystem, browse to the myzen theme folder at `sites/all/themes/myzen`.

10. Navigate into its `templates` subfolder.

11. Create a new file with the chosen candidate filename—`views-view-table--tracker--page.tpl.php`.

12. Open this file in an editor and paste the code copied earlier into it.

Alternatively, we could have also copied the file `views-view-table.`
`tpl.php` from the Views module's theme folder at `sites/all/modules/`
`views/theme` and pasted it into the myzen theme's templates folder.
We could then have subsequently renamed it to `views-view-table—`
`tracker—page.tpl.php`.

13. Amend the code as per the following highlighted segments so that the file now looks something like this:

```php
<?php
// $Id: views-view-table.tpl.php,v 1.8 2009/01/28 00:43:43
merlinofchaos Exp $
/**
 * @file views-view-table.tpl.php
 * Template to display a view as a table.
 *
 * - $title : The title of this group of rows.  May be empty.
 * - $header: An array of header labels keyed by field id.
 * - $fields: An array of CSS IDs to use for each field id.
 * - $class: A class or classes to apply to the table, based on
settings.
 * - $row_classes: An array of classes to apply to each row,
indexed by row
 *   number. This matches the index in $rows.
 * - $rows: An array of row items. Each row is an array of
content.
 *   $rows are keyed by row number, fields within rows are keyed
by field ID.
 * @ingroup views_templates
 */


  // Calculate rowspans and store in an array.
  // This code should ideally be inside a preprocess
  // function.
  foreach ($rows as $row) {
    // Initialize tracking variables.
    if (!isset($groups)) {
      $groups = array();
      $current = $row['type'];
      $count = 0;
      $total = 0;
    }

    if ($row['type'] == $current) {
      $count++;
```

```php
    }
    else {
      $current = $row['type'];
      $groups[$total] = $count;
      $total += $count;
      $count = 1;
    }
  }
  $groups[$total] = $count;
?>
<table class="<?php print $class; ?>">
  <?php if (!empty($title)) : ?>
    <caption><?php print $title; ?></caption>
  <?php endif; ?>
  <thead>
    <tr>
      <?php foreach ($header as $field => $label): ?>
        <th class="views-field views-field-<?php print
$fields[$field]; ?>">
          <?php print $label; ?>
        </th>
      <?php endforeach; ?>
    </tr>
  </thead>
  <tbody>
    <?php foreach ($rows as $count => $row): ?>
      <tr class="<?php print implode(' ', $row_classes[$count]);
?>">
        <?php foreach ($row as $field => $content):
          // Only group the type column.
          if ($field == 'type'):
            // Add rowspan attribute only if the current
            // row is the first of a series. If not, do not
            // display any content.
            if (isset($groups[$count])): ?>
              <td class="views-field views-field-<?php print
$fields[$field]; ?>" rowspan="<?php print $groups[$count]; ?>">
                <?php print $content; ?>
              </td>
            <?php endif; ?>
          <?php else: ?>
            <td class="views-field views-field-<?php print
$fields[$field]; ?>">
              <?php print $content; ?>
            </td>
```

```
        <?php endif; ?>
      <?php endforeach; ?>
    </tr>
  <?php endforeach; ?>
  </tbody>
</table>
```

14. Back in the browser, click on **Rescan template files** at the bottom of the **Theming information** section. This is the equivalent of clearing Drupal's cache which should be performed as a matter of course whenever template files are newly introduced or removed.

15. Note that **views-view-table--tracker--page.tpl.php** is now in bold next to the **Style output** link as in the following screenshot:

⊚ **Page: Theming information**

This section lists all possible templates for the display plugin and for the style plugins, ordered roughly from the least specific to the most specific. The active template for each plugin -- which is the most specific template found on the system -- is highlighted in bold.

My Zen　▾　[Change theme]

- Display output: **views-view.tpl.php**, views-view--tracker.tpl.php, views-view--default.tpl.php, views-view--page.tpl.php, views-view--tracker--page.tpl.php
- Style output: views-view-table.tpl.php, views-view-table--tracker.tpl.php, views-view-table--default.tpl.php, views-view-table--page.tpl.php, **views-view-table--tracker--page.tpl.php**

16. Click on the **OK** button.

17. Click on the **Save** button to save the changes to the view.

How it works...

Refreshing the tracker page should now display a cleaner representation of its contents with node types occupying multiple rows as in the following screenshot:

Type	Title	Author	Replies	Last Post
	Blandit Facilisis Cogo Populus Dolor	Karthik	24	05/09/2010 - 02:03
Story	Exerci Oppeto Loquor Paratus Consequat Neque Nimis	Anonymous	12	05/09/2010 - 01:58
	Premo Proprius Mos Inhibeo Amet	Karthik	2	05/09/2010 - 01:48
Page	Qui Loquor Verto Wisi Nulla Commodo	Anonymous	14	05/08/2010 - 21:55
Story	Ad Wisi Brevitas Usitas Nimis Capto	Anonymous	8	05/08/2010 - 20:17
Page	Ludus Ad Commodo Abico Abigo Wisi	Anonymous	24	05/08/2010 - 18:23
	Nobis	Karthik	27	05/08/2010 - 17:28

Looking at the PHP used in the template file, we can see that we made two passes through the `$rows` array. The first iteration was expressly used to analyze the node type of each row, and to create the `$groups` array which was used to keep track of contiguous blocks of identical node types. Using this information in the second iteration, we selectively displayed the type only once for each of these contiguous blocks and, through the use of the `rowspan` attribute, achieved our grouping effect.

There's more...

Through the use of particular naming conventions, Views allows us to narrow our changes only to specific instances of a view.

Naming conventions

If the Theme developer module is enabled, we can confirm that the template file being used is indeed the one we have created, by clicking on the table with **Themer info** enabled.

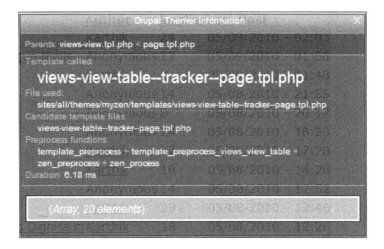

The file `views-view-table—tracker—page.tpl.php`, due to its chosen naming convention, will be triggered only for the **Page** display of the **Tracker** view when styled as a **Table**. The following table illustrates the range of the other options in the candidate template list:

Candidate template filename	Applies to ...
`views-view-table.tpl.php`	All views styled as tables.
`views-view-table--tracker.tpl.php`	The tracker view when styled as a table.
`views-view-table--default.tpl.php`	Only the default displays of all views styled as tables.
`views-view-table--page.tpl.php`	Only the page displays of all views styled as tables.
`views-view-table--tracker--page.tpl.php`	Only the page display of the tracker view styled as a table.

Adding a class to a Views style

While the Views module generously sprinkles `class` and `id` tags throughout its markup, they might not be perfectly suitable from a styling point of view with respect to our custom themes. In this recipe, we will look at using a preprocess function to add a class to the row of a view styled with the table plugin which, in this example, is the tracker view we have been working on throughout this chapter.

Getting ready

We will be using the myzen theme created earlier in this book to hold our template and styling customizations. We will also be using the Theme developer and Devel module while we peer under the hood. These modules are assumed to be installed and enabled.

The tracker view is assumed to be enabled. This recipe carries on with the customizations made to the tracker view earlier in this chapter.

How to do it...

First, let us use the Theme developer to get an idea of what we are dealing with. Browse to the tracker page at URL `tracker` and enable **Themer info**. Subsequently, clicking on the tracker table should provide us with template information as in the following screenshot:

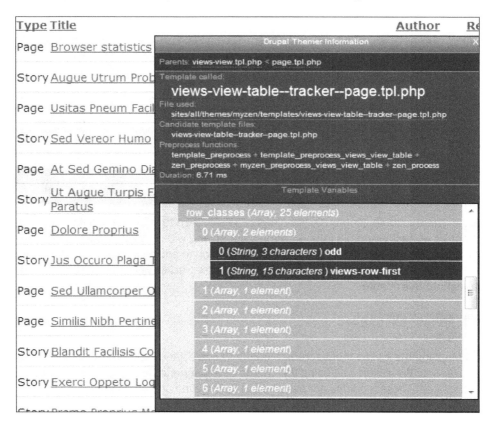

The screenshot confirms that we are overriding the default table template with our own custom file. Furthermore, looking at the table's markup and the actual template file, we can see that each row in the table has its class attribute populated by way of a variable named `$row_classes`. This is further corroborated in the previous screenshot where we can see that the `$row_classes` variable as an array that does indeed hold the classes for each row. In other words, adding our class to this array is pretty much all we need to do to accomplish our task.

Since we are talking about a template variable here, modifying it can be done via a template preprocess function. Looking at the Theme developer module's recommendations for **Preprocess functions** in the previous image, `myzen_preprocess_views_view_table()` seems a likely candidate as it targets the table style particular to a view display. However, it should also be noted that this table style is not confined solely to the tracker view and will also affect other views using the same style. This will need to be addressed in the preprocess function.

We can now add our classes and style the table by following these steps:

1. Navigate to the myzen theme folder at `sites/all/themes/myzen`.

2. Open the file `template.php` in an editor.

3. Scroll down to the bottom and add the following function:

```
/**
 * Preprocess function to add row classes for the tracker
 * view.
 */
function myzen_preprocess_views_view_table(&$vars, $hook) {
  // dpm($hook);
  // Restrict our customizations to the tracker view alone.
  if ($hook == 'views_view_table__tracker__page') {
    foreach ($vars['view']->result as $id=>$row) {
      $vars['row_classes'][$id][] = 'tracker-' . $row->node_type;
    }
  }
}
```

In the code that we just saw, the Devel module's `dpm()` function has been used to verify the view being modified. This allows us to restrict our changes solely to the tracker view.

4. Save the file and exit the editor.

5. Now, browse into the `css` subfolder.

6. Locate the file `views-styles.css` and open it in an editor. This file is loaded by default by the myzen theme via its `.info` file.

7. Add the following code which sets the background color for each row based on its node type:

```
/* Tracker */
.view-tracker .tracker-page {
  background: #FC0;
}

.view-tracker .tracker-page .active {
  background: #A80;
```

```
}

.view-tracker .tracker-story {
  background: #A90;
}

.view-tracker .tracker-story .active {
  background: #890;
}
```

The rule for the `.active` classes overrides the background color set for the column being sorted.

8. Save the file and exit the editor.

9. Clear the Drupal cache to rebuild the theme registry as we have added a new template function.

10. Refresh the tracker page to confirm that our changes have taken effect.

How it works...

The tracker page should now display something like the following:

Type	Title	Author	Replies	Last Post
Page	Browser statistics	Karthik	0	05/09/2010 - 17:25
Story	Augue Utrum Probo	Anonymous	19	05/09/2010 - 15:34
Page	Usitas Pneum Facilisis Si Nostrud Duis Eros Persto	Karthik	26	05/09/2010 - 15:02
Story	Sed Vereor Humo	Karthik	25	05/09/2010 - 14:35
Page	At Sed Gemino Diam Vulpes	Anonymous	3	05/09/2010 - 14:17
Story	Ut Augue Turpis Facilisis Accumsan Secundum Utinam Paratus	Karthik	19	05/09/2010 - 14:16
Page	Dolore Proprius	Anonymous	10	05/09/2010 - 13:48
Story	Jus Occuro Plaga Te Ullamcorper Nimis Euismod	Anonymous	14	05/09/2010 - 12:53
Page	Sed Ullamcorper Odio Abdo	Anonymous	10	05/09/2010 - 10:11
	Similis Nibh Pertineo Tum	Anonymous	8	05/09/2010 - 08:10
	Blandit Facilisis Cogo Populus Dolor	Karthik	24	05/09/2010 - 02:03
Story	Exerci Oppeto Loquor Paratus Consequat Neque Nimis	Anonymous	12	05/09/2010 - 01:58
	Premo Proprius Mos Inhibeo Amet	Karthik	2	05/09/2010 - 01:48

As in the previous image, rows pertaining to the **Page** node type are colored differently from those of the **Story** node type.

There's more...

It is important to ensure that we do not overcrowd our template files with PHP logic.

Preprocess functions versus template files

Instead of using a preprocess function, we could have simply added our code and classes directly to the template file. However, this is not recommended for the sole reason of maintaining a distinction between logic and presentation. By keeping all our logic in preprocess functions, either in the `template.php` file of the theme or if need be, within a module and just exporting the required variables to the template file, we keep the template file cleaner and simpler thereby making it less cumbersome while customizing the markup.

Creating a custom Views style plugin

Views style plugins such as tables and lists are used to render the view in a variety of display formats. The inbuilt plugins are often all that are needed for basic displays and the ability to override their template files via the theme tends to be a straightforward answer for most customization requirements. However, more complex display scenarios, especially those which are frequently reused, necessitate a better solution—a custom style plugin.

In this recipe, we will create a custom style plugin which will render a view as an HTML definition list and use it to display a list of taxonomy terms along with their descriptions.

Getting ready

Create a view named **definitions** to display taxonomy terms which displays two fields—the taxonomy term and its description—and optionally also takes the vocabulary ID as an argument as in the following screenshot.

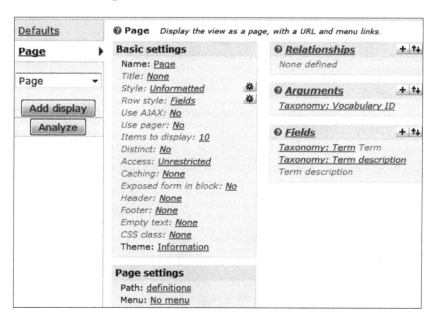

As in the previous image, a **Page** display also needs to be created and made accessible at the URL **definitions**.

We will be using the mysite module created earlier in this book to hold our custom style plugin.

How to do it...

Browse to the mysite module folder at `sites/all/modules/mysite` and perform the following steps:

1. Open the file `mysite.module` in an editor and add the following code which declares to the Views module that we are going to be specifying some customizations.

    ```
    /**
     * Implementation of hook_views_api().
     */
    function mysite_views_api() {
      return array(
        'api' => 2,
        'path' => drupal_get_path('module', 'mysite') . '/views'
      );
    }
    ```

2. Save the file and exit the editor.

3. Create a folder named `views`.

4. Within it, create four files named `dlist.views.theme.inc`, `mysite.views.inc`, `views_plugin_style_dlist.inc`, and `views-view-dlist.tpl.php` respectively.

> The term `dlist`—short for *definition list*—in the filenames above indicates the internal name for our new plugin.

5. Add the following PHP which declares our new plugin to the file `mysite.views.inc`:

    ```
    /**
     * Implementation of hook_views_plugins().
     */
    function mysite_views_plugins() {
      return array(
        'style' => array(
          'dlist' => array(
            'title' => t('Definition list'),
    ```

```
            'type' => 'normal',
            'path' => drupal_get_path('module', 'mysite') . '/views',
            'handler' => 'views_plugin_style_dlist',
            'uses fields' => TRUE,
            'uses row plugin' => FALSE,
            'uses options' => TRUE,
            'uses grouping' => FALSE,
            'theme' => 'views_view_dlist',
            'theme path' => drupal_get_path('module', 'mysite') . '/
views',
            'theme file' => 'dlist.views.theme.inc',
            'help' => t('Render a view as a definition list.')
          )
        )
      );
    }
```

6. Add the following PHP code which adds custom options to our plugin to the file
   `views_plugin_style_dlist.inc`:

```
/**
 * Style plugin to render each item in a definition list.
 *
 * @ingroup views_style_plugins
 */
class views_plugin_style_dlist extends views_plugin_style {
  function options_form(&$form, &$form_state) {
    parent::options_form($form, $form_state);

    // Create an array of allowed columns.
    $field_names = $this->display->handler->get_field_labels();

    // The term field indicates the definition term.
    $form['term'] = array(
      '#type' => 'select',
      '#title' => t('Term field for the definition list
&lt;DT&gt;'),
      '#options' => $field_names,
      '#default_value' => $this->options['term']
    );

    // The definition field indicates the definition content.
    $form['definition'] = array(
      '#type' => 'select',
      '#title' => t('Definition field for the definition list
&lt;DD&gt;'),
    '#options' => $field_names,
```

```
          '#default_value' => $this->options['definition']
      );
  }
}
```

7. Add the following PHP code which preprocesses the variables made available to the template to the file `dlist.views.theme.inc`:

```
/**
 * Make variables available to the definition list template.
 * file.
 */
function template_preprocess_views_view_dlist(&$vars) {
  template_preprocess_views_view_unformatted($vars);
  // Filter fields to only contain the term and definition.
  $vars['rows'] = $vars['view']->style_plugin->rendered_fields;
}
```

8. Add the following theme markup to the file `views-view-dlist.tpl.php`:

```
<div class="definition-list">
  <?php if (!empty($title)): ?>
    <h3><?php print $title; ?></h3>
  <?php endif; ?>
  <dl>
    <?php foreach ($rows as $id => $row): ?>
      <dt class="views-field views-field-term-<?php print $id;
?>">
        <?php print $row[$options['term']]; ?>
      </dt>
      <dd class="views-field views-field-definition-<?php print
$id; ?>">
        <?php print $row[$options['definition']]; ?>
      </dd>
    <?php endforeach; ?>
  </dl>
</div>
```

This file can eventually be overridden just like any other template file.

9. Save all the files and exit their editors.

10. Rebuild the theme registry by clearing the Drupal cache.

11. Navigate to the Views management page at `admin/build/views` (**Home | Administer | Site building | Views**).

12. Locate the custom view named **definitions** and click on its **Edit** link.

13. In the resulting page, select the **Page** display.

14. Edit the displays style setting by clicking on its current style which in the following screenshot is **Unformatted**.

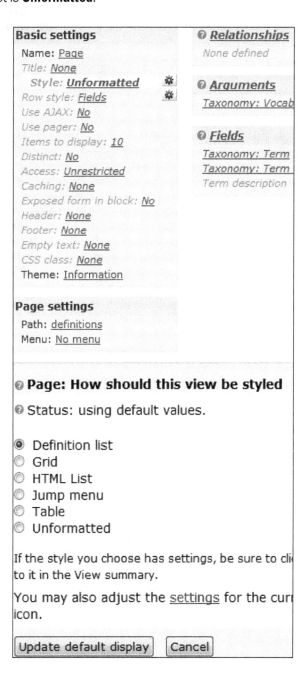

15. Set the style to the newly available **Definition list** option.

16. Click on **Update default display**.

17. With the **Style** set to **Definition list**, click on the configuration icon—a gear—next to it to customize it further.

18. Set the **Term field** to **Term** and the **Definition field** to **Term description**.

19. Click on **Update default display** again.

20. Finally, click on the **Save** button to save the changes to the View.

How it works...

Accessing the page display at URL `definitions/3`, where 3 represents a vocabulary ID, should now display the terms for said vocabulary along with their descriptions as a definition list. The following screenshot displays the view with its title set and a pager enabled:

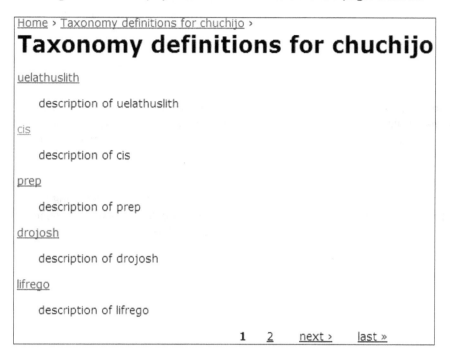

Generally speaking, the key to constructing a custom plugin is to declare it correctly. Looking at the declaration of the `dlist` plugin in `mysite_views_plugins()`, we can see that there are a myriad options available to be set as per our requirements.

```
/**
 * Implementation of hook_views_plugins().
 */
function mysite_views_plugins() {
  return array(
    'style' => array(
      'dlist' => array(
        'title' => t('Definition list'),
        'type' => 'normal',
        'path' => drupal_get_path('module', 'mysite') . '/views',
        'handler' => 'views_plugin_style_dlist',
        'uses fields' => TRUE,
        'uses row plugin' => FALSE,
```

```
            'uses options' => TRUE,
            'uses grouping' => FALSE,
            'theme' => 'views_view_dlist',
            'theme path' => drupal_get_path('module', 'mysite') . '/
    views',
            'theme file' => 'dlist.views.theme.inc',
            'help' => t('Render a view as a definition list.')
          )
        )
      );
    }
```

For example, we have set the `path` and `theme  path` values to point to the `views` folder within the mysite module since that is where we have located our files. We have also indicated that the plugin `uses  fields` from the view and also `uses  options` to specify the term and definition fields to be used during output.

More information on the plugin API can be gleaned from the Views documentation which can be accessed by installing the `Advanced  Help` module. Furthermore, browsing through the code pertaining to the inbuilt plugins tends to be very educational as well. These files can be found within the Views module's `plugins` and `theme` subfolders.

12
Rapid Layouts with Panels

We will be covering the following recipes in this chapter:

- ▸ Using Panels to create a front-page layout
- ▸ Embedding content in a panel
- ▸ Styling a panel with rounded corners
- ▸ Creating custom styles with the Panel stylizer module
- ▸ Changing the layout of a panel
- ▸ Creating a custom panel layout
- ▸ Replacing the site contact page with a panel
- ▸ Embedding tabbed panels in blocks

Introduction

The **Panels** module is, at its heart, a visual tool for layout design. Layered on top of this core is a sometimes overwhelming myriad of features and suite of modules that give a new meaning to flexibility and ease of use. In this chapter, we will be concentrating on the layout and theming aspects of this module.

Panels are useful for everything from creating complex landing pages such as the front page of a site, to overriding system pages and replacing them with a custom layout. Besides being used to lay out the content of a page, they can just as easily be embedded within nodes or even within other panels. This enables us to design and implement complex layouts virtually at the click of a few buttons.

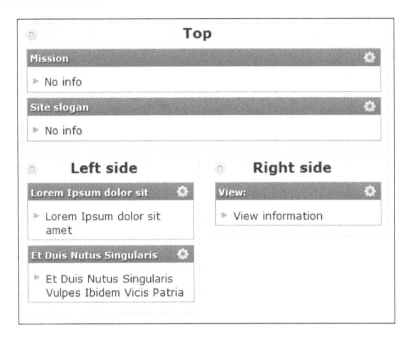

The previous screenshot illustrates a typical panel layout. In the screenshot, **Top**, **Left side**, and **Right side** represent **regions** within the panel. Each region can contain an unlimited number of **panes** which are not restricted in what they can contain. For example, the **Top** region contains two panes named **Mission** and **Site slogan**, which as their names suggest, display the site mission and slogan statements. On the other hand, the panes within the **Left side** region contain two nodes. Lastly, the **Right side** region contains a view which displays a list of recent comments submitted to the site.

The layout designer supports dragging and dropping panes from one region to another and within the same region. In other words, reordering or reorganizing the content within a layout becomes a painless exercise. The content itself can be chosen from a variety of sources. For example, in the previous screenshot, we have embedded site elements, nodes, and even a view.

Panels also come with style plugins which can be applied to entire regions or to individual panes. Furthermore, we can tweak region and pane properties, such as their CSS classes, to assist during any additional theming or for use by JavaScript.

All in all, Panels are a lot of fun as the recipes which follow will demonstrate!

 The version of Panels covered in this chapter is *6.x-3.5*, the latest stable at the time of writing. The interface for future releases of the *6.x-3* branch should largely be unchanged.

Using Panels to create a front-page layout

Panels are useful in a variety of scenarios. But their most common use case is in implementing complex front-page designs which draw input from a number of sources, and attempt to display them in a cohesive layout.

In this recipe, we will look at using Panels to create a basic front-page layout.

Getting ready

It is assumed that the Panels module and its dependencies which include the **Chaos tools** and the **Page manager** modules are installed and enabled. The Panels module controls access to its features via the **Permissions** page at `admin/user/permissions` (**Home | Administer | User management | Permissions**). In cases where the Panel's administrator is not logged in as **user ID 1**, it is assumed that relevant permissions for the Panels module are assigned appropriately.

How to do it...

The following steps are performed on the Panel management page at `admin/build/panels` (**Home | Administer | Site building | Panels**):

1. Click on the **Panel page** link.
2. In the resulting form, set the **Administrative title** to **Frontpage dashboard**.
3. Set the **Machine name** to **frontpage_dashboard**.
4. If the title is not sufficiently indicative of the type of panel we are creating, add a description in the **Administrative description** textarea.
5. Configure the URL where the panel is to be accessible by setting the **Path** to **dashboard**.

6. Check **Make this your site home page** as this page is going to be used as the front page of the site.

7. Click on the **Continue** button.

8. In the next step, select the layout for the panel, which in this case is the one titled **Two column stacked**.

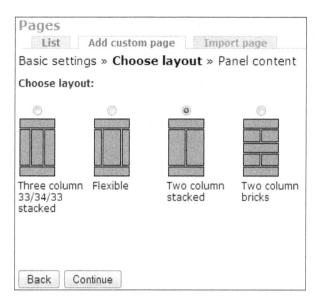

9. Click on the **Continue** button.

10. On the Panel content step, set the **Title type** to **No title** as the front page requires no title.

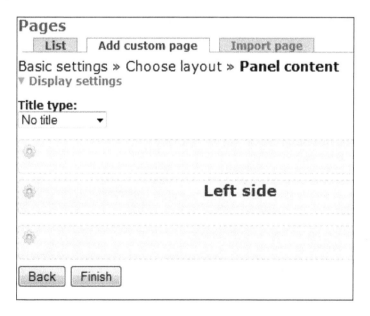

While we can also specify content in this step, it is recommended that we complete creating the panel before doing so.

11. Click on the **Finish** button.

12. In the ensuing panel management page, click on **Save** to complete the creation process as in the following screenshot:

13. Click on the **Content** tab on the left to confirm the layout of our panel and to add content, if necessary.

14. Browsing to the front page of the site or the URL dashboard should now display a valid albeit empty page, with tabs titled **View** and **Edit Panel**.

How it works...

The **Content** tab of the Panel management page should now look something like this:

Each of **Top**, **Left side**, **Right side**, and **Bottom** are the regions of the panel layout which can each contain one or more panes added by way of the configuration icons available in the form of gears pinned to the top left of each region.

Embedding content in a panel

Now that we have a layout ready for our front-page panel, we can look into adding content to it. In this recipe, we will be embedding the site's mission statement into the `Top` region of the `frontpage_dashboard` panel.

Getting ready

We are going to be using the `frontpage_dashboard` panel created in the previous recipe. Since we will be using the site's mission statement as a field, it is expected to be filled in via the **Site information** page at `admin/settings/site-information` (**Home | Administer | Site configuration | Site information**).

Furthermore, in order to avoid duplication, turn off support for the mission statement in the `page.tpl.php` template file of the current theme since we are going to be embedding it directly into the panel.

How to do it...

It is possible to access the management page for a panel in a number of ways. Here, let us do so by navigating to the front page of the site, which should now have the `frontpage_ dashboard` panel, and click on the **Edit panel** tab at the top. This should bring up the panel management interface where we can perform the following steps:

1. On the Panel management page, click on the **Content** tab on the left.

2. The two-column stacked layout should now be visible with four regions—**Top**, **Left side**, **Right side**, and **Bottom**—each with its own configuration icon in the form of a gear. Click on the configuration icon for the **Top** region.

3. In the context menu that appears, click on **Add content**.

4. In the resulting pop up, select the **Page elements** tab on the left.

5. As in the following screenshot, click on **Mission** which should add the mission statement to the **Top** region as a pane.

6. Back in the **Content** page, click on **Update and preview** to preview our changes.

7. Once satisfied, click on the **Update and save** button to save our changes.

8. Repeat the previous steps to add content to the other regions of this panel as necessary.

How it works...

Visiting the front page should now display the mission statement of the site as content within the **Top** region. The following screenshot demonstrates the `frontpage_dashboard` panel with a number of panes added to its regions using the similar steps to the ones we followed in this recipe. The site's mission statement, as per this recipe, is a pane in its **Top** region, a View displaying a list of recent comments as a pane in the **Right side** region, and two nodes have been inserted as separate panes inside the **Left side** region. Additionally, the **Bottom** region contains the standard contact form provided by the contact module.

Reorganizing the panel

Panes within a panel can be reorganized by dragging and dropping them at will either within or between regions.

There's more...

Just as with a Panel region, the panes within each region come with their own configuration icon which can be used to configure them further.

Editing existing content

Just like configuration icons exist for each region, each content pane can be configured by clicking on its own configuration icon which is also a gear residing on the right-hand side of the pane. Configuration options include editing CSS properties, such as ID and class values of the pane, styling and performance options, and a host more, as in the following screenshot:

Views support for Panels

Views support for the Panels module can be achieved by enabling the **Views content panes** module which is a part of the **Chaos tools** suite. Once enabled, available views can be added and configured via the Panel region's configuration pop up.

If the Views option is unavailable even once the **Views content panes** module has been enabled, visit the Panel modules configuration page at `admin/build/panels/settings` (**Home | Administer | Site building | Panels | Settings**) and click on the Panel pages tab at the top. Make sure that the **New View Panes** and **New All Views** checkboxes are enabled. Empty the Drupal cache in cases where the Views module was installed after Panels.

Styling a panel with rounded corners

With our layout created and content added, we can look at using the Panel module's style plugins to pretty things up a little bit. In this recipe, we will be styling the **Mission** pane, created earlier in this chapter, by containing it within a box with rounded corners.

Getting ready

We will be working with the `frontpage_dashboard` panel created earlier in this chapter and it is assumed that a **Mission** pane has been added as per the previous recipe.

How to do it...

All page panels are listed in the page manager table at `admin/build/pages` (**Home | Administer | Site building | Pages**). Locate the `frontpage_dashboard` panel and click on its **Edit** link to perform the following steps:

1. In the resulting panel management interface, click on the **Content** tab on the left.

2. In the content layout page, click on the configuration icon for the **Top** region.

3. Click on the **Region style: Default** link in the resulting context menu as in the following screenshot:

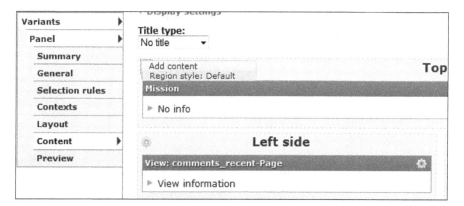

4. In the **Panel style** popup, select **Rounded corners** from the list of available styles.

5. Click on the **Next** button.

6. In the **Box around** drop down, select **Each region** as we want the entire region to be encased in a box with rounded corners. In cases where multiple panes are contained within the region, we might need to choose **Each pane** instead.

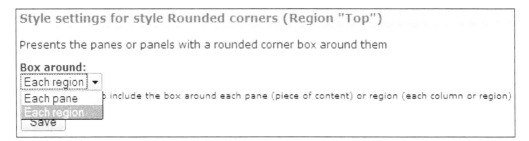

7. Click on the **Save** button.

8. Back on the content layout page, click on **Update and save** to save our changes.

9. Repeat this process for each panel region as necessary.

10. Refresh the site's front page in a browser to confirm that our new style settings have taken effect.

How it works...

The following screenshot demonstrates the front-page panel with its regions and panes styled with the rounded corners effect:

The effect is provided by a Panels style plugin which injects its own markup when the pane or region is set to be the output. The plugin also includes its own CSS file and images to create the rounded corners effect.

There's more...

Just as we styled a panel region, we can also similarly style individual panes.

Styling individual panes

While we have looked at how we can apply styles to regions and all panes within a region, individual panes can be also be styled similarly via their configuration screens as shown in the following screenshot:

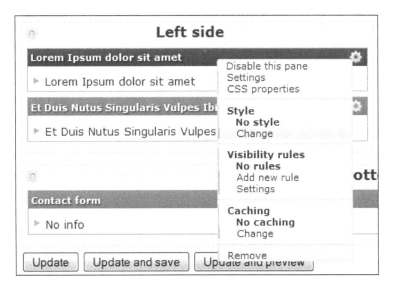

Creating custom styles with the Panel stylizer module

While we learned how to apply styles to panel regions and panes earlier in this chapter, this recipe will outline how we can utilize the **Panel stylizer** module to easily create and apply our own custom styles. We will create a style using the Panel stylizer module and apply it to the mission pane which is part of the `frontpage_dashboard` we have been working on through this chapter.

Getting ready

Panel stylizer comes with the Panels module and is assumed to have been enabled along with its dependencies. The module exposes a permission named **administer panels styles** which is required to add and manage our custom styles.

While we will be using the `frontpage_dashboard` panel created earlier in this chapter as an example panel to implement our styles, it is not a prerequisite. This recipe can be easily adapted to work with any available pane.

How to do it...

The Panel stylizer module enables us to create styles particular to panel regions and panes. These styles can either be created on-the-fly from region or pane configuration screens, or as recommended in the following steps, created via the Stylizer management interface and then applied to the regions and panes as appropriate.

1. Navigate to the Panels management page at `admin/build/panels` (**Home | Administer | Site building | Panels**).

2. Click on the **Styles** tab at the top.

3. Click on the **Add pane style** tab on the Stylizer management page.

4. In the resulting page, select the **Rounded shadow box** style and click on **Continue**.

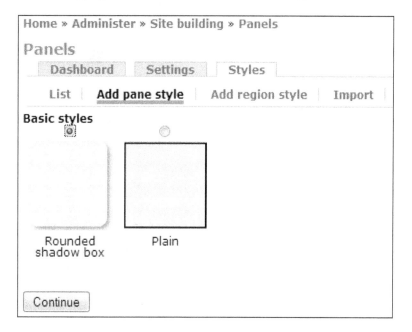

5. In the next page, use the color module's color form to choose the scheme for the pane, and the font and padding fieldsets for additional styling. The values for the mission pane can be seen in the following screenshot:

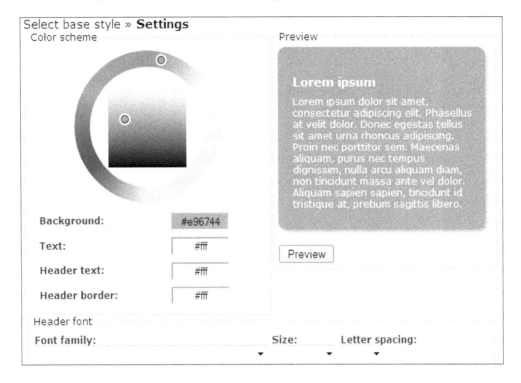

Since the mission pane does not have a header field, these fields can be left as is.

6. Use the **Preview** button to preview the new style using the provided sample of text.

7. Once satisfied, scroll down to the bottom and add a meaningful title to the **Administrative title** field. This will be used to identify the style later on. Since we are going to use this style to prominently project the mission pane, we can run with **Prominent** as the title.

8. Similarly, fill in the internal **Machine name** for this style and add a suitable description in the **Administrative description** textarea.

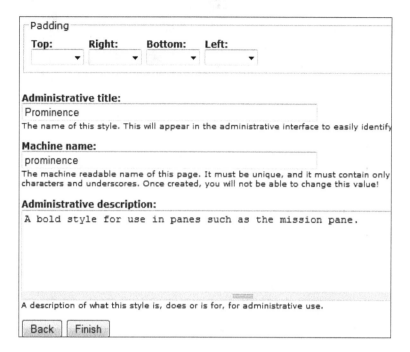

9. Finally, click on the **Finish** button to save the style.

   Now that we have created the style, we can use it to style our panel panes.

10. Browse to the `frontpage_dashboard` panel on the site's front page and click on its **Edit panel** tab.

11. On the Panel management page, click on the **Content** tab on the left.

12. Click on the configuration icon of the **Mission** pane and, in the ensuing context menu, click on **Change** under the **Style** menu.

13. In the resulting pop up, select **Stylizer** and click on **Continue**.

14. Choose the **Prominence** style from the **Select a preconfigured style** drop down.

Style settings for style Stylizer (Pane "Mission")

Allows choice of a stylizer style

Select a preconfigured style:

- None selected -
- None selected -
Prominence   style...

Save

15. Click on the **Save** button.

16. Back in the Panel management page, click on **Update and Save** to save our changes.

17. Refresh the site's front page to confirm that the new style has taken effect.

How it works...

In this recipe, we have created and applied a pane style named **Prominence** to the mission pane. This transforms what was a simple line of text into a block with rounded corners, a drop shadow, modified background and foreground colors, text alignment, font styling, and if need be, a lot more. The end result is demonstrated in the following screenshot:

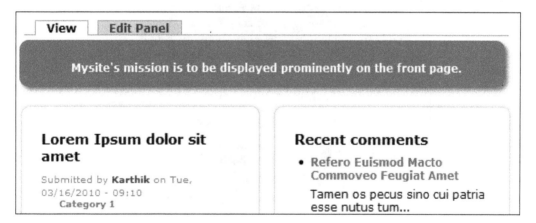

There's more...

The Panel stylizer module can be very effective when styling both regions and panes. Furthermore, updating the Stylizer preset will also automatically update the styles of associated regions and panes.

Stylizer for regions and panes

The Panel stylizer module allows us to create specific styles for regions and panes. As their names suggest, region styles affect entire panel regions whereas pane styles affect individual panes. In the following screenshot, we can see the **Mission** pane styled with the `Prominence` style situated within the `Top` region, which is unstyled. Below it, we can see the `Left` region styled with a region style and two panes within which are both styled individually with pane styles.

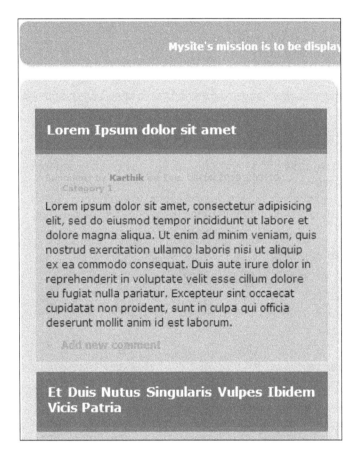

Changing the layout of a panel

Plans are seldom perfect and during the development of a site, there is an inevitable stage where things are chopped and changed leading to a lot of wasted time and effort. The Panels module, however, eases these concerns due to its modular nature, making nudges, tweaks, and even large-scale modifications relatively pain free.

In this recipe, we will be looking at changing the entire layout of a panel from a **Two column stacked** layout to a simpler **Single column** layout. Since we are effectively losing a column, we will see how the module allows us to intelligently merge the content from the two columns into the single column.

Getting ready

We will be using the `frontpage_dashboard` layout created earlier in this chapter to serve as an example panel in this recipe.

How to do it...

Navigate to `admin/build/pages` (**Home | Administer | Site building | Pages**) and locate the `frontpage_dashboard` panel. Click on its **Edit** link to perform the following steps:

1. Click on the **Layout** tab on the left.

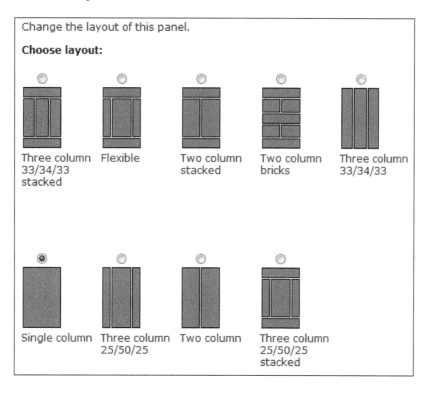

2. As in the previous screenshot, change the layout from the **Two column stacked** layout to the **Single column layout**.

3. Click on **Continue**.

    The next screen provides us an opportunity to migrate content from our existing layout to the new layout which might not retain a similar structure. In this case, we are moving from a layout with five regions to a layout with a single region.

4. As in the following screenshot, since there is only one region titled **Middle column**, all the content from the original **Bottom**, **Left side**, **Right side**, and **Top** regions can be migrated and merged into the **Middle column** region.

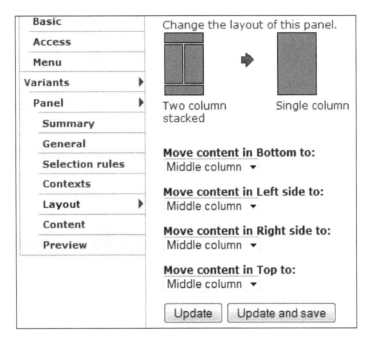

5. Click on **Update and Save** to complete the migration.

6. Back in the Panel management page, confirm that our layout is now a **Single column** layout.

How it works...

Layout migration is a painless procedure that allows us to make changes at will without losing any of the styles or customizations applied to panes. In the following screenshot, we can see that the new **Single column layout** has now been activated and all the panes from the five regions now reside in a single region named **Middle column**.

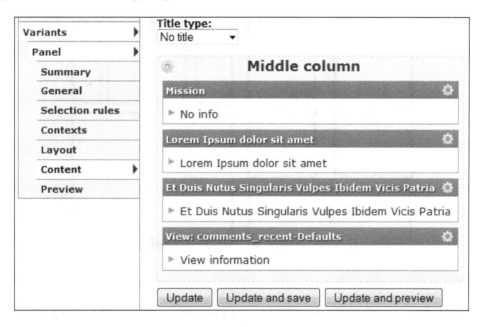

Creating a custom panel layout

The myriad of layouts that the Panels module comes packaged with are usually sufficient for most requirements. That said, themers wanting to display content using more interesting and complex layouts can also roll their own. While it used to be the case that custom panel layouts needed to be added in as a plugin, this is no longer needed.

In this recipe, we will make use of the Panel module's `Layout designer` to create our own custom layout designed for a page requiring a lot of regions.

Getting ready

It is a good idea to sketch an outline of our layout either on paper or in a graphics editor to get an idea of what we want prior to fiddling with the layout designer. For example, the layout that we are looking to create in this recipe will be based on the rudimentary sketch in the following screenshot which was created using Microsoft Paint.

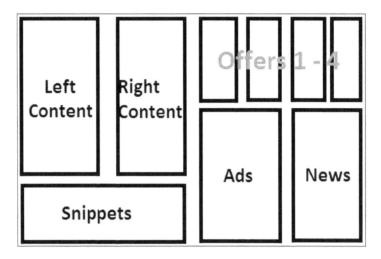

How to do it...

Create an empty panel page named **blurbs** with particular care taken to choose **Flexible** as its layout during creation. Once this layout has been selected, we gain access to the layout designer and can create our layout as follows:

1. Navigate to the `blurbs` Panel management page and click on its **Content** tab.

2. Click on the **Show layout designer** button which should be visible above the sole visible region titled **Center**.

3. Click on the **Region** link which contains the **Center** region and select **Region settings**.

Note the presence of the **Remove region** option which will come in handy while reworking the layout, if necessary.

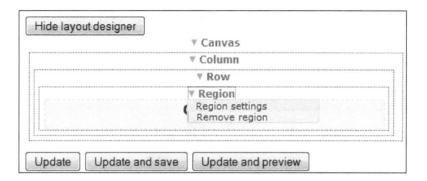

4. In the region configuration pop up, set the **Region title** to **Snippets**.

5. Optionally, add a class to enable easy access to the region from CSS or JavaScript.

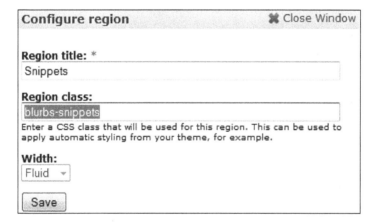

6. Click on the **Save** button to save our changes.

7. Back in the designer, click on the **Columns** link and select **Add row on top**.

8. In the **Add row** pop up, select **Columns** in the drop down and click on **Save**.

9. Click on the newly created row and select **Add column**.

10. In the **Add column** pop up, set the value of the **Width** drop down to **Fluid** and click on **Save**.

11. Repeat this process to add a second column to the right which should result in our layout looking like the one in the following screenshot:

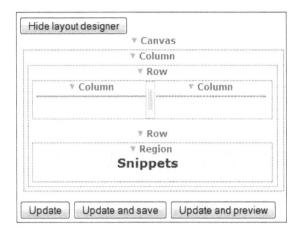

Note the presence of the resize handles between the two columns which allow us to adjust the width of the two columns, if required.

12. Click on the **Column** link and click on **Add row**.

13. This time, however, select **Regions** in the **Add row** pop up and click on **Save**.

14. Click on the newly created row and select **Add region**.

15. In the resulting pop up, set the **Region title** to **Left Content**.

16. Set the **Width** to **Fluid** and click on **Save**.

17. Similarly, add a row and a region named **Right Content** to the second column as well, which should result in our layout looking like the following screenshot:

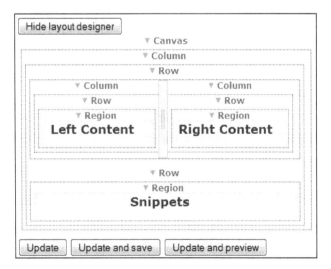

It is a good idea to **Update and save** our progress after any significant changes have been made to the layout.

18. Now that we have the first column from our sketched layout up and running, we can create the second column by clicking on the **Canvas** link and selecting **Add column to right**.

19. In the ensuing pop up, set the **Width** to **Fluid** and click on **Save**.

20. As we did earlier, add two rows to the column which are set to contain regions.

21. In the top row, add four regions named **Offers 1** through **4** respectively.

22. In the bottom row, create two regions named **Ads** and **News** respectively so that our layout now resembles the following screenshot:

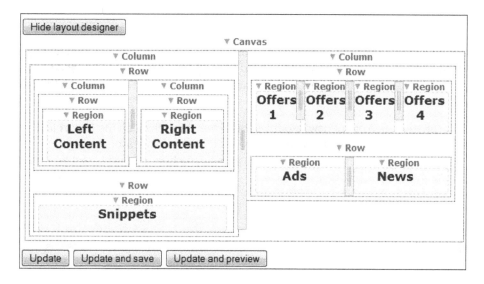

23. Finally, click on **Update and save** to create our custom layout.

How it works...

Looking at our newly created panel from the **Content** tab of the Panel manager, with the **Layout designer** switched off, results in a layout as in the following screenshot:

The layout designer uses a JavaScript-based frontend to allow the user to design the layout. Once done, the specifics of the layout are saved in the Drupal database and loaded during runtime to provide us with our layout. The layouts which come with Panels are, on the other hand, stored as code.

The PHP representation of our new layout can be viewed by clicking on the **Export** link at the top of the Panel management page. For our more involved endeavors, it might be worth exporting our layout into a module especially in situations where we might want to reuse the layout elsewhere.

There's more...

The layout designer can take some getting used to and we will initially find ourselves doing a lot of chopping and changing in order to get our layout just right.

Removing regions, rows, and columns

While working with the layout designer, it is often necessary to remove elements to rework or tweak the layout. This, however, is not always a simple process. The rule of thumb with removing elements in the Panel layout designer is that the element being removed has to be empty. Since columns contain rows, and rows contain regions, removing a row requires that any regions within will need to be removed first. Similarly, removing a column requires that any rows contained within will need to also be removed first, and consequently, all regions within said rows!

Replacing the site contact page with a panel

The Contact module's contact form is, by default, rather static and plain with no straightforward option to add new content or to reorganize it. In this recipe, we will replace the standard contact page with a panel thereby allowing us to take advantage of the power of Panels.

Getting ready

The Contact module is assumed to be enabled as we will be embedding the default contact form in one of our new panel's panes. To demonstrate how using panels allows us to easily add new content, we will be embedding a view into one of its panes. The view is to be titled **Addresses** and should return a list of nodes containing sample contact information. It is assumed that the view has been created and is available for use by the panel.

How to do it...

The Page manager module allows the overriding of specific Drupal pages. These pages are listed along with custom panels on the page management interface accessible at `admin/build/pages` (**Home | Administer | Site building | Pages**). The contact page can be overridden by following this procedure:

1. Locate the entry for the site contact page in the table and enable it by clicking on its **Enable** link.

Type	Name	Title	Path	Storage	Operations
System	search-node	Content	/search/node/!keywords	In code	**Edit** Enable
System	search-user	Users	/search/user/!keywords	In code	**Edit** Enable
System	search-advanced_help	Help	/search/advanced_help /!keywords	In code	**Edit** Enable
System	node_edit	Node add/edit form	/node/%node/edit	In code	**Edit** Enable
System	user_view	User profile template	/user/%user	In code	**Edit** Enable
Custom	page-frontpage_dashboard	Frontpage dashboard	**/dashboard**	Normal	**Edit** Disable
Custom	page-fp2	fp2	/fp2	Normal	**Edit** Enable
Custom	page-blurbs	blurbs	/blurbs	Normal	**Edit** Disable
System	contact_site	Site contact page	/contact	In code	**Edit** Enable

2. Once enabled, click on the same entry's **Edit** link.

3. By default, there are no panels available and Drupal uses the standard contact form. To remedy this, let us create a panel by clicking either on the **Add a new variant** link or the **Add variant** tab at the top.

4. Give the variant a title such as **Contact** or, as in the following screenshot, **Contact with addresses**.

5. Click on **Update and save**.

6. In the resulting layout page, choose a suitable layout. In our case, a simple **Two column** layout will suffice.

7. Click on **Continue**.

8. In the Panel content step, set the **Title type** to **No title**.

9. Click on **Update and save** to complete the creation process.

10. Back on the **Content** tab, click on the **Left side** region's configuration icon and click on **Add content**.

11. In the ensuing pop up, click on the **Widgets** tab on the left.

12. Choose the **Contact form** on the right.

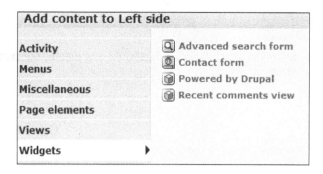

13. Click on the **Finish** button on the next page.

14. Similarly, add content to the right side column which, in this case, is the **Addresses** view which returns a list of addresses of offices around the world.

15. Finally, click on **Update and save** to save our changes.

How it works...

Browsing to the contact form at the URL `contact` should now display our panel as displayed in the following screenshot:

Contact

Contact us!
You can leave a message using the contact form below.

Your name: *
Karthik

Your e-mail address: *
mysite@example.com

Subject: *

Category: *
- Please choose - ▼

Message: *

☐ Send yourself a copy.

[Send e-mail]

Our offices

India
1234, Example avenue
Example city,
Example State,
Example PIN code
India
Ph: +91 12-3456-7890

United Kingdom
1234, Example avenue
Example city,
Example county,
Example Post Code
United Kingdom
Ph: +44 123-4567-8901

United States
1234, Example drive
Example city,
Example ZIP
USA
Ph: +1 123-456-7890

We can see that, along with the standard contact form, we now have the Addresses view also displayed alongside. Since the form as well as the view are both panes, we can now also style them at will.

Embedding tabbed panels in blocks

This recipe demonstrates the power and flexibility of Panels by exposing a panel as a block and jazzing it up by using jQuery's **Tabs** module.

Getting ready

This recipe uses the **Mini panels** module which is part of the Panels suite. For the tabs styling, this recipe utilizes the **Tabs panel style** module which can be downloaded at `http://drupal.org/project/panels_tabs`. This in turn depends on the **Tabs** module which can be downloaded from `http://drupal.org/project/tabs`.

It is assumed that the above modules have all been installed and are enabled. Furthermore, the Mini panels module controls access to its administrative features by way of permissions. It is assumed that they are enabled for the current user.

How to do it...

Navigate to `admin/build/panel-mini` (**Home | Administer | Site building | Mini panels**) to perform the following steps:

1. Click on the tab titled **Add**.
2. On the **Add** page, select the **Single column** layout.
3. In the resulting form, add **Activity monitor** as the **Mini panel title**.
4. Set the **Mini panel name** to **activity**.
5. Set the **Mini panel category** to **tabs**.

6. Click on **Save and proceed** to complete the creation process.

7. Next, click on the **Content** tab at the top of the page.

8. Click on the configuration icon of the **Middle column** region and click on **Add content**.

9. In the resulting pop up, click on the **Activity** tab on the left.

10. Click on **Who's new** from the list of available content as in the following screenshot:

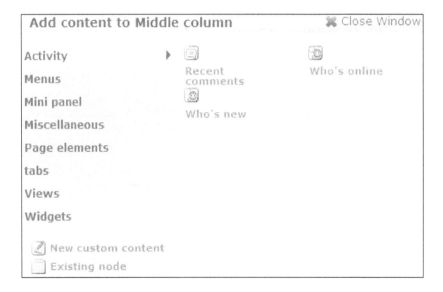

11. Complete the procedure by clicking on the **Finish** button in the ensuing step.

12. Similarly, add **Who's online** as another pane in the **Middle column** region.

13. To achieve the tab effect, click on the configuration icon of the region and click on **Region style: Default** in order to change the style plugin in use.

14. Set the **Style** to **Tabs** and click on **Next**.

15. Click on **Save**.

16. Back in the **Content** tab, click on the **Save** button to save our changes.

17. Click on the **Preview** tab at the top to confirm that the tabs are functioning satisfactorily.

18. Next, head to the block administration page at `admin/build/blocks` (**Home | Administer | Site building | Blocks**).

19. Under the section titled **Disabled**, locate the block which should be titled **Mini panel: "Activity monitor"** and enable it.

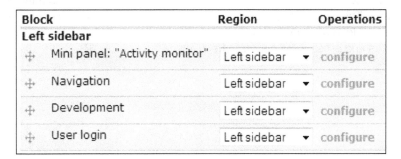

Block	Region	Operations
Left sidebar		
⊹ Mini panel: "Activity monitor"	Left sidebar ▾	configure
⊹ Navigation	Left sidebar ▾	configure
⊹ Development	Left sidebar ▾	configure
⊹ User login	Left sidebar ▾	configure

20. Click on the **Save blocks** button to save our changes.

How it works...

Mini panels are automatically exposed as blocks. Once enabled, our mini panel should be visible as a tabbed block as demonstrated in the following screenshot:

In the previous screenshot we can see that the two panes within the Middle column region have both been styled as tabs. The Tabs module inserts the requisite markup into the region and each pane which triggers the jQuery UI tabs plugin to take effect.

There's more...

Mini panels allow developers to create complex nested layouts comprising content from a variety of sources.

The flexibility of Mini panels

Mini panels are not restricted to blocks. Once enabled, they become just another piece of content that can be embedded anywhere. For example, a panel could add a mini panel into one of its panes. This mini panel, on the other hand, could already be embedding a mini panel of its own thereby leading to nested panels. This modular aspect allows us to easily create complex layouts and present our content effectively.

Index

Symbols

rows attribute 222
rowspan attribute 312
RTL 66

S

Save button 193
screenshot image, theme
  changing 40, 41
search_box variable 145
search textfield
  default text, adding to 177-179
secondary links menu 202
settings
  modifying, for myzen theme 76-79
show() function 182
simple view
  creating 283
site contact page
  replacing, with panel 353-356
site maintenance page
  maintenance template 108
  styling 107, 108
slogan
  adding, to theme 16, 17
Smarty 36
standard submit button
  replacing, with image button 232, 234
STARTERKIT folder 63
static variable 161
  URL 161
style sheet, base theme
  overriding 43
submitted date
  displaying, instead of last updated date 151-154
sub-theme
  layout, selecting for 65
sub-theme, of existing core theme
  chaining 36
  creating 34, 35
Suckerfish method 206
Superfish 206
switch block 150

T

tabbed panels
  embedding, in blocks 356-359
tables
  column-sort functionality, adding 183-187
template file
  documentation 101
  used, for theming CCK field 266-270
  variables, listing 99-101
template files
  importing, from Zen to myzen 66, 68
  versus preprocess function 317
template.php file 56
templates/ folder 56
test content
  generating, Devel Generate module used 117-120
textarea
  columns, altering 222, 223
  height, changing 221, 222
  replacing, with WYSIWYG HTML editor 226-228
  resize feature, turning off 223, 224
t() function 143
theme
  background image, adding 71-73
  creating, from scratch 59-61
  JavaScript, including from 167, 168
theme_ 81
theme_breadcrumb() 207
Theme developer module
  compatibility issues 98
  Drupal API documentation 98
  Enable Theme developer link 96
  hook_theme_registry_alter() function 97
  Themer info checkbox 96
  theme_username() function 98
  URL, for downloading 95
  used, for theme overrides 95
theme_fieldset() 243
theme_fieldset() function 244
theme function
  finding 111
theme_get_setting() 147

Z

Thank you for buying
Drupal 6 Theming Cookbook

About Packt Publishing

Packt, pronounced 'packed', published its first book "*Mastering phpMyAdmin for Effective MySQL Management*" in April 2004 and subsequently continued to specialize in publishing highly focused books on specific technologies and solutions.

Our books and publications share the experiences of your fellow IT professionals in adapting and customizing today's systems, applications, and frameworks. Our solution based books give you the knowledge and power to customize the software and technologies you're using to get the job done. Packt books are more specific and less general than the IT books you have seen in the past. Our unique business model allows us to bring you more focused information, giving you more of what you need to know, and less of what you don't.

Packt is a modern, yet unique publishing company, which focuses on producing quality, cutting-edge books for communities of developers, administrators, and newbies alike. For more information, please visit our website: www.packtpub.com.

About Packt Open Source

In 2010, Packt launched two new brands, Packt Open Source and Packt Enterprise, in order to continue its focus on specialization. This book is part of the Packt Open Source brand, home to books published on software built around Open Source licences, and offering information to anybody from advanced developers to budding web designers. The Open Source brand also runs Packt's Open Source Royalty Scheme, by which Packt gives a royalty to each Open Source project about whose software a book is sold.

Writing for Packt

We welcome all inquiries from people who are interested in authoring. Book proposals should be sent to author@packtpub.com. If your book idea is still at an early stage and you would like to discuss it first before writing a formal book proposal, contact us; one of our commissioning editors will get in touch with you.

We're not just looking for published authors; if you have strong technical skills but no writing experience, our experienced editors can help you develop a writing career, or simply get some additional reward for your expertise.

www.ingramcontent.com/pod-product-compliance
Lightning Source LLC
Chambersburg PA
CBHW062046050326
40690CB00016B/2996